Mergers and Acquisitions Security

MERGERS AND ACQUISITIONS SECURITY

Corporate Restructuring and Security Management

Edward P. Halibozek
Dr. Gerald L. Kovacich

ELSEVIER
BUTTERWORTH
HEINEMANN

AMSTERDAM • BOSTON • HEIDELBERG • LONDON
NEW YORK • OXFORD • PARIS • SAN DIEGO
SAN FRANCISCO • SINGAPORE • SYDNEY • TOKYO

Elsevier Butterworth–Heinemann
30 Corporate Drive, Suite 400, Burlington, MA 01803, USA
Linacre House, Jordan Hill, Oxford OX2 8DP, UK

∞ Recognizing the importance of preserving what has been written, Elsevier prints
its books on acid-free paper whenever possible.

Library of Congress Cataloging-in-Publication Data

Halibozek, Edward P.
  Mergers and acquisitions security : corporate reorganizations and security
management / Edward P. Halibozek, Gerald L. Kovacich.
      p. cm.
  Includes bibliographical references and index.
  ISBN 0-7506-7805-4 (alk. paper)
  1. Consolidation and merger of corporations. 2. Corporate divestiture.
  3. Confidential   business information. 4. Security consultants.
  5. Corporations–Security measures. I. Kovacich, Gerald L. II. Title.
  HD2746.5.H354 2005
  658.1′62–dc22

                                                                    2004029369

British Library Cataloguing-in-Publication Data
A catalogue record for this book is available from the British Library.

For information on all Elsevier Butterworth–Heinemann publications
visit our Web site at www.books.elsevier.com

Printed in the United States of America
05 06 07 08 09 10   10 9 8 7 6 5 4 3 2 1

Other Butterworth-Heinemann Titles Authored or Co-Authored by Dr. Gerald L. Kovacich

- *Information Systems Security Officer's Guide: Establishing and Managing an Information Protection Program*, First Edition and Second Edition (Czech translation of First Edition also available)
- *I-Way Robbery: Crime on the Internet* (Japanese translation also available) with William C. Boni
- *High-Technology Crime Investigator's Handbook: Working in the Global Information Environment* with William C. Boni
- *Netspionage: The Global Threat to Information* with William C. Boni

Other Books Co-Authored by Dr. Gerald L. Kovacich and Edward P. Halibozek

- *The Manager's Handbook for Corporate Security: Establishing and Managing a Successful Assets Protection Program*
- *Security Metrics Management: How to Manage the Costs, Successes and Failures of an Assets Protection Program*

This book is dedicated to the security professionals around the world who must protect corporate assets in a time of trials, tribulations, and turmoil when companies are being acquired, merging with other companies, or acquiring other companies.

Contents

Preface

As we enter the twenty-first century, we see a continuation of rapid changes occurring throughout the world. Nations are changing from an industrial base to an information-based economy. Changes that once took generations to make now occur much more rapidly with the use of, and advances in, technology, particularly information systems technology and telecommunications technology. Businesses, while using these advances in technology to become more productive, competitive, and advanced, have also become dependent on them. Increased global economic competition, increased dependency and use of technology, and rapid and technology-driven changes on a global scale have changed the global marketplace in just a few short years.

In reaction to these changes, companies develop many business strategies to increase their competitiveness and improve profitability. Companies regularly reshape themselves to the needs of the future marketplace. They explore new markets and develop new products. When they can't expand into new markets or develop new products on their own, they seek alternatives including merging with or acquiring other companies to create a single, more capable company. Companies acquire other companies for a variety of reasons including, but not limited to, the following:

- Adding additional product lines
- Gaining market share
- Gaining distribution capabilities
- Acquiring newer or different technologies
- Expanding the customer base
- Increasing business assets
- Buying additional experience

Business conditions drive companies to engage in mergers, acquisitions, and divestitures. Globalization of competition, deregulation, industry downsizing and consolidation, and financial market conditions are just some of the many drivers causing CEOs and company Boards of Directors to seek ways to improve the competitiveness and profitability of their companies. In some cases, the pursuit of mergers and acquisitions is driven by an even more fundamental need than that of increased competitiveness or profit. Company survival may actually be the intended goal.

During the decade of the 1990s, the number of mergers and acquisitions grew dramatically. In 1991, there were more than 3,600 mergers, acquisitions, and divestitures involving companies from the United States, with an estimated value of $140 billion. By the end of the decade, these numbers were dwarfed. In 1999, nearly 8,700 mergers, acquisitions, and divestitures occurred within the United States, with an estimated value of $1.4 trillion.[1] Clearly CEOs and Boards of Directors see mergers and acquisitions as a powerful business strategy for success.

What does this condition mean to the security professional? In the course of mergers and acquisitions, security plays a vital role in helping to make the endeavor successful. In this book, we focus on the role security plays in helping to make a merger, acquisition, or divestiture successful.

We address the fundamental security elements that are required to support the effort; provide an integrated "how to" approach to implementing mergers and acquisitions security complete with methods and processes that the reader can use and implement immediately. The methods and processes discussed have been successfully implemented on numerous occasions. Thus, the reader is provided information as to some of the security tools that can be implemented quickly and cost effectively.

The intent of this book is to provide security professionals or merger and acquisition specialists with clear security guidelines for any merger, acquisition, or divestiture. The reader is provided with methods, processes, and procedures that can be used for immediate implementation. Moreover, delivery of these services through proprietary security organizations and/or security consultants is discussed.

The book is divided into three sections:

Section I: An Introduction to Mergers and Acquisitions: This section addresses what mergers and acquisitions are and why they occur. Moreover, the current global business environment within which mergers and acquisitions occur is discussed. Finally, the role of security and the security manager in supporting mergers and acquisitions is addressed.

Chapter 1: What Are Mergers and Acquisitions? This chapter provides an explanation of the different types of mergers and acquisitions. It further provides information relevant to why they occur. Merger and acquisition trend data are presented, helping to explain why so many mergers and acquisitions occurred over the past decade.

Chapter 2: The Current Global Business Environment: Is It Merger and Acquisition Friendly? This chapter addresses the global business climate

---

[1] See http://www.tfsd.com/home.asp

within which mergers and acquisitions occur. It also addresses how the current business environment compares with the recent past business environment and suggests what may be expected in the near future in terms of merger and acquisition activity.

Chapter 3: The Role of Security and the Security Manager in Mergers and Acquisitions: This chapter discusses the importance of security in the process of mergers and acquisitions.

Section II: Premerger and Preacquisition Support: The section describes the role of security in the premerger and acquisition phase. From the time a decision is made by a company to pursue a merger or acquisition until the day it is actually and officially accomplished, security must be part of the effort. Issues such as ensuring the effort itself is not compromised—that is, its existence discovered by the competition—to the participation of security in assessing the security condition of the target company all require the support of the security organization and will be addressed in much detail.

Chapter 4: Gathering Information and Producing Corporate Intelligence. This chapter focuses on the gathering of information to produce corporate intelligence. Corporate intelligence is used to assist in the decision-making process for any merger or acquisition. Corporate intelligence can be produced through the gathering of information from a variety of open sources. These sources are discussed and the process for developing useful intelligence is addressed.

Chapter 5: Why Premerger and Acquisition Support? This chapter discusses the importance of protecting the effort to merge with or acquire another company. Ensuring that the merger and acquisition strategy is not compromised is paramount, as it may adversely affect the competitive situation of the company.

Chapter 6: Security's Role in the Due Diligence Assessment: In this chapter we discuss why security is an important part of the due diligence assessment. Furthermore, we examine how the security professional should conduct an assessment of the targeted company's security condition and security capabilities.

Section III: Postmerger and Postacquisition Support: This section addresses the role of security once the "deal is done" and the newly acquired or merged company is integrated into the acquiring company. The expectations of executive management regarding security during the integration process are also presented.

Chapter 7: Short-Term Postmerger Security: This chapter addresses security's role in integrating the newly merged or acquired company into the existing acquiring company. For example, how will the acquiring company's security manager ensure that the newly acquired company's security organization becomes fully integrated? What issues will exist, and what synergies can be gained?

Chapter 8: Long-Term Postmerger Support: This chapter addresses one of the most complicated issues facing any merger or acquisition: creating a new company culture. How does the new culture affect the security organization in terms of its role of providing support to the company and in integrating the security department of the newly acquired or merged company into the acquiring company?

Chapter 9: Divestitures: This chapter discusses security support for divestitures. When a company chooses to sell off a portion of its business, what role does the security organization play? How can the security organization contribute to a successful divestiture? What are some of the key security issues faced during a divestiture? All of these questions are addressed in this chapter.

Chapter 10: Mergers, Acquisitions, and Divestitures Summary by Checklists: This chapter reviews the major activities and responsibilities that security has in any merger, acquisition, or divestiture. The chapter provides checklists for each major activity that can be used as a guide by any security manager or business executive tasked with supporting a merger or acquisition.

We believe that this book provides an exceptional foundation for security professionals or business executives involved in providing security for mergers and acquisitions. The material contained in this book was taken from public sources; under no circumstances was any information obtained or used that fell under the rules of trade secrets, proprietary information, or national security (classified) information.

This book was written based primarily on the knowledge and actual experience of the authors. Together the authors have a long and experienced record of managing large and complex security organizations. For example, since 1994, Mr. Halibozek has provided security support for eight different mergers, acquisitions, or divestitures. The largest involved an acquisition worth several billion dollars and with more than 100,000 employees. Dr. Kovacich has also been been involved in many mergers and acquisitions as both an international security consultant and business security manager.

Acknowledgments

This project has taken the time and effort of more people than just its authors. It has taken the support and understanding of our families; professional input of our security colleagues, friends, and those involved in mergers and acquisitions; and the publisher's team assigned to this project.

We are grateful to all of them for their support not only on this project but also on our other projects. We send a special thanks to:

- William C. Boni, Vice President and CISO Motorola Corporation, one of the "best and brightest" of the CISOs in the profession today
- Don Evans, who continues to be the InfoSec Conferences' "workhorse" and security professional even before computers used punchcards
- Dr. Andy Jones, Ph.D., Professor, University of Glamorgan, Wales, U.K., leader in the European security arena, computer forensics, and security expert
- Steve Lutz, international security consultant and President, Waysecure.Com, the best in the global InfoSec consulting business today
- Motomu Akashi, business security expert, mentor, and fellow author

To the staff and project team of Butterworth-Heinemann—Mark Listewnik, Chris Nolin, Jenn Soucy, Pam Sosnowski, and Pam Chester—thanks for another great effort and for your continued support and guidance, which made this and our other books possible. We look forward to your continued professional support and expertise.

And, of course, a special thanks to Phillis Halibozek and Hsiao-yun Kovacich for their decades of continued support and for giving us the "space" to get this book written.

About the Authors

Dr. Gerald L. Kovacich has more than 40 years of counterintelligence/counterespionage, business security, criminal and civil investigations, antifraud, information warfare, and information systems security experience in the U.S. government as a special agent and in the international business sector. He has also worked for numerous technology-based, international corporations as an information systems security manager, information warfare technologist, investigations and security audit manager, and antifraud program manager, as well as an international lecturer and consultant on these topics. Dr. Kovacich is currently living on an island in Washington State, where he continues to write and conduct research relative to these topics. More information about Dr. Kovacich, as well as numerous security-related articles can be found on his web site: http://www.ShockwaveWriters.Com.

Edward P. Halibozek has been employed by a Fortune 100 corporation for more than 20 years and is currently their Corporate Director of Security. Mr. Halibozek is currently a member of the Board of Directors for the Chief Special Agents Association in Los Angeles California. He also served four years (1997–2000) as an Industry member to the National Industrial Security Program Policy Advisory Committee (NISPPAC). Mr. Halibozek holds a Bachelor of Science degree and Master of Science degree in criminal justice from California State University, Long Beach. He also earned an MBA from Pepperdine University, Malibu, California.

Foreword

When I first began studying security and the management of this important corporate function in the last part of the twentieth century, it seemed to be a rather forthright set of responsibilities. As a security professional, it would be my duty to advise and assist business or organization management teams on the optimum combination of protection mechanisms that best managed risks to our legitimate interests. It was well understood that for retail organizations that meant "loss prevention" techniques. If a high-rise office complex was the client, then premises protection would be key and so forth. Little did that young man of those days appreciate how much the world would change over the next 25 years or how the security professional's role would grow, adapt, and "morph" into the complex array of duties now characteristic of the early twenty-first century.

We now live in an era of unprecedented and rapid changes. The mind often boggles at the vast increase in functional accountabilities that challenge even the most adept practitioner of the traditional protection arts. No longer is a solid grounding in law enforcement, investigations, intelligence, and security/protection technologies/techniques sufficient to accomplish the work at hand. Indeed, although such foundational skills and experience are excellent preparation, today's global business environment virtually guarantees that security staff, managers, and executives will be confronted with many requests for their support that go well beyond their core competencies of "hard" security skills.

Indeed, the security professional must now commit to a lifelong effort to educate themselves on issues that will impact secure operations but originate from the nature of the chaotic pace of global businesses.

To help prepare for what has become one of the most stressful of these challenges, Dr. Kovacich and Mr. Halibozek have prepared an excellent guidebook. They have distilled the essential and relevant experience from their own careers, as well as the insights from many other skilled security practitioners to help advise you on how to be of service to your company and succeed during the tectonic shifts that so often precede and accompany a merger, acquisition, or divestiture. As one who has experienced these shifts with increasing frequency during my own 25+ years of security assignments, I can tell you that there is rarely a "minor" merger, acquisition, or divestiture. Even an event that is otherwise considered "financially immaterial" to the bottom line of the organization by the finance managers is fraught with peril as well as opportunity, *if* the essential elements can be executed with skill and precision.

To that end, I believe you will find this book to be relevant, timely, and extremely helpful. Acting almost as a "personal coach" in tone and substantive recommendations, Dr. Kovacich and Mr. Halibozek lay out a cogent approach that will first help you understand the business/organizational dynamics that encourage and support mergers, acquisitions, and divestitures. Then they explain what you and the security organization must do before, during, and immediately after the event(s) to minimize risks and increase the odds of a wholly successful transaction.

Although such efforts may have been relatively infrequent in the past century, I believe they are a common response of organization management to the sweeping nature of changes in the global marketplace. If my assessment is correct, security professionals at every point in their careers would be prudent to school themselves on the unique elements of these events so as to ensure that transactions occur as smoothly and risk free as possible.

Of special value to many readers are the insights the authors share regarding how to support the due diligence process before executing a transaction. The advice on how to minimize the often bumpy process of integrating an acquired company's security team to create a cohesive and effective new security organization is also useful.

Taken in whole, this volume is one of a number of essential references that will allow the committed security professional to achieve new levels of professional excellence and contribute to managing the high-impact risks of today and the near future. Even if you do not anticipate any major mergers, acquisitions, or divestitures in your organization, the book provides additional business knowledge that will improve your ability to articulate risks and plan management processes and to manage those risks.

Although we can anticipate some of the changes ahead, it's important to accept that rapid, unpredictable, and frequent changes are part of the current business environment. With that as backdrop, my recommendation is that you formulate a personal strategy for success by learning as much information as possible that is relevant to your organization/industry, practice to improve your personal leadership skills, and be prepared to accept new challenges as they develop. The knowledge and insight you will gain from this book will help you have confidence and perform well when/if you are called on to support mergers, acquisitions, or divestitures.

William Boni
Vice President, Information Security and Protection
Motorola, Inc.

Section I

An Introduction to Mergers and Acquisitions

This section defines mergers and acquisitions: what they are, why they occur, and why security plays such an important role in the planning and execution of any merger or acquisition.

Mergers and acquisitions occur for a variety of reasons, although the expected result of improving a company's competitiveness or somehow adding value to a company is generally the ultimate objective of any merger or acquisition. The activities that precede a merger or acquisition may vary greatly. From an early decision to engage in a merger or acquisition, through the due diligence phase and into the integration of two separate companies, the actions that each company goes through may differ greatly depending on the size and complexity of the effort.

Mergers and acquisitions may be large or small. They may involve a single product, single or multiple technologies, or an entire company. They may help one company expand its market-share or help another company just survive in its chosen business. As often as some mergers and acquisitions succeed, others fail. Nearly four of five mergers and acquisitions fail to meet their objectives.[1]

Failure generally means that the merger or acquisition did not achieve what it was expected to achieve. In spite of a high rate of failure, investors and business executives continue to use mergers and acquisitions as strategic tools for reshaping their businesses, and have done so for more than a century. Since the late nineteenth century, mergers and acquisitions have played an important role in national and global business environments.

---

[1] see http://www.corporatetrends.com.au/pmachine/comments.php?id=189_0_1_0_M19

In this section, a history of mergers and acquisitions will be presented to help the reader understand this environment in which security professionals must work. In addition, the current global business environment within which mergers and acquisitions occur is discussed. Finally, the role of the security staff and the security manager in supporting mergers and acquisitions is addressed.

Security professionals may wonder why this topic is important to them. More than ever before, security professionals must understand the world in which they work. Security professionals can no longer rely on just doing the physical security job of days gone by. They can no longer work "in their own little world," as so much of what is happening in today's world impacts, generally negatively, their ability to support the companies for which they work and successfully protect the companies' assets.

Chapter 1

What Are Mergers and Acquisitions?

The first rule of life is also the first rule of business: Adapt or die. – Alan M. Weber

INTRODUCTION

This chapter explains the different types of mergers and acquisitions. For a security professional to fully understand why mergers and acquisitions are important, they first must understand what they are and why they occur.

As supporting evidence, trend data are presented, helping to explain why so many mergers and acquisitions occurred over the past decade. Moreover, the security professional needs to understand why mergers and acquisitions are important to any business, the executives that manage the business, and the investors who own the business. As with any element of a business, it is easier to provide an appropriate level of protection if the protectors—the security professionals—understand what company assets they are protecting and why they need to protect them.

Black's Law Dictionary *defines mergers and acquisitions as the following:*
- Merger: *The union of two or more corporations by the transfer of property of all, to one of them, which continues in existence, the others being swallowed up or merged therein. . . .*
- Acquisition: *The act of becoming the owner of a certain property. . .*
- Divestiture: *to deprive; to take away; to withdraw*

TYPES OF MERGERS, ACQUISITIONS, AND DIVESTITURES

Beyond the definitions provided above from *Black's Law Dictionary*, what are mergers, acquisitions, and divestitures? In a very basic sense, they are the purchase of a company, in whole or in part, or the sale of a company, in whole or in part. Each transaction differs in size and complexity. Some transactions are very large, involving whole companies and billions of dollars, sometimes referred to as mega-mergers. Some transactions are very small, perhaps involving only the purchase of a product line, a start-up company, or a new technology, often gaining little notice or attention.

In today's national and global business environments, mergers and acquisitions are frequently taking place as companies compete with one another. Thousands of mergers and acquisitions may occur in a single year. Companies often use these methods to grow their business (e.g. combining with other companies). Ultimately, all mergers and acquisitions occur for the same basic reasons: to improve the immediate, short-term, and/or long-term financial position of both companies or to provide a strategic advantage to one or both of the companies involved. In the long run, the transaction is at least expected to improve the long-term financial position and competitive position of the newly formed company; and it obviously is expected to benefit the company owners. These owners may be private individuals owning their own company, or they may be groups of shareholders owning stock in a corporation.

Mergers and acquisitions can be very large and complex, engaged in for a variety of reasons. Therefore, they can be further characterized into different categories that better describe the nature of the transaction.

Acquisition of Total Assets

Acquisition of total assets, as the phrase implies, is a transaction in which one company purchases the total assets of another company. In other words, one company acquires another company to do with it as it sees fit. The acquiring company may liquidate the purchased company, selling off all of its assets for their individual value. This type of acquisition occurred during the early 1980s when the economy was growing and interest rates were high, making assets more valuable. An acquiring company may break up the company it purchases into different business units or product lines and sell some or all of them.

This break-up is usually done because an assessment is made that the individual business unit or product line is not part of the strategic direction of the company. It may also mean that the company may need an immediate cash infusion, and selling a business unit or product line may add cash to the company treasury. It may also be a method of eliminating a competitor, providing that such a transaction, as applicable, is approved by the country's government regulators.

The acquiring company may choose to keep the entire company it purchased and integrate it into itself, creating a larger company from the two smaller companies. The intent here is to capitalize on the capabilities of both companies as they are shaped into a single new company. Here the new company expects to take advantage of any synergies created from this acquisition and leverage them to create a financial gain.

New technologies, expanded product lines, or increased knowledge capital can be used to improve the existing capabilities of the new company, thereby increasing its current and future market value. In fact, an acquiring company may purchase another company for the sole purpose of adding another specific capability. For example, a distributor of consumer products may acquire another distributor of consumer products because the acquired company has better developed distribution channels. Acquiring this capability would be expected to expand and improve the distribution capabilities and network of the acquiring company.

Acquisition

With a product line or business unit type of acquisition, the acquiring company is interested only in obtaining a specific business unit or product line. There is no intention to acquire a whole company. The acquiring company makes a determination that it would benefit from the addition of a new technology, a new product, an expansion of its existing product line, or a new business area to become more competitive in its chosen marketplace. Purchasing an established product line or newly developed technology is a much more expedient way to expand market-share or add capabilities than growing or developing it from within (internal growth is often referred to as organic growth).

Merger

As defined earlier, a merger brings two companies together to form a single new company. In this instance, both companies agree to come together, generally as equal partners, with each bringing something unique to the union. Generally, each company brings something the other lacks, thereby improving the capabilities of the newly created company. Neither company has an advantage after the merger, as both companies combine their people, assets, and capabilities to form a new entity. The new company expects to capitalize on synergies—efficiencies gained from two companies working together and producing something greater than either could have produced by themselves—eliminate redundancies, and become a more capable, efficient, and profitable company.

Ultimately, it is expected that the owners of the two merging companies will financially benefit from this union. The newly created company is expected to be better positioned for future growth and earnings than the two individual companies that combined to form this new union. At least this is the theory; as the cliché states, however, "it is much easier said than done." The long-term success rate of mergers and acquisitions in recent history is not very good. We will explore this phenomenon later in this chapter because, in spite of a high rate of failure, mergers and acquisitions continue to be used as an important strategic tool by business executives and are supported by investors and owners.

Divestiture

A divestiture is a transaction that results in the sale of a business unit or product line. For example, a divestiture may occur when a company chooses to sell one of its product lines to another company. The selling company may conclude that it no longer chooses to be in the business of producing that particular product, or it may need cash and can best raise it by selling one of its business units or product lines. Never forget, in business cash is king. It may be a strategic decision to divest a particular product line or business unit where the seller changes its direction or focus and sells a product line or business unit which no longer fits into its strategic plans.

PITTSBURGH—Generic drug maker Mylan Laboratories Inc. (MYL) is buying branded drug maker King Pharmaceuticals Inc. (KG) for about $4 billion in stock, company officials said Monday. Mylan has pursued a stronger position in the branded drug market and believes King can accelerate that goal. "The significant expansion of our branded business advances our long-term strategy," said Robert J. Coury, Mylan's vice chairman and chief executive officer. Bristol, Tenn.-based King and Mylan, which is based in Pittsburgh, will create a company with combined annual revenues of about $3 billion and a work force of 6,000 people.[1]

---

[1] http://www.foxnews.com/printer_friendly_story/0,3566,127016,00.html

DIVESTITURES, MERGERS, OR ACQUISITIONS: NOT AN EASY TASK

In 1999, Thomson Financial Securities Data indicated the value of world merger and acquisition activity to be $2.2 trillion. With crowded markets and intense competition, many companies look for ways to strengthen their position. Mergers and acquisitions seem to be a popular approach.[2]

Benefiting from a merger, acquisition, or divestiture is not as easy as it appears. In fact, considering that their overall success rate is not very high, one has to wonder why they continue to occur as frequently as they do. It is important for us to understand why they occur. What is it that drives any company to pursue divesting, acquiring, or merging with another company? They are actions that should not be taken lightly, as they will require the use of much of the company's resources to plan and execute. Time, energy, and capital are all expended in pursuit of a merger or acquisition. Well-managed companies do not lightly pursue these endeavors. Nevertheless, there are conditions that drive management and owners down the path of divestitures, mergers, or acquisitions, as discussed next.

The Globalization of Competition: The Market Share Driver

Market share is the key driver here. Companies seek new markets as existing markets become saturated, mature, or as the competition within those markets becomes far too intense. Within highly mature markets or markets where there is a downtrend in business (the market is actually contracting), competition for growth can be fierce. With no growth in the overall market, the only way for a company to grow its share of that market is to take it away from its competitors.

Unless a company is very capable, developing and maintaining a significant advantage over its competitors is difficult to accomplish. In this environment, internal growth becomes so difficult that companies must attempt to achieve growth by entering into or creating new markets. Often, this means that companies must expand from their domestic marketplace and pursue growth in international markets. These international markets are new areas (to those companies) where they can sell their products and services because there are no similar or equal products available for sale there, but there is an excessive business or consumer demand. These new markets may also be places where a company is in a much stronger position and thus able to produce similar products and services much more competitively (generally this means produced for a lower cost and sold at a lower price).

---

[2] See http://www.managementfirst.com/strategy/curves/merger.html

In his book,[3] Kenichi Ohmae provides a chart that clearly shows the two primary factors (cost and value) that differentiate companies from one another. Such factors, as is alluded to throughout this book, drive divestitures, mergers, and acquisitions. See Figure 1.1 for a view of the dynamics in mature domestic markets.

The Regulatory Change Driver

The changing of government regulations can drive, enable, and even encourage companies to pursue divestitures, mergers, or acquisitions. Government regulations exist for many reasons. In the marketplace, their goal is generally to ensure fairness and maintain competition; in some countries, government regulations may be used to stifle foreign or even national competition. Regulation is generally developed in response to market conditions and to control or shape the behavior of companies within many different markets.

When market conditions change, governments often react with changes in regulations. These changes may be new regulations, which attempt to implement greater controls, or deregulation, which, in effect, lessens market controls. Deregulation can make it more conducive for companies to pursue mergers or acquisitions. Recent history has shown that

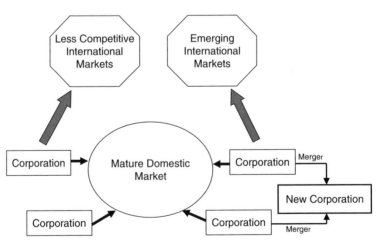

Figure 1.1   Fierce competition in mature domestic markets drives compotitors to seek alliances through mergers or acquisitions, or to enter new markets.

[3] *The Mind of the Strategist, Business Planning for Competitive Advantage*, New York, McGraw-Hill, Inc., 1982.

deregulation within the media, telecommunications, utilities, and health care industries has led to increased merger and acquisition activity. Ironically, at the end of periods of heavy merger and acquisition activities, new regulations are often enacted to deal with activities that were unanticipated and are causing problems in the affected market. Usually, that means consumers or investors were injured and new regulations need to be developed to protect against future occurrences.

An example of deregulation that affected banks in the United States occurred in 1999, with the repeal of the Glass Steagal Act. This action allowed commercial banks and investment banks to own each other with no limits on income.[4] This practice was prohibited by the initial regulatory legislation.

Another example of the impact of deregulation occurred within the United States' electric power industry as it underwent major restructuring through mergers and acquisitions resulting from deregulation in the 1990s. With the passage of the Energy Policy Act (EPACT) of 1992, mergers and acquisitions were set to increase with the deregulation of the electric power industry in many states. Essentially, the passage of EPACT allowed the Federal Energy Regulatory Commission to allow non-utility power producers to have access to the transmission grid to sell power in an open market. The intent of the U.S. Congress was to promote competition in the electricity generation sector. More competition drives efficiency and helps to eliminate barriers to entry generally associated with limited competition or monopolistic conditions.

However, the intended results are not always achieved. In 2003, a study conducted by the University of New Hampshire and the University of Miami concluded that mergers and acquisitions made in the electric power industry in response to deregulation did not create value for company shareholders or investors. Moreover, synergistic benefits leading to operating efficiencies did not develop. The study did not address the impact on consumers, but one needs only to look at the state of California and its energy-related problems in 2002 and 2003, which contributed to the recall of the state's governor, to see where government's intent did not match reality. Clearly, consumers of electricity, many of whom happen to be voters who expressed their dissatisfaction with their votes, were not pleased with the results of this government change.

Industry Downsizing and Consolidation

When downtrends within a market or industry occur, businesses usually experience reductions in sales, revenue, and growth. Even their share of

---

[4] http://www.emporia.edu/~chenyika/fi448_fall2002/solutions/chapt14.pdf

the market may be affected as competitors aggressively try to find ways to increase their sales, revenue, and profits. In this environment, the loss of market-share is not uncommon. These conditions negatively impact the earnings capabilities of a company doing business in this type of environment. To combat these negative effects, companies are presented with few alternatives to continue on the path of profitability. Generally, the initial reaction under these difficult conditions is to cut costs.

Cutting costs usually begins with cutting jobs. Employees are often let go based on numbers of jobs to eliminate. This can lead to the elimination of employees who are key to the successful completion of tasks. When key employees are gone, the processes and tasks may not be as easily accomplished; this increases costs by delaying crucial processes, and so forth. If this situation turns into a major, across-the-board problem, it may contribute to not meeting the goals of a merger or acquisition. Quite often, this detail is overlooked in the wholesale effort to slash costs.

As a security manager, it is important to keep the preceding scenario in mind so that if you are in a similar position to cut costs by cutting employees, you look first at the key employees who must be retained. If the number that should be retained is more than your directed budget, it would behoove you to look at the consequences of such actions on meeting the overall asset protection goals. If job elimination has a negative impact, executive management should be advised of the negative results. Generally, management will say to cut anyway; however, if the negative aspects of such cuts are realized, you can at least have the satisfaction of saying to executive management, "I told you so," although that will be of little help to you in meeting the asset protection goals.

The counteraction to cost-cutting is to expand market-share. Generally, in a downward market, companies are unable to increase their market-share, as the competition in a shrinking market can be severe. One effective way to increase market-share is to acquire another company operating in the same marketplace. The acquisition is not limited to a company in the acquiring company's country, as more and more companies are targeting foreign companies. One obvious reason is that the acquired company may be native to the marketplace in which the acquiring company wishes to penetrate and has a greater market-share in that marketplace than the acquiring company.

When one company acquires another, along with the acquired company comes its market-share. An excellent example of this condition occurred within the United States' aerospace business between 1989 and 2002. Within 14 years, ten of the largest companies operating in the aerospace market in 1989 were reduced to only four as a result of the merger and acquisition process (see Figure 1.2).

U. S. government spending on defense was rapidly decreasing as a result of changes in the geopolitical environment. Former adversaries were now allies. Money usually spent on defense was being diverted to more

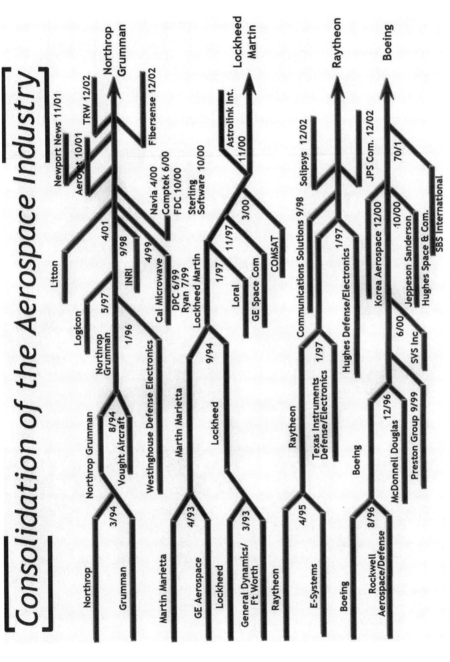

Figure 1.2 Results of mergers and acquisitions in the U.S. aerospace business.

peaceful projects. The market for products and services within the aerospace business was rapidly shrinking, and in a rapidly shrinking market it is difficult not only to maintain market-share but also to survive. Many companies sought out the path of mergers and acquisitions purely for survival. During this period in the aerospace marketplace, companies were driven to mergers and acquisitions as market conditions forced them to downsize and consolidate their businesses.

Technological Changes and Developments

Major technological changes can have a disruptive impact on businesses. With rapid changes in technology, particularly information technology, the need to advance technological capabilities can drive companies down the merger and acquisition path. To improve technological capabilities or develop and maintain a technological edge, companies have two choices:

- Develop technological capability from within. This takes time and much money, as research and development is costly. Moreover, as time passes, the risk of losing strategic and entrepreneurial opportunities increases.
- Acquire the desired technology. Find a company that possesses the desired technology or has the capacity to quickly develop the desired technology and purchase that company; however, purchasing an entire company may be costly and unnecessary. In some cases, it may be necessary to acquire only a portion of a company to obtain a new technology. It is not uncommon for a company to sell off a new technology or product line. It may do this for sorely needed cash or perhaps its strategic business objectives have changed. In any event, there are options.

Northrop Grumman's purchase of Teledyne Ryan. Teledyne Ryan was a manufacturer of unmanned air vehicles (UAV). Teledyne Ryan successfully competed against other much larger unmanned air vehicle developers and manufacturers and did so with lower development costs and more advanced technological and design capabilities. This became apparent during a competition for a U.S. military contract to develop and produce an advanced unmanned military surveillance aircraft. Teledyne Ryan successfully out-performed all other major producers of military aircraft and was awarded the contract for the Global Hawk unmanned air vehicle. One of the companies Teledyne Ryan competed against was Northrop Grumman. To reenter this market, after having been nearly eliminated from it, Northrop Grumman acquired Teledyne Ryan. Thus, Northrop Grumman again became a dominant player in the UAV business.

Financial Marketplace Conditions

Purely financial marketplace conditions may drive companies down the merger and acquisition path. Companies looking to achieve long-term (5 to 10 years) high rates of return may target other companies for acquisition when their analysis indicates that they can achieve significant growth in value at the end of this period. This is particularly true when other investment opportunities offer much smaller potential for returns on investment. For example, during periods of low interest rates, the cost of money is low, thus making the option of leveraging capital for acquisitions much more attractive.

When an acquisition is made solely for financial objectives as opposed to longer term strategic marketplace objectives, often the intent is not to integrate the acquired company into the acquiring company but rather leave it as a stand-alone company. The objective is to improve the cash flow of the acquired company, thereby increasing its total market value. Once the target financial objectives are achieved, the stand-alone company is often divested.

Consolidation

When companies consolidate, they are implementing a strategy to bring together companies in similar businesses but possibly from a wider geographical area. The focus is to achieve greater brand recognition in a broader marketplace along with improved operational efficiencies. Brand recognition means having the company name or brand become more recognizable with a product and thus a more powerful marketing tool. Brand recognition helps a company develop consumer brand loyalty. For example, consider a common household product, the facial tissue. Think about this product in terms of how you identify or refer to it. Do you call it *facial tissue*, or do you find yourself, like many others, referring to it as *Kleenex*? Kleenex is a brand name; facial tissue is the product. Another example is the Xerox corporation. Often people will not ask others to make copies of documents but to "Xerox" copies for them. These examples illustrate the power of a brand name when it becomes interchangeable or synonymous with a product.

Furthermore, operational efficiencies are expected to come from capitalizing on synergies when two different companies come together as one. Synergies are achieved when companies bring different strengths together, enabling them to improve or eliminate their individual weaknesses and maximize their strengths. The synergistic effect of bringing two companies together allows them to achieve that which neither could achieve independently. Combining strengths helps position newly created companies to better achieve improved operational performance. The elimination of redundant systems and the adoption of best practices and processes help the original companies transform into a new, more competitive company.

> *The American Heritage Dictionary of the English Language* defines synergism as the following: The action of two or more substances, organs, or organisms to achieve an effect of which each is individually incapable.

External Investment Alternative to Internal Growth

When companies recognize that the cost of internally growing their business exceeds the cost of achieving growth through the acquisition of other companies, they often turn to acquisitions. After all, achieving growth in a cost-effective way is the desired outcome. It is even more desirable when it can be accomplished swiftly. Growth through acquisition is a swift process compared with developing growth from within. When markets are shrinking and economic conditions stifle market expansion, to achieve real growth in the marketplace a company may only have the option of acquisition.[5] It may be difficult or impossible to achieve growth any other way.

Divestment of Non-Core Businesses

Companies change their strategic direction and objectives for a variety of reasons. Changes occurring within the marketplace may cause a company to change its strategic direction. The development of new technologies or the maturing of old technologies and products may also lead a company to change its strategy.

During the late 1980s and early 1990s, as a result of an industry downturn and cuts in government spending, many government contractors doing most of their business with U. S. government agencies explored developing commercial products for commercial markets. Using technology developed for their government customers' products, these companies now sought commercial applications for their technologies. This was an attempt to exploit their existing capabilities and technologies and expand business opportunities into new markets. Most believed if they were to achieve any growth at all, this transition was necessary as the traditional markets for their core capabilities and technologies were contracting.

---

[5] Copeland, Tom; Koller, Tim; Murrin, Jack. "Valuation, Measuring and Managing the Value of Companies," McKinsey & Company, Inc., New York, John Wiley & Sons, 1995.

Their efforts were met with limited success. Ultimately, many of the aerospace companies divested themselves of these newly formed business units.

The companies discovered they were unable to successfully operate within commercial markets. Their ability to efficiently develop products and services for commercial markets just was not there. Essentially, the commercial business ventures were not part of their business set of core competencies and expertise. For many companies, it turned out to be a costly lesson, causing them to migrate away from commercial expansion and back to their areas of expertise.

One of the major problems of expanding into new markets is the lack of knowledge about how these markets operate. Commercial markets are very different from government markets. Perhaps the best approach a company can take when seeking to expand into new and unfamiliar markets is to develop an alliance with a company already well established in the desired market. The market expertise offered by a partner or an alliance, coupled with new or advanced technologies that have great potential for application within that market, may create the synergy needed to benefit both companies.

WHAT COMPANIES EXPECT TO ACHIEVE WITH MERGERS AND ACQUISITIONS

In a strategic merger or acquisition, a company attempts to position or change itself to be more competitive in its future marketplace. Purchasing another company or companies in related businesses, where the chance of achieving economic synergies is high, is usually the chosen path. The primary objective of strategic mergers and acquisitions is to achieve a competitive advantage for the future by aligning a company in such a way so that its strategic capabilities are consistent with the future anticipated performances and expectations of the marketplace. In other words, a company anticipates what the future marketplace will be like and then shapes itself to operate effectively and efficiently within that marketplace.

Mergers and acquisitions are methods by which companies can pursue business strategies designed to enhance their future capabilities and grow revenue and/or market share. They are a strategic option when a company can't develop new growth, revenue, or capabilities from within, or the cost of doing so is not practical. Mergers and acquisitions have the potential of adding value to companies, in many ways enabling them to accomplish strategic moves such as the following:

- Attain greater market-share and/or reach new markets. Reaching new markets may include expanding the business into international markets thus adding new geographical capabilities

- Create new synergies such as enriching the existing company talent pool with new talent from the acquired or merged company
- Capitalize on efficiencies through economies of scale
- Diversify the existing product line by acquiring additional brands and/or complementary or competitive products

It may also help realize improved company infrastructure:

- Through acquisition of new technology
- With the selection and implementation of best practices, business systems, and processes
- Through the expansion of knowledge capital (Knowledge capital is the knowledge and experience possessed by employees.)
- By capturing and protecting existing intellectual property that includes patents, trademarks, copyrights, and proprietary processes and knowledge
- By expanding distribution channels that may provide a competitive edge, as established distribution capabilities and channels may assist a company in reaching new markets, growing its share within the current marketplace, and help drive down its cost. Use of an acquisition process allows for the immediate use of a capability that otherwise could take years to develop.
- Integrating management experience: This is particularly important to buyers who plan to leave the acquired company as a stand-alone operating business unit. If there is no intention to integrate the acquired company into the acquiring company, having a skilled and experienced management team in place is critical. If such a team does not exist, the acquiring company must provide one. To achieve this goal, talent from the acquiring company must be diverted to the management of the acquired company. There are two problems with this approach: (1) The management team from the acquiring company may not have the necessary understanding of the operations of the newly acquired company to be effective immediately, thereby reducing the opportunities for immediate cost reductions; and (2) outside management experts and consultants may need to be hired to support the management of the new entity.

WHY MERGERS AND ACQUISITIONS FAIL

As discussed in the preceding paragraphs, there are many reasons why companies pursue the path of mergers and acquisitions . In all cases, they include the objective of adding value to the acquiring company or the merging companies. That value benefits the company owners and stakeholders. Mergers and acquisitions are carefully chosen strategic actions undertaken to enhance the capabilities of a company with the intent of improving immediate or long-term profitability. Mergers and acquisitions are obviously never done to reduce value, increase costs, or decrease profits.

As counterintuitive as this may seem, sometimes it is what actually occurs. Even the best-planned efforts sometimes fail. It is difficult to plan and execute a successful acquisition or merger. Each transaction has many unknown conditions. Regardless of how much analysis goes in to the evaluation of the deal, future conditions always remain unknown. The following addresses some of the more significant reasons why mergers and acquisitions fail:

Bad Management and Personality Problems at the Senior Level

Much energy is often expended preparing for the deal. Executives expend considerable time and effort working to successfully plan the merger or acquisition, taking it up to the closing of the deal. Some of this energy is negative. During the acquisition process, management teams don't always agree on strategy or tactics. Disagreements ensue and animosity can develop. If this condition is not properly managed early in the process, it could develop into an obstacle later during the integration phase. It may also create a situation in which more attention and effort are spent on dealing with these problems and conflict than is spent on the successful integration of the two companies or working to develop a new company culture. The merger or acquisition cannot be successful until the integration of the acquired company is complete. Conflict among the management team may inhibit its ability to properly perform the integration effort. Until full integration is accomplished, the maximum value of the merger will not be realized.

Inability to Successfully Integrate the Newly Acquired Business Unit into the Acquiring Company

Once an acquisition or merger is completed, the integration of the new business unit into the acquiring company must be accomplished swiftly and completely. Failure to do this will affect the management team's ability to achieve cost reductions in the short and long run. Failing to move quickly to integrate the two companies into a new company will limit all early gains or successes. Furthermore, and just as problematic, acquiring another company and then leaving it to continue on its own denies both parties the advantage of eliminating redundancies, creating synergies, and ultimately attaining maximum value from the merger or acquisition.

How does one know if and when the integration of both companies into one is a success? The only effective method to assess performance is to measure. Remember the old adage, what gets measured, gets done. The acquisition team must establish early on the criterion for success. How will the elements of success be defined? Once established, the team must develop an appropriate set of metrics to measure progress and success; as well as monitor them throughout the process.

Reviewing metrics as the integration progresses will provide regular indicators on how successful the team is in working toward its goals. Moreover, knowing about a problem or issue early in the process allows for corrective action before the problem becomes too serious. When developing meaningful metrics to assess success, one that may be useful in helping to assess the long-term progress is the measurement of output per employee, that is, how productive were employees before the merger or acquisition, and how productive are they after the two companies integrate to form a new company?

Remember that as a security manager of the newly formed or acquiring company, the responsibilities of assets protection and ensuring the security of the merger or acquisition is not the only job that must be successfully accomplished. There is also the responsibility, like all other managers in the company, to ensure the total integration of security staff, elimination of redundancies, implementation of best practices, and increasing the productivity of the "new" security organization.

Overestimation of Synergies

A miscalculation of the ability to capitalize on synergies and eliminate redundancies will negatively impede the achievement of expected or established goals and objectives. Miscalculations generally fall into the overly optimistic category as opposed to being understated. Acquisition teams can easily get caught up in the euphoria or energy of making the deal and make an overly optimistic assessment of the potential benefits of the merger or acquisition. They may overestimate the gains they expect to achieve by capitalizing on synergies and eliminating redundancies. When this happens, expectations are difficult to achieve as optimism slams right into reality.

Combining two companies always creates opportunities to benefit from combined strengths and to eliminate redundancies. Part of the value of any merger or acquisition is assessed on this expectation. But when the expected gains are misstated, achieving them becomes difficult, if not impossible. Recent studies indicate that approximately 50% of all mergers failed to produce the synergistic benefits that were expected of them.[6] This failure can be attributed to many reasons: lack of leadership, poor communications, cultural differences, and over-estimation of synergies.

Paying Too Much

During the valuation phase of the merger or acquisition effort, an overly optimistic estimate of future earnings potential is made. This is easy to do. When the target company is highly desired, management may let its desires influence their analysis, thus presenting an overly optimistic assessment of future earnings potential and the total value of the target company. This is a case of wanting it so badly that you are willing to do anything to make it happen, including paying too much. Paying too much may also occur when one company worries that one of its competitors may successfully outbid it for an acquisition. Fearing the worst situation, losing the deal that may cause a loss of market-share instead of a potential gain, a company may willingly overbid, thereby not just acquiring the target company but also preventing a competitor from acquiring that company.

Achieving accurate valuation of a target company is exceptionally difficult. Valuation is a subjective science and subject to the changes in supply and demand. The complexities of valuing a target company can confound and even intimidate the inexperienced executive. An inadequate valuation can lead to overpaying or underselling. Depending on how much is overpaid or to what extent a company is undersold, the deal has the potential of being a disaster. Furthermore, the company being acquired may also try to overestimate its value (e.g., value of its assets to increase the purchase price of the company being acquired and not coincidentally, increase the buy-out money to be paid to the executives being bought out!) In today's business world, one must remember that sometimes it is not the good of the company that the management executives have in mind but what they can personally get out of it.

You may also have seen that when companies are bidding on other companies, the stock price of the bidding companies goes down. This often occurs because the stockholders or potential stockholders of one or both of the companies do not believe that it is a worthwhile endeavor. You may also have seen that when a merger or acquisition deal has not occurred as planned, stock prices of one or both of the companies goes up. Sometimes, the stock market is more objective and realistic than the management teams of one or both of the companies involved in the merger or acquisition.

---

[6] See http://thesius.emeraldinsight.com/vl=11924345/cl=33/nw=1/rpsv/cgi-bin/mfirst.pl?viewpoint=30

Cultural Differences

Global research shows that four of five mergers or acquisitions fail to meet their objectives.[7] This does not necessarily mean the merger or acquisition was a complete failure. It does mean that the merger or acquisition did not achieve planned objectives, and therefore less than expected value was created. In the United States, two of three acquisitions are likely to be sold within five years.[8] Cultural integration is a major factor in these failures. Bringing two different companies together, each with its own distinct culture, calls for the creation of a new culture. The intent should be to maximize the strengths from each of the heritage company cultures and minimize the limitations. This process must take into consideration the desired culture of the new company.

What culture does the organization's leadership want to develop? Company leadership should have a clear idea of the desired new culture it hopes to create. That message should be communicated to all employees and a plan created to develop that culture. The message employees need to hear and understand is that they are no longer the company they were before the merger or acquisition but are now part of a new enterprise with a different vision and strategy. It is not business as usual anymore. Change is the new order. The old companies are gone and a new company has been formed. How it moves forward, what its values are, and management's expectations of all employees need to be clearly communicated by senior management to all employees early and often. Failure of the acquiring company to establish a plan for a new culture and the failure of the acquired company to accept and recognize this necessary condition will at best inhibit full integration, thereby delaying cost reductions and savings and potentially creating culture clashes. At worst, it will lead to a failed merger.

Corporate Identity

Creating a new identity for the new company is essential. When two companies merge, to some varied extent (depending on many factors) they become a new company. This change needs to be recognized and accepted by all employees, from senior management to the rank-and-file employees. Company leadership must establish the new identity and foster its development. That action is a significant and necessary step toward full and successful integration. Failure to recognize the need for shaping a new identity ignores the importance of acknowledging a new company identity and

---

[7] See http://www.corporatetrends.com.au/pmachine/comments.php?id=189_0_1_0M19
[8] See http://www.corporatetrends.com.au/pmachine/comments.php?id=189_0_1_0_M19

culture. On its own, a new identity will probably develop over time, but will it be what was envisioned by management? If not, is it better or worse than what was envisioned? The answers to these questions may indicate whether the merger or acquisition was a success or failure, or something in between.

In the earliest stages of integrating the two companies, leadership has the best opportunity to shape a new identity into one it desires. It then must nurture the new identity into existence. Failure to do this leaves in place multiple identities operating separately and, perhaps, even in conflict. This conflict can directly and negatively affect employee morale and job satisfaction.[9] Failure to integrate into a single identity creates a condition of segregation within the company as elements of the company hold onto their earlier and separate identity. Eventually, as stated earlier, a new company identity will develop on its own; however, it may not be the identity desired by the leadership or stakeholders.

Corporate Communications and Trust

An essential component of successful integration of one company into another is trust. The senior management of the acquiring company must gain the trust of all employees, particularly those employees who were part of the acquired company. Perhaps the best way to accomplish this goal is through open, frequent, and honest communications. Communications that is shaped and properly directed by company leadership is essential. Moreover, communication needs to flow up, down, and across the company hierarchy. Questions, concerns, and issues raised by the rank-and-file need to be heard and answered by management and leadership.

To be effective, communication should be made through many mediums such as corporate announcements, communications sessions or forums with large groups of employees (the corporate equivalent of town hall sessions), and smaller chat sessions reinforced by frequent messages. In addition, it may be useful for the training department to create a special class or workshop, one for management and one for non-management employees, that provides information not only about the new company being formed and their part in it but also what is expected of them as this integration takes place.

To be most effective, this process is long term and ongoing. Too often companies focus on short-term priorities such as financial issues, and they neglect such issues as corporate identity, culture, and open communications. These issues have a great impact—probably the primary driving

---

[9] See http://gessler.emeraldinsight.com/v1=18519227/cl=43/nw=1/rpsv/cgi-bin/mfirst.pl?viewp

impact—on the financial success of the newly-formed company and, ironically, are not given as much attention as the financial issues. Remember, it is the employees who get things done and financial matters are only one indication of their productivity.

Technology Problems

When two different companies come together, each brings with it its own operating infrastructure. If the infrastructures—primarily information systems infrastructures—are similar or compatible, then the problem may only be a connectivity challenge. When the infrastructures are significantly different, the problem becomes an integration nightmare. For example, imagine two companies merging together with two completely different financial information systems. As a new company, they only need one. How do they get from two systems to one system? Can they be effectively connected? If not, can one system be selected as the system of choice and all business units make the transition to that system? Transitioning from one major system to another is costly. These costs lie not only in hardware, software, training, and experience, but also with the performance and cultural issues associated with any major change. There will be those who resist change and impede the efficient transition to any new system. This creates delays and unnecessary additional costs.

MERGERS AND ACQUISITIONS: A HISTORY

Mergers and acquisitions are not a new phenomenon in business. During the last century they occurred with great frequency. These occurrences were generally grouped into well-defined periods representing different trends and market conditions.

During the later portion of the nineteenth century and the very early part of the twentieth century, a wave of mergers and acquisitions occurred. Approximately 3,000 U. S. companies disappeared as a result of this activity. Since this was the Industrial Age, most activity occurred within heavy industries such as petroleum, chemical, transportation, metals, and various heavy machinery industries. Significant factors driving these events were the following:

- Technological developments in transportation, with the emergence of transcontinental railroads shifting the mode of transportation for goods to rail
- The expanding use of electricity as a source of inexpensive power
- Innovations in production processes (e.g., Ford Motor Company's car assembly line)

- Rapid national economic expansion
- Lax antitrust enforcement

In the United States, this period saw companies engaging in mergers or acquisitions to position themselves as monopolies within their respective industry. In reality, many mergers failed, as they were unable to achieve the necessary improvements in efficiency and reductions in operating costs. Other factors contributed to the high rate of failure. An economic recession in 1903 followed by a stock market crash in 1904 created a difficult environment for businesses to succeed. Furthermore, the U. S. Supreme Court ruled that the Sherman Act, which passed Congress in 1890, could be used to attack anticompetitive mergers. This decision led to the break-up of large companies, (e.g., Standard Oil Company in 1911). Additional factors contributing to the economic conditions of the period were poor social conditions. There existed a great separation between the few very rich and the many very poor; added to this were conditions of extensive poverty leading to disruptions within the entire social structure.

The next wave of mergers and acquisitions occurred in the United States after World War I. Between 1926 and 1930 alone, more than 4,500 mergers occurred. During this period, there were continued technological developments:

- The railroads continued to expand.
- Motor vehicle transportation was rapidly expanding.
- Technology producing the radio was developed, improving communications and the ability of companies to advertise their brands.
- Economies of scale were achieved.
- Airplane passenger and cargo travel were becoming more popular.
- A lax regulatory environment existed as the encouragement of companies to work together during World War I continued into the early 1920s.

Unlike the prior period of mergers and acquisitions, this trend was not toward the establishment of monopolies but toward the establishment of oligopolies. This period came to an end in 1929 as the United States stock market crashed and the Great Depression began in the United States. Some of what followed led to new legislation designed to prevent market manipulation, provide greater financial controls, and create the Federal Securities and Exchange Commission.

Over the next 30 years, mergers and acquisitions activities slowed significantly. Much of this was due to the war efforts during the 1940s and 1950s. Furthermore, changes in antitrust laws strengthened the U.S. governments' ability to block mergers and acquisitions.

The next wave of mergers and acquisitions occurred during the mid- to late 1960s. Here the focus was on conglomerate (a collection of unrelated companies) mergers. As a result of enforcement of antitrust laws, companies sought to diversify their holdings. Gone was the pursuit of monopolies or oligopolies. Most of this activity was equity financed and investment banks did not play a key role. This merger trend was driven by the following factors:

- Booming economy
- Rising stock prices in a booming market
- High interest rates
- New financial structures
- Tough antitrust enforcement preventing monopolies
- Wall Street looking for growth

An example of acquisitions for the purpose of becoming a conglomerate was International Telephone and Telegraph (ITT). Between 1959 and 1969, ITT made 350 acquisitions in 80 countries. By 1969, their conglomerate portfolio included the following diverse companies:

- Avis Rent-A-Car
- Sheraton Hotels
- Continental Banking
- Aetna Finance
- Hartford Insurance
- Levitt & Sons

As with prior mergers and acquisition trends, problems developed with conglomerates. They did not perform as expected. Moreover, the market saw through the new financial structures that were to some degree just sophisticated financial manipulations. Another problem was the inability of companies to manage these acquisitions. With all of the mergers and acquisitions of this period, the most active industry was the aerospace industry. This activity would again occur in the late 1980s and 1990s. Industrial machinery, auto parts, railway equipment, textiles, and tobacco were also very active.

In 1968, the U. S. Attorney General announced plans to crackdown on conglomerates. Along with new legislation (Williams Act and Tax Reform Act) and poor performance of these companies, this wave of mergers and acquisitions had nearly ended. Mergers and acquisitions slowed down in the 1970s; however, some important trends developed during this time.

One study showed that roughly 60% of the cross-industry mergers and acquisitions that occurred between 1970 and 1982 were divested by 1989.[10] This clearly suggests that the success of these mergers and acquisitions was quite limited.

---

[10] See http://www.mergerforum.com

The next wave of mergers and acquisitions occurred in the early 1980s. The conditions that launched this new wave of mergers and acquisitions were similar to those conditions that existed during previous periods. Again, we see an expanding economy as a primary driver. Economic conditions were good and the economy was growing. Inflation was high, which translated to high asset values.

Technological developments also contributed to this wave of mergers and acquisitions just as they did during the first part of the century. Deregulation, financial innovations, and the failure of conglomerates all contributed to the new wave of mergers and acquisitions. None of these factors were really new, as all played a role in prior waves of mergers and acquisitions. What was different about this wave was the sheer size and prominence of the acquisition targets.

Early in the decade, oil and gas industries were dominant in merger and acquisition business strategy. Later in the decade this trend changed, and pharmaceuticals, airlines, and banking dominated. This new period of mergers and acquisitions was also influenced by global competition. Foreign takeovers became common, as did hostile takeovers. Corporate raiders, arbitrageurs, investment banks, and law firms all became active during this period. Investment bankers played an important role here because unlike the 1960s, when equity was used to finance mergers and acquisitions, this wave saw the heavy use of debt incurred to pay for acquisitions.

Much of this debt was in the form of junk bonds, which became an important financial tool in the 1980s. They were used to finance company growth and then to finance takeovers. Companies used junk bonds as a tool when other financial means were not readily available. Moreover, Wall Street was less adverse to the pitfalls of junk bonds. Many of these deals were complicated and required involvement of legal expertise, which was more common during this period than in other periods of mergers and acquisitions.

This "party" started to come to an end in 1987 with the crash of the stock market. This condition was followed by the collapse of the junk bond market. In 1989, Michael Milken, a well-known junk bond trader, was indicted; and his company, Drexel Burnham Lamert, filed for bankruptcy the next year. These conditions again caused the U. S. Congress to enact legislation intended to change the regulations governing mergers and acquisitions and their enabling conditions. In 1989, the Financial Institutions Reform, Recover, and Enforcement Act was passed. Moreover, many of the states of the United States now got into the act with their own anti-takeover legislation. And, as if this was not enough to dampen the merger and acquisition activity, along came the Gulf War.

It did not take long for mergers and acquisition activity to begin again. In 1992, shortly after the Gulf War, the economy began to expand again. Rising stock prices, technological developments, continued globalization, and new deregulation all contributed to the next wave of mergers and acquisitions, which differed from the previous period. The new mergers and acquisitions were financed more often with equity than with debt, much like that of the 1960s. Moreover, the emphasis was placed on longer term strategies than had been the prior practice. Short-term or immediate financial gains did not dominate. What was much the same though was the continuation of mergers and acquisitions in the banking and telecommunications sectors.

The 1990s saw the reemergence of mergers and acquisitions fuelled by a booming stock market and an effort to consolidate major industries such as telecommunications, banking, and health care. Banking was particularly active. During the decades of the 1980s and 1990s, the U. S. banking industry experienced a never-before-seen period of sustained merger activity. This activity led to a large decline in the actual number of banks and banking organizations.[11] However, an increase in the number of banking offices and the number of automated teller machines (ATM) occurred. There was also a greater concentration of bank deposits among the larger banks.

If this activity increases the cost of banking for consumers, we could see a public policy remedy driving divestitures to increase competition. Until that time, bank mergers and acquisitions appear to be alive and well. In October 2003, the Bank of America announced a $47 billion acquisition of FleetBoston Financial. This combination made Bank of America the second largest bank in the United States (in terms of assets), just behind Citigroup. It also gave Bank of America the largest number of retail outlets in the United States.[12] This event sparked a new round of takeover speculation, recalling the merger mania that swept through the industry five years earlier.[13] In 1998, there were three major banking deals:

- Citicorp and Travelers merged to form Citigroup
- Bank One acquired First Chicago NBD and
- Bank of America and NationsBank combined.

Shortly thereafter, Wells Fargo and Norwest agreed to a deal. It appears that the Bank of America and FleetBoston acquisition could mark the start of another round of mergers and acquisitions. It is expected that several more deals will be announced in the coming years, but expectations for similar investment opportunities and profits seem to be more subdued. Bank stocks are currently trading at a much lower earnings ratio than they did during the 1998 period that was considered far too high.[14]

---

[11] See http//ideas.repec.org/p/fip/fedgss/174.html
[12] See http://money.cnn.com/2003/10/27/news/companies/ba_fleet/index.htm
[13] CNN/Money (October 27, 2003) (Paul R. La Monica) "Bank Merger Mania Is Back"
[14] See http://money.cnn.com/2003/10/27/markets/banks/index.htm?

FOCUS ON MERGERS AND ACQUISITIONS DURING THE 1990s

The 1990s has been referred to as the decade of the customer. It was also the decade when companies focused on "increasing shareholder value." Thus, many chief executive officers shifted their focus to operational and financial performance. Mergers and acquisitions provided another business tool for the company executives to use in this effort.

From the end of the 1990s and into the early 2000s, the economic downturn and the bursting of the "dot-com" bubble contributed to the slowdown of the mergers and acquisitions wave. By 2003, this trend began to change. With companies hedging their bets on an economic turnaround and stocks still cheap, mergers and acquisitions suddenly picked up steam. Auto parts maker Arvin Merito got the ball rolling with its unsolicited $2.2 billion tender offer for Dana Corporation.[15] This offer was followed by many other deals ranging from the $600 million purchase of Nautica Enterprises by apparel maker VF Corporation to the $3.91 billion hostile takeover offer for France's Pechiney SA by Canadian aluminum maker Alcan. In July 2003 alone, nearly $26 billion of mergers were announced.

Mergers and acquisitions activities are again occurring in many industries. Real estate mega-brokers are experiencing such activity. According to Stefan Swanepoel, Chairman and CEO of RealtyU, industry consolidation through merger and acquisition ". . . peaked in 2002, but it is very likely to continue beyond 2003, albeit, at a somewhat slower pace.[16] Furthermore, in a recent white paper, "Real Estate Confronts Profitability," co-authors Swanepoel and John Tucillo suggest the next three to five years will have a significant impact on the stand-alone residential real estate company, perhaps leading to its demise.

NEW YORK—Carnival Corp. (CCL), *the world's biggest cruise group, on Friday said quarterly earnings rose sharply, citing the merger with P&O Princess Cruises* (search) *last year.*[17]

Over the last three years, the number of mergers and acquisitions slowed significantly from a high in 1999; however, that trend appears to be reversing itself. A 2002 survey conducted by Rutgers University School of Business reported that within companies with annual revenue between $5 million and $100 million (middle market companies), 39% of the owners expected to see their companies sold or merged within the next three years. This is particularly significant, as there are about 300,000 middle market

---

[15] *Wall Street Journal* (07/09/03) P. C1 (Sidel, Robin) "Merger Activity Sizzles Again"
[16] http://www.rismedia.com/index.php/articleview/3361/1/345/
[17] http://www.foxnews.com/printer_friendly_story/0,3566,132739,00.html

companies in the United States alone accounting for close to one third of all U.S. employment.[18] Table 1-1 reinforces this trend, as it shows that between July 2001 and July 2002, there were more than 3,000 companies sold within 48 different industries within the middle market alone. During this period, General Electric had been one of the busiest companies in this market. Between July 2000 and July 2002, GE reported 40 acquisitions.[19]

Table 1-1   Transactions Completed in 12 Months Ending July 2002: Estimated Deals <$100Million

Industry	Deal Count	Industry	Deal Count
Aerospace & Defense	33	Health Services	154
Agricultural Production	16	Household Goods	36
Apparel	16	Industrial & Farm	113
Automotive Products	37	Equipment & Machinery	
Auto & Trucks	10	Instruments & Photographic	112
Banking and Finance	267	Equipment	
Beverages	36	Insurance	239
Broadcasting	84	Leisure & Entertainment	218
Brokerage, Investments	389	Mining & Minerals	35
& Consulting		Miscellaneous Manufacturing	28
Building Products	3	Miscellaneous Services	697
Chemicals, Paints	97	Office Equipment &	72
& Coatings		Computer Hardware	
Communications	225	Oil & Gas	90
Computer Software,	1225	Package & Containers	12
Supplies and Services		Paper	34
Construction Contractors &	162	Plastics & Rubber	55
Engineering Services		Primary Metal Processing	71
Construction, Mining &	21	Printing & Publishing	168
Oil Equipment		Real Estate	82
Drugs, Medical Supplies	205	Retail	227
& Equipment		Stone, Clay & Glass	39
Electric, Gas, Water	134	Textiles	18
& Sanitary Services		Timber & Forest Products	14
Electric Equipment	162	Toiletries & Cosmetics	13
Electronics	110	Toys 7 Recreational Products	34
Energy Services	41	Transportation	73
Fabricated Metal Products	74	Valves, Pumps & Hydraulics	13
Food Processing	89	Wholesale & Distribution	270
Furniture	13		

Source: Cherry Tree: www.cherrytree.com Middle Market Mergers & Acquisitions, Outlook Report, Research Report September 2002.

---

[18] Cherry Tree, September 2002. Middle Market Mergers and acquisitions. Outlook report.
[19] Cherry Tree, September 2002. Middle Market Mergers and acquisitions. Outlook report.

During the ten-year period from 1990 to 1999, mergers and acquisitions steadily grew. According to Thomson Financial Securities Data Co., mergers, acquisitions, and divestitures priced at $5 million or more, as well as purchases of partial interest that involved at lease a 40% stake in the target company or an investment of at least $100 million, increased from a value of $206.5 billion in 1990 to $1393.9 billion in 1999. (See Table 1-2.)

The 1990s, especially 1994 to 1998, was a period of numerous large bank mergers, including a few that were among the largest mergers in U. S. history; however, mergers and acquisitions were also happening on a global scale.

PUBLIC CRITICISM OF MERGERS AND ACQUISITIONS AND MARKET-DRIVEN CORPORATE GOVERNANCE

Not everyone is enamored with mergers and acquisitions and market-driven controls. Public opinion does not hold the same favorable perspective as much of the leadership of corporate management, regardless of its global locations. In particular, corporate raiders receive much of the public's attention and concern. They are viewed as using their control to strip assets from acquired companies for the purpose of quick profits while destroying the company in the process and putting people out of work.

Much of the public resentment is directed toward corporate raiders and sympathy toward displaced workers who the public sees as entitled to

Table 1-2 10-Year Merger Completion Record: 1990–1999[20]				
Year	Number of Deals	% Change	Value ($Billion)	%Change
1990	4,324	—	206.5	—
1991	3,621	−16.3	140.6	−31.9
1992	3,778	4.3	125.1	−11.0
1993	4,193	11.0	177.6	42.0
1994	5,060	20.1	277.9	56.5
1995	6,427	27.0	388.5	39.8
1996	7,333	14.1	562.6	44.8
1997	8,525	16.3	778.9	38.4
1998	10,092	18.4	1,342.8	72.4
1999	8,695	−13.9	1,393.9	3.8

Source: Thomson Financial Securities Data.

---

[20] See http://www.findarticles.com/cf_dls/m6402/2_35/60599708/p1/article.jhtml

a greater say in the decision-making process. The workers (the real producers of products and services) are not seen as the great benefactors of mergers and acquisitions. Consequently, they receive much public sympathy and support. Mergers and acquisitions are generally viewed as destroying value and damaging the morale and productivity of workers.

Markets are viewed by the general public as shortsighted and only interested in short-term financial gains as opposed to long-term growth. Companies' executive management are seen as willing to leverage companies to dangerous levels of debt while protecting themselves with "golden parachutes" (millions of dollars of a company's money paid to them when they leave a company, even if fired). These actions create the perception of all company management executives enriching themselves on the backs of workers. In general, the public maintains a somewhat harsh view of mergers, acquisitions, and market-driven governance exercised by companies' executive management.

Needless to say, corporate leadership and the investment community (Wall Street) don't hold a similar view. Markets are viewed by corporate leadership as fairly efficient, properly valuing firms based on performance that includes rewarding higher levels of research and development investment and cautiously evaluating or avoiding high levels of debt. The investment community has the direct opportunity to express its pleasure or displeasure through decisions to invest.

SUMMARY

It is imperative that today's security professionals understand the reality of the new, global marketplace and some of its major components: mergers, acquisitions, and divestitures. This is necessary if the security professional is to be a key contributor to the success of such actions.Generally there are two types of mergers and acquisitions:

- Acquisition of an entire company by another
- Acquisition of a portion of another company such as a product line, business unit, or technological capability

Mergers and acquisitions occur for many reasons. In all cases, each company believes the transaction will benefit its owners and shareholders.

During the last 100 years, there have been four periods of major mergers and acquisitions activities. Each was driven by many of the same conditions:

- Strong economy
- Technological change such as improvements in transportation and infrastructure

- Less or changing emphasis on government regulation
- Need to generate growth or new market share through external means when internal growth is too difficult.

Despite the large number of mergers and acquisitions, more than half are unsuccessful, failing to achieve the anticipated or planned results. Yet they continue to occur. They can fail for a variety of reasons:

- The acquiring company does not properly assess the value of the target company
- Inability of the acquiring company to successfully integrate the target company that leads to a failed acquisition

In any event, mergers and acquisitions appear to be a high-stakes game that is here to stay. The security professionals must understand this "game," and, like it or not, they are and will continue to be a "player" in the mergers and acquisitions game. After all, it is the working environment of all security professionals who are employed by companies in the global marketplace today and into the future, regardless of the part of the global marketplace where they live and work.

Chapter 2

The Current Global Business Environment: Is It Merger and Acquisition Friendly?

Globalization has served to undermine the role of the nation-state as the sole determinant of a society's well-being.—Henry Kissinger[1]

INTRODUCTION

This chapter addresses the global business climate within which mergers and acquisitions occur, particularly in the United States, Europe, and Asia, where most of the world's mergers and acquisitions take place. It also addresses how the current business environment compares with the recent past, what trends are developing, and suggests what may be expected in the near future in terms of mergers and acquisitions activity.

Understanding the current trends in mergers and acquisitions and learning the lessons of the past are useful to security professionals as they support and protect these efforts. Knowing what to expect is useful when planning for and supporting these often fast-paced activities. In this environment, any advantage is welcome and, in fact, is aggressively sought.

THE GLOBAL ECONOMY AND BUSINESS ENVIRONMENT

Many factors contribute to the overall condition of the United States and the global economy. These factors range from routine changes in normal business cycle conditions to the confidence of investors and consumers. Levels of personal savings, the growth of foreign economies, and government policy all have an impact on the national and global economic

---

[1] Kissinger, Henry, *Does America Need a Foreign Policy? Toward a Diplomacy for the 21st Century.* New York, Simon & Schuster, 2001.

conditions that we experience in our daily lives. This is no different for businesses. They too are obviously impacted by the national and global economic conditions. Economic conditions influence the strategic decisions and plans made by successful and unsuccessful companies alike.

National and global economic conditions are also affected by geopolitical activities. Conditions and uncertainties such as the current war on terrorism, the recent war in Iraq, and the effort to transform Afghanistan and Iraq from oppressed societies to free political and economic states all have an impact on economic conditions. One only has to look at the fluctuations in the cost of a barrel of oil to see that. Even lesser events like the many regional conflicts occurring throughout the world, such as the conflict between the Israelis and Palestinians, can and do have an impact on a national and even global economy. The political unrest in Haiti not only affects the Haitian economy and its social stability but also had an immediate negative impact on the surrounding Caribbean countries.

War, terrorism, and political unrest are not unique in having an effect on national or global economic conditions. Health concerns also have the potential for adversely affecting global economic activity. The recent outbreak of severe acute respiratory syndrome (SARS) in 2003 had an immediate and severe impact on the geographic regions affected. International business activities, along with tourism and personal travel to parts of Asia and Canada, experienced an immediate and adverse economic impact. Not until the SARS outbreak was under control and many businesses lost large amounts of revenue did economic conditions return to a normal state. However, with every new case of SARS or even a possible SARS case, these negative economic effects are immediately felt. For example, if a business team is about to travel to Asia (e.g., China) to finalize some mergers or acquisitions activities, that trip is immediately put on hold indefinitely until the "all clear" is sounded when the business team is again safe to travel to meet with the other company's representatives. Such unplanned events can cause major disruptions and thus possible loss of revenue as the mergers or acquisitions are held in temporary limbo.

Another example of health concerns affecting the economy occurred recently in the United Kingdom and North America with the discovery of mad cow disease in Canada and the United States. Even without government action to restrict or ban imports and exports of beef, consumer reaction to the potential danger immediately threatened to curtail trade in the beef industry. Several years ago, European countries stopped importing beef from the United Kingdom when it experienced an outbreak of mad cow disease. The resulting losses were devastating to the United Kingdom's beef industry. The ripple effects reverberated throughout the overall economy of Great Britain.

Suppose discussions were being held regarding merger or acquisition between two meatpacking companies. You can imagine the impact a mad cow disease outbreak would have on such talks, especially if one of the companies involved in the discussion had discovered mad cow disease at one of its plants.

Globalization, according to the American Heritage Dictionary, *is the act, process, or policy of making something worldwide in scope or application.*

Doing business in today's economic environment can be tricky indeed. Globalization of business means that any company may be affected by distant and seemingly unrelated economic conditions. Does the cost of labor in China affect the price of jeans in the United States? How does the strategic sourcing of computer programming from a company in the United States to a company in India affect union membership in the United States? The actions of government leaders, company executives, investors, and consumers all have an impact on global economic conditions. Their decisions and choices are also affected by those same conditions.

How Has the Global Economy Been Doing Recently?

After growth of less than 2% in 2001 and 2002[2], the global economy began to gain momentum in 2003. Significant increases in economic activity occurred within the last half of 2003 led primarily by the United States' economy but also with an important contribution from China, Japan, and much of East Asia. After nearly a decade of stagnation, Japan's economy has begun to experience a recovery. Its economy has shown improvements in corporate profits along with increased exports, industrial activity, and improvements in the stock market.

The developing trend of improving economic activity in 2003 extended far beyond North America and Asia. Even some of the significant economic difficulties facing Latin American countries seemed to lessen, which helped to improve the overall global outlook for economic growth. Western Europe, particularly France, Germany, and the United Kingdom, lagging behind in its economic recovery, started to show positive signs toward the end of 2003 and early 2004. In early 2004, the U.S. Congressional Budget Office (CBO) reported that world trade grew by 4.75% in 2003 and is expected to grow by 7.5% in 2004. Global economic conditions started to look much better as the world moved into the beginning of the middle period of the decade.

---

[2] http://www.un.org/esa/policy/wess/index.html World Economic Situation and Prospects 2004.

What does all this mean for mergers and acquisitions? As the global economy improves, so do companies' product sales; therefore, more revenue is realized. More revenue generally means more profits and that means more cash to use to look for business growth opportunities. And as we discussed earlier, growth these days often occurs through mergers or acquisitions.

The impact, then, on the security professional may be substantial. The security professional should keep informed of matters pertaining to the global economy and how their company is doing in this arena. They should also look at their company's competitors and suppliers. They should also become friendly with their business managers who would be involved in any company mergers or acquisitions. By doing so, the security professional can prepare to support such endeavors in a proactive and not reactive mode. At the very least, in case your company is the object of a merger or acquisition, you have sufficient warning so that you can update your resumé, just in case. After all, it is easier to find a job when you have one!

In the United States

According to the U. S. Federal Reserve Board, economic activity continued to expand in early 2004. Consumer spending rose; manufacturing output continued its rise; tourism increased, reaching levels comparable to the pre-September 11, 2001 levels; and the service sector (information technology, business and financial services, transportation, health–care, and insurance) expanded as well. Overall employment, along with wages and salaries, increased slowly, slower than White House predictions or expectations; however, the U.S. Department of Labor reported a continued reduction in the overall unemployment rate, with a slight increase in the overall hourly wage rate.

Also, household spending increased, as did other indicators, suggesting that commodity prices were moving up and thus contributing to heightened concerns of inflation and the potential for increased interest rates. This is a particularly important concern, as the strength of the global economy is still largely affected by low interest rates and expansionary fiscal measures. Expansionary fiscal measures are actions taken by any government to stimulate economic growth. When expansionary fiscal measures are implemented by the U. S. government, the impact is global. Changing interest rates and implementing expansionary fiscal measures are always a dangerous balancing act for any country, as an improper balance of the two can lead to either stifling economic recovery and growth or overheating the economy leading to higher rates of inflation. All these events have an impact on the willingness of companies to engage in mergers, acquisitions, and/or divestitures.

In the late 1970s during President Carter's administration, the American economy experienced both higher interest rates and stifled economic growth. This condition proved fatal to President Carter's run for a second term; it also had a major impact on mergers, acquisitions, and divestitures. If a company was able to profit from this type of economy, it was in a position to acquire those that could not.

Additional economic indicators support data provided by the U.S. Federal Reserve Board. The United States CBO forecast for the years 2004 and 2005 indicate an expected increase in real gross domestic product (GDP) (4.8% and 4.2%, respectively) along with a continued decrease in the unemployment rate and a decrease in the Consumer Price Index. The CBO also forecast that the total economy should grow at a healthy rate over the next two years as the recovery from the economic downturn of the early 2000s has taken hold. Furthermore, between 2004 and beyond 2010, the CBO forecasts modest growth in potential output for the overall economy. Rapid productivity growth has led to strong capital investment by businesses contributing to the overall economic growth potential (see Figure 2.1).

Longer term forecasts by the CBO and the United Nations shows slow, steady growth, both in GDP and productivity. The COB projects between 2% to 3% growth in the United States after 2010, but labor productivity has been exceptional since the downturn of 2001, with rates as high as 5.6% in late 2003. This rate is higher than any since the 1950s for a similar time span. The unknown element is whether this rate of growth is an anomaly or an indication of the potential for growth in the economy's productive potential. Nevertheless, most economic indicators suggest that the U.S. economy is growing at a steady rate. These are good signs for businesses. When the economy grows and interest rates remain low, business in general prospers. It is during periods of economic growth that mergers and acquisitions most frequently occur.

If you are a security professional employed by a business in the United States or affected by the U.S. economy, you may want to consider the potential increase in mergers and acquisitions that may favorably or negatively impact your company. Furthermore, you will want to consider how you as an individual security professional will be affected.

Outside the United States

The rate of recent economic growth was greater in developed countries than in developing countries, with the highest rate of growth in North America followed by East Asia. The growth rate increases in East Asia occurred in large part due to Japan's return to positive growth after a decade of economic struggle. Both China and India, the two most populous countries in the world, have experienced recent growth at a rate of more

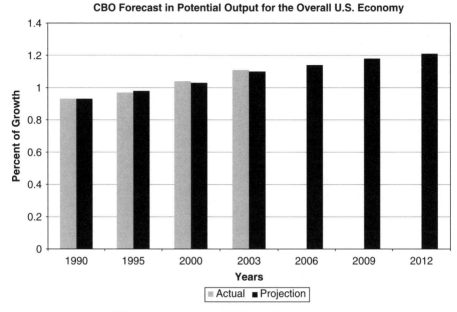

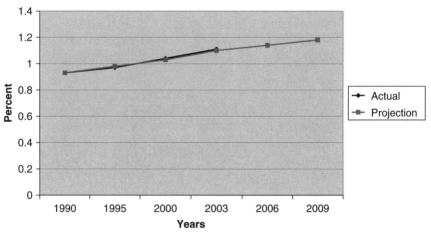

Figure 2.1   The CBO forecast in potential output for the overall U.S. economy.

than twice the world average. Considering the size of these two economies, their rate of growth should have far-reaching implications for international patterns of trade and production, as well as on the total global supply and demand for energy (e.g., oil, and commodities)—two areas with the potential to significantly impact global economic conditions.[3]

---

[3] http://www.un.org/esa/policy/wess/index.html

China, with its large labor pool and low-cost work force, has become very attractive to many international corporations, causing some to relocate production facilities and operations there. India, with its increasingly skilled and low-cost labor force (particularly in the area of information technology) has become very attractive to international companies as a location for competitive sourcing (outsourcing work to a lower cost provider).

This trend has, and will continue to have, increased international competition and globalization driving many businesses to greater efficiencies. Greater efficiencies ultimately lead to increases in productivity and output. Increased productivity growth and international competition are essential ingredients for higher wages and better living standards of workers. For many of the world's developed countries, where production has migrated off-shore, the net effect has been a short-term loss of jobs. Essentially, jobs are exported from high-cost producer countries to countries that are low-cost producers. Naturally, any exporting of jobs has political and social consequences. In some cases, the loss of production jobs has even led to increases in overall poverty rates.

In Eastern Europe, the Russian Federation continues to be the economic engine for the region. Africa and Latin America experienced some growth in 2004, but, along with West Asia, they are still among the slow-growth nations.

With the global economic engine warming up, there is a concern that inflation will develop. At this time, worldwide inflation remains at an almost nonexistent rate, so it is really not an immediate problem. However, continued increases in worldwide consumer demands may lead to a reversal of this trend. If that occurs, we can expect to see a shift in worldwide monetary policy, at least in the United States, from the period of low interest rates of the past three years to a tightening of monetary policy and an increase of interest rates.

The raising of interest rates is most often associated with periods of economic growth and much less likely to occur during periods of economic stagnation. When interest rates increase, the cost of capital also increases. In essence, money becomes more expensive to borrow. Expensive borrowing cost will influence the willingness of business to allocate funds for capital spending and investment. It may even affect their desire to leverage mergers and acquisitions. When money is more expensive to borrow, the willingness of businesses to spend decreases.

In summary, the world economy is changing rapidly. Many of these changes have been in large part driven by changes in the political economy over the past decade. Evidence of this exists in much of Eastern Europe and in East Asia. Advances and developments in technology, along with intensified interdependencies of countries and businesses operating within the world economy, particularly in trade and finance, will continue to influence long-term global economic development. At this time, conditions seem to be improving. For many reasons, this is a desired trend.

Remember, as a security professional, you have a professional and personal stake in all this. As the global, national, and your employer's economic conditions change, so does the potential for mergers, acquisitions, and divestitures. And as we stated earlier, that also impacts your responsibilities as a security professional and may even impact your own job security.

CURRENT ECONOMIC ENVIRONMENT FOR MERGERS AND ACQUISITIONS: IS IT BUSINESS FRIENDLY? IS IT MERGER AND ACQUISITION FRIENDLY?

In business, mergers and acquisitions are a fact of life. According to the U.S. Federal Trade Commission, in the United States alone there were more that 8,700 mergers and acquisitions in 1999, up from 3,600 in 1991. This trend suggests that mergers and acquisitions are an increasingly used business strategy.

The 1990s may very well come to be known as the decade of mergers and acquisitions in addition to the strongest bull market in the history of the United States. However, in the first two years of the new millennium, that trend was reversed, perhaps even overcorrected, as we saw a significant drop in the dollar value and total number of mergers and acquisitions in the United States[5] (see Figure 2.2).

During the early 2000s, many companies focused on organic growth (the term *organic growth* is the act of growing a company from within as opposed to growing a company through acquisition), thus avoiding taking on large debt for mergers or acquisitions. One advantage of an economic downturn is that many companies are forced to go back to the basics. Going back to the basics means looking internally at how a company operates. When a company does this, it focuses on improving processes, changing market strategies, cutting costs, and improving management teams. In other words, it focuses on the basics. Some would argue that these should be regular management practices and not just something to fall back on during difficult economic periods. Yes, well, one can always hope.

> *The Chamberlain Group, Inc., has acquired Elite Access Systems Inc.: "The acquisition will expand Chamberlain's line of perimeter access control products."*[6]

---

[4] See http://www.findarticles.com/cf_dls/m6402/2_35/60599708/p1/article.jhtml
[5] See http://www.bkd.com/docs/about/MergersAarticle.pdf
[6] ASIS Magazine, *Security Management*, January 2004, page 119

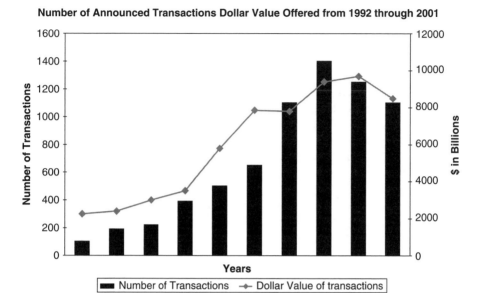

Number of Announced Transactions Dollar Value Offered from 1992 through 2001

Figure 2.2   The number and total dollar value of merger and acquisition transactions in the United States between 1992 and 2001.

Those companies and investors that did venture into mergers and acquisitions did so cautiously, often looking for a specific opportunity, or niche, within a market. Even in a mature market, there may be a niche that offers an opportunity for expansion of market-share or product line. In the early 2000s, the business services, financial services, and specialized technology sectors offered some of the best opportunities for niche markets.

The consolidation of the banking industry during this period also contributed to the reduction of mergers and acquisitions. As banks were focused on improving their capabilities and competitiveness, less capital was available for investors.

As we progress further into the new decade, a reversal of the short-lived economic downward trend of the early 2000s took hold. In the month of July 2003 alone, nearly $26 billion in mergers had been announced. A *Wall Street Journal* article declared that with companies hedging their bets on an economic turnaround and stocks still cheap, activity had suddenly picked up steam."[7] Early indications are that the current environment for mergers and acquisitions is in fact becoming friendly, very friendly. This is primarily due to the continuation of low interest rates and recent economic growth.

---

[7] See http://www.afponline.org/ohc/071603/214_article_7/214_article_7.html-"Merger Activity Sizzles Again" *Wall Street Journal* (07/09/03) p.C1 (Sidel, Robin)

Mergers and Acquisitions Outside the United States

Cross-border mergers and acquisitions are an increasingly important occurrence in international business. With increased pressures in globalization, many countries have liberalized their trade and investment regulations, making mergers and acquisitions more accessible and more common. The need to be more competitive and productive within the global marketplace is the primary driver. Keep in mind, greater productivity and competitiveness generally should lead to higher rates of employment, higher wages, and higher standards of living. Politically, these are good reasons for countries to adopt policies more friendly to mergers and acquisitions.

Mergers and acquisitions are still relatively less important in developing countries. However, there are exceptions, such as when a government moves to privatize government-owned industries such as telecommunications, utilities, and transportation. Recently, this type of activity took place in South America and in a few African nations.

Merger Trends in the United Kingdom and Continental Europe

Peak periods of European mergers and acquisitions activity occurred in 1968, 1972, 1989, and again in the late 1990s.[8] Within the United Kingdom, there was an increase in corporate takeovers in the late 1980s, primarily due to increasing stock prices and the permissive governmental attitude of the Thatcher period toward mergers and acquisitions and other financial innovations.

July 26, 2004: 7:17 AM EDT
MADRID (Reuters) – Spain's Santander Central Hispano struck Europe's biggest cross-border bank takeover deal on Monday, agreeing to buy Britain's Abbey National for about £8.25 billion, or about $15.1 billion.[9]

On the European continent, mergers and acquisitions were relatively uncommon before the 1990s. Two important events helped change this condition:

- Deregulation of the financial service markets in the late 1980s led to increased privatization and increased mergers and acquisitions.
- Since the introduction of the Euro as a common European currency, a large number of deals have been made.

---

[8] http://www.som.hw.ac.uk/somjdb/malectures/Lecture%207.doc
[9] http://money.cnn.com/2004/07/26/news/internioal/abbey_santander.reut/index.htm

The United Kingdom, France, and Germany have been the most active countries in Europe involved in mergers and acquisitions. In 1998, the United Kingdom actually surpassed the United States as the largest purchasing country. Many conditions led to this change, but the primary driver was the British desire to protect business sectors where the United Kingdom's competitive advantage had been threatened.

A common characteristic of European mergers and acquisitions in the late 1990s was the effort to protect national interests. Although mergers and acquisitions activity significantly increased, few of the deals were actual cross-border deals. Most deals focused on preserving business sectors within the country. For example, the French government made it clear that it would block any attempt by a foreign company to buy Renault in which it owned 44% of the shares. Furthermore, in Italy, Fiat was not accessible to investors, as the Agnelli family maintained firm control through a network of affiliated companies.[10] The danger in this control lies in the potential for losing a competitive edge to more progressive companies less focused on national interests (or pride) and more focused on growing their business and increasing their competitiveness.

Moreover, in 1997, the Union Bank of Switzerland and Swiss Bank Corp. agreed to merge operations in a transaction valued at more than $25 billion, creating one of the world's largest financial services companies. The combined bank was named United Bank of Switzerland and included the world's leading money management concern, with 1.32 trillion Swiss francs (equivalent to $912.8 billion) in assets under their management. This transaction was clearly an attempt to preserve and enhance national strength within the Swiss banking sector. Banking has been a long-time Swiss tradition and as much a part of Switzerland's national identity as mountains, watches, and chocolate (see Figure 2.3).

Although merger and acquisition activity throughout Europe has increased, European companies face strong anticompetitive restrictions and controls established and managed by the European Union (EU). Holding a dominant position within any market as a result of internal competitive strength, capabilities, and effectiveness is not illegal. However, obtaining a dominant position by acquiring competitors may be a violation of EU competition law. Normally, companies that create dominant positions are forced to adjust through divestiture. Competitiveness is closely watched. Just ask Bill Gates of Microsoft (an American-based international corporation) as he challenges the multimillion dollar penalty imposed by the EU for anticompetitiveness practices. Of course, Microsoft is having similar difficulties with the U. S. federal and state governments.

---

[10] See http://www.siue.edu/~bzhou/europe-mergers.html

On December 8, 1997, Cable News Network (CNN) reported the following European Business transaction:

Union Bank of Switzerland and Swiss Bank Corp. agreed to merge operations in a transaction valued at over $25 billion, creating one of the world's largest financial services companies, both banks said early Monday.

This combination will create a bank with 1.32 trillion Swiss Francs ($912.8 billion) in assets under management. The combined bank will employ about 56,000 workers following an extensive restructuring, including layoffs of approximately 13,000 people over the next several years. Cost of restructuring is expected to reach nearly $5 billion resulting in a net loss in the fiscal year.

Figure 2.3   The Swiss banks' merger.

"Honeywell Security Products Group acquires Olympo Controls s.r.o and Olympo Bratislava spol s.r.o: This acquisition will allow Honeywell to solidify its distribution base in central Europe."[11]

Within the EU is an independent commission charged with regulating competition. This commission is armed with strong merger regulations and seeks to oversee merger and acquisition activities, prohibiting any transaction that may create a dominant position for one company within the Common Market. Only large transactions are closely watched as EU merger regulations that have established thresholds for engagement. For global transactions to warrant their attention, the value of the deal must exceed EUR 5000 million.[12]

Within Central and Eastern Europe, the most active business sectors have been the manufacturing sector, which, in 2002, accounted for more than 21% of all deals followed by the financial services sector, which represented 15% of all deals. In 2002 there were more than 1,000 deals, with an estimated total market value of $17.7 billion. Russia leads this group in the number and size of deals, closing just short of 300 with a value of

---

[11] ASIS Magazine, *Security Management*, January 2004, page 119.
[12] See http://www.europa.eu.int/comm/competition/citizen/citizen_mergers_en.html

nearly $7.5 billion. They were followed by the Czech Republic and Poland with roughly $2.0 billion each.

Mergers and Acquisitions Trends in Asia

Within Asian cross-border mergers and acquisitions, there are encouraging long-term economic policy reforms that could have an impact on operational efficiency and the overall competitiveness of the Asian domestic economy. Moreover, the presence of external capital and financial strength can help Asian companies withstand domestic financial and economic crises. However, these mergers and acquisitions can be problematic, as companies struggle with attempts to reduce cost and improve efficiency between entities with significantly different cultures.

> *Cross-border mergers and acquisitions are defined as mergers and acquisitions of domestic firms by international firms.*

Changes in the business environment resulting from mergers and acquisitions may also have unintended results. Recent trends indicate that the once independent and dynamic Asian automobile industry will remain Asian only in a geographical sense. In terms of ownership, it may become only a branch of a European or U.S. automobile industry. During the period of slow growth within the Japanese economy (1990s) and the financial crises in East Asia, Western automobile companies acquired large chunks of the Asian automobile industry's companies.

In some cases, ailing Asian automobile producers actually sought alliances with Western companies as a means of improving the strength of their ailing firms. Excess capacity and weak profits in the Western automobile market caused Western firms to set their sights on the Asian market. In hopes of a creating a strong rebound from the depressed conditions of the 1990s, Asian automobile producers, along with their host countries, were also willing to invite them in.

Asian automobile manufacturers, the once frightening challengers to the powerful Western automobile producers, may now be on a path of becoming outsourcing subsidiaries of the same Western producers. Since the 1998 DaimlerChrysler merger, a wave of mergers, acquisitions, and alliances have occurred in the international automobile industry. As a result, nearly 75% of the global automobile market is currently controlled by six big players.[13] This is quite a change from the days when Detroit was viewed as rapidly on its way to the rust-heap.

---

[13] See http://www.macroscan.com/cur/jul00/print/prnt140700Automobile_Trends.html

> *According to the* American Heritage Dictionary, *alliance is a union, relationship, or connection by common interest. Business alliances can be quite complicated as each company brings to the agreement its own assets, agendas, and proposals. Until operating processes, performance indicators, and problem resolutions methods are established, conflict can develop. This conflict, if uncontrolled, can erode trust and the partnership.*

Three major groups of producers are expected to dominate the global industry of automobile production. General Motors (GM), Ford, and DaimlerChrysler are the big three. Considering alliances, GM is estimated to control 20% of the world's market, with Ford a very close second.

In terms of the global automobile industry, both the Japanese and American markets are mature and very competitive. In Japan, between 1990 and 1998, automobile sales fell from 7.8 million to 5.9 million per year,[14] with no reduction in automobile production capacity and capability. For an automotive manufacturer to be profitable, it must have success in the United States. Moreover, it is helpful to have a global infrastructure where cheap labor can be obtained and where production facilities are located close to where the products are being sold. Having a global presence contributes to successfully coordinating design, manufacturing, and marketing in all markets. In essence, to be a success in the world market of automobile manufacturing and sales, a company must have a global operating presence. As previously shown, this is often done through mergers and acquisitions.

Although the previous example describes the automobile industry, the same can be said for various other industries. As you read through this section, look at the commonality of the rationale for the changes, mergers, and acquisitions in the automobile industry, as they will continue to form the basis for additional mergers and acquisitions in the future.

As a security professional employed in a company with global business interests, would the conditions and rationale for the mergers and acquisitions in the automobile company apply to your company's business sector? Your company? Are you prepared in advance to support your company's merger or acquisition efforts?

China

The long-time hostile mergers and acquisitions regulatory environment in China is changing. Mergers and acquisitions activity, virtually nonexistent

---

[14] Economist.com: "The also-rans: Mitsubishi and Mazda struggle, despite western partners" (March 7, 2004)

ten years ago, is now becoming common. For investors and international companies seeking opportunities in China, much progress has been made; however, there is still a long way to go. The Chinese government contends there are political and economic reasons for maintaining strong controls in some economic sectors, but they are relaxing regulation in other sectors. This makes mergers and acquisitions in China more accessible and attractive to foreign and domestic investors, but does not eliminate all obstacles.

The Chinese government, in terms of foreign investment, categorizes different industry sectors into the following: "Permitted," "Encouraged," "Restricted," and "Prohibited." Knowing the category of the targeted investment is essential before proceeding with any merger and acquisition transaction.

With China joining the World Trade Organization, it is required to open its marketplace. However, it is expected that this will continue to be fought by the Chinese government through the use of various rationales for its protectionist decisions. Regardless, gradually China is expected to be less protective of its business base. As a result, there will be increased opportunities for foreign businesses to look to Chinese companies as targets of opportunity for mergers or acquisitions, and vice versa.

This change in direction is largely attributed to efforts by the Chinese government to stimulate foreign investment. The need for foreign investment and the desire to become a part of the world economic community have led the Chinese government to grudgingly relax many restrictions. Consequently, it is now somewhat easier for foreign companies to purchase Chinese businesses and restructure their investments through mergers, acquisitions, and divestitures. Transactions that just a few years ago were nearly impossible are now becoming more common.

Multinational corporations seeking to restructure their businesses to improve efficiency and profitability can now move more freely within China. Changes in the Chinese legal structure have lessened the impact of China's preference for state planning of the economy on the ability of companies to engage in relatively quick and simple mergers and acquisitions. It is not just international or foreign companies that benefit from these regulatory changes. Chinese domestic companies are also participating in the merger and acquisition game and are now often buying out foreign investors in Chinese companies.

The Chinese government strategy, in conjunction with China's domestic companies, has been one of inviting in foreign businesses as long as they share their proprietary information and processes, establish joint ventures with a Chinese business, and train the Chinese employees. Of course, foreign businesses have little choice if they are to have a piece of the Chinese marketplace action. After all, over one billion potential customers! Once Chinese employees are trained and skilled, the Chinese business may try to buy out its foreign partner or even start a new competitive business, thereby using the mergers and acquisition strategy after it has squeezed all it can from its foreign partners. Many of these Chinese businesses have Chinese government "shareholders" and are thus in a position to favorably leverage their government connections in any mergers and acquisitions.

The Chinese regulatory system is becoming more sophisticated and flexible, making more complex merger and acquisition transactions now possible. Even with the relaxation of foreign investment legislation and regulation on mergers and acquisitions, direct investment in a Chinese business can be a complicated and problematic process. The most effective way for foreign investors to engage in mergers and acquisitions with Chinese businesses is through an offshore company, ideally, a Hong Kong or Cayman Islands holding company. The Chinese government applies fewer controls and regulation to offshore transactions than it does to direct transactions. This is particularly true if the offshore company already owns an interest in a Chinese enterprise. Using offshore holding companies makes the various transactions much easier for international or foreign investors, as it involves much less legal and regulatory scrutiny.

In China, the recent development of mergers and acquisition activity has played a positive role in privatizing and revitalizing the country's inefficient state enterprises and attracting foreign investment. The potential for economic development and expansion is tremendous, particularly in the telecommunications, insurance, and banking industries. Consequently, much attention in the Western and Asian investment banking community is focusing on China. While global mergers and acquisitions slowed down in 2002, merger and acquisition activity in China almost doubled.

Chinese corporations participated in partnerships, mergers, and acquisitions deals exceeding $27 billion. That figure represented one quarter of all such deals in Asia.[15] Chinese investors see mergers and acquisitions as a means to becoming more competitive in the global marketplace. U. S. and other Western investment bankers see China as a market with great potential for growth. There are limitations on foreign investors as the Chinese government continues to maintain some restrictions on foreign investment. Moreover, infrastructure issues exist. Inadequate financial controls, communications issues, and cultural differences make participating in Chinese markets difficult. Nevertheless, considering the size of the Chinese population and its potential for rapid expansion, there will undoubtedly be continued interest in mergers and acquisitions for quite some time.

---

[15] See http://browne.com/newsletters/newsletter.asp?storyID=694

Japan

On February 24, 2004, Reuters reported that Yamanouchi Pharmaceutical Co. Ltd reported its intent to purchase rival Fujisawa Pharmaceutical Co. Ltd in a stock deal worth nearly $7.8 billion.[16] This acquisition would create Japan's second-largest drug maker. The initial reaction of the market was reflected in a rise in stock price for both companies. Overall the market expectation is that this mega-merger will trigger other merger and acquisitions activities within this market. This transaction is important for several reasons:

- It is an important strategic merger within the Japanese Pharmaceutical industry with the potential to contribute to the overall competitiveness of Japanese companies in this business sector.
- It is another example of a change in the willingness of Japanese businesses to engage in merger and acquisition activity.

If you are a security professional employed by a pharmaceutical company, were you aware of this merger? Do you see an impact on your employer? If so, is it a positive or negative impact? How will it affect your company and your security responsibilities now and in the future if your company is competing with this new Japanese pharmaceutical giant?

Until recently, Japan has been notably subdued in merger and acquisition activity. In large part, this lack of activity was due to the Japanese view that most mergers and acquisitions were predatory and did not benefit the buying company. In general, Japanese businesses still remain quite skeptical about mergers and acquisitions. More recently, however, managers and owners of Japanese companies have come to realize that there are strategic benefits associated with mergers and acquisitions. Large companies with significant international business are more apt to recognize the strategic value of mergers and acquisitions. Smaller companies appear to be considering mergers and acquisitions for different reasons. Their reasons are more focused on the competitiveness in local markets.

Korea and Thailand

Since the financial crises of 1997, both Korea and Thailand have introduced various measures to encourage business consolidation through mergers and acquisitions, as well as moving to liberalize foreign investment. These policy changes have led to a rise in cross-border mergers and acquisitions bringing in much needed foreign capital.

---

[16] See http://forbes.com/home_europ/newswire/2004/02/24/rtr1274634.html

Korea has adopted international accounting standards and introduced new requirements for domestic companies to increase involvement of outside (non-Korean) directors on their companies' boards of directors. Both moves are seen to increase corporate transparency and accountability. In 1999, Thailand moved to amend its bankruptcy code that opened up its economy to market forces, making it easier for creditors to gain control of debtor's assets to obtain payment of debt due.[17]

All things considered, it is clear that the environment for mergers and acquisitions in Asia has greatly changed. Relaxation of government regulation, a large and growing population of consumers, and a more skilled and educated work force all contribute to the shifting trend toward a more friendly atmosphere for merger and acquisitions.

MERGER AND ACQUISITION ACTIVITY IN THE RECENT PAST

As 2004 arrived, the merger and acquisition momentum that began building in mid-2003 continued. Deals developed in many major business sectors. The travel, defense, entertainment, media, information technology, and telecommunications industries all saw large transactions occurring early in the year. The reasons for these deals varied from an effort by JetBlue to expand its market share, to the quest for new products by Comcast.

In January 2004, American Airlines and JetBlue Airways emerged as contenders to purchase the Boston-New York-Washington shuttle service from an ailing US Airways. Since its bankruptcy in 2003, US Airways has struggled to emerge from its severe financial troubles. Competition with discount providers makes this struggle to recover even more difficult. JetBlue, a three-year-old, low-fare airline has experienced success and is looking for an opportunity to expand.[18] In spite of the post-September 11, 2001 slump in air travel, JetBlue has managed to prosper and is seeking rapid expansion.

Also in January 2004, Alliant Techsystems agreed to purchase Mission Research Corporation (MRC) a Santa Barbara defense company, for approximately $225 million. MRC holds contracts with the Department of Homeland Security and is developing "next generation" weapons technology. Unlike the airline industry, the U.S. defense sector is doing quite well in the post-September 11 global environment, as the war on terrorism continues to be a priority for the United States and many of its allies. With the acquisition of MRC, Alliant expects to leverage its ability to secure more

---

[17] See http://www.imf.org/external/pubs/ft/fandd/201/03/mody.htm
[18] See http://www.philly.com/mld/inquirer/business/7811837.htm- "American, JetBlue vying for shuttle" *The Philadelphia Inquirer* (01/28/04) (Belden, Tom)

government contracts with the new advanced weapons technology developed by MRC.

In one of the year's most high profile acquisition attempt, Comcast attempted to purchase Disney. On February 12, 2004, the *Wall Street Journal* headline read "Disney, Struggling to Regain Glory, Gets $48.7 Billion Bid from Comcast." Comcast, the nation's largest cable company in terms of both subscribers and revenue offered $48.7 billion in stock to acquire Disney.[19] Interestingly enough, the next business day, the value of Comcast stock dropped 8% and the value of Disney stock increased by nearly 15%. This change suggested that investors expect another bidder for Disney may appear, or that Comcast will need to increase its offer for Disney to accept. A combination of Disney and Comcast would have created a rival similar in size to Time Warner and Viacom, two giants in media and communications. This action by Comcast follows their 2002 acquisition of AT&T Broadband for $51 billion.

On April 28, 2004, CNN Money reported "Comcast drops Disney offer: No. 1 cable operator withdraws $48B merger bid. . . ."[20] This change in strategy came as no surprise to most, as the offer had been valued below the Disney stock price for some time. Comcast executives indicated the change in strategy was primarily due to Disney's lack of interest in combining the two companies. Apparently Wall Street agreed with the move by Comcast. Shortly after the Comcast announcement, its stock rose by more than 2% while Disney stock dropped by nearly 2%.

Comcast's effort to acquire Disney was driven primarily by changes in technology. Digital technology, which is the digitization of sound, words, and images, allows for transmission via satellite at a cost that is now competitive with cable. Satellite television continues to put pressure on the cable companies that have been allowed to monopolize within their areas of operation, thus driving them to seek alternative business models to maintain or grow their business. Cable companies, facing a shrinking market for their distribution capabilities, as new technology threatens its very existence, are looking at using their cable infrastructure for high-speed Internet access (competing with phone companies) or ownership of media content. (Media content is the product—for example, movies, music—that is delivered over the distribution channels of cable and satellite.)

Although recent technology-driven media mergers and acquisitions have not been very successful, mega-media mergers and acquisitions are likely to continue. Comcast's aborted effort to acquire Disney seems to be one of the more recent examples of a media company ignoring the lessons of history. However, Comcast is not alone. In 2000, Vivendi SA of France

---

[19] *Wall Street Journal* (02/12/04) P.A1 (Orwall, Grant) "Disney, Struggling to Regain Glory, Gets $48.7 Billion Bid From Comcast"
[20] See http://money.cnn.com/2004/04/28/news/fortune500/comcast/index.htm

acquired Universal Music Group's parent company, Seagram Co. By 2002, Vivendi was suffering from excessive debt levels that threatened its very survival. Closer to home, the America Online Inc. and Time Warner Inc. merger ultimately destroyed billions of dollars in stock market value, creating very unhappy shareholders.

The Comcast effort to acquire Disney also demonstrated that hostile takeover attempts are alive and well. Not all merger and acquisition activity is friendly. In March 2004, PeopleSoft Inc. shareholders were asked by its CEO to reject a $9.4 billion takeover offer from Oracle.[21] Clearly the PeopleSoft board of directors and CEO were not pleased with Oracle's move to take over their company. They weren't alone. Within the U.S. Department of Justice and the European Commission, concerns of damage to competitiveness of the business software market was considered as possibly leading to the U.S. government's rejection of Oracle's takeover attempt. They were concerned that, if the takeover was successful, only two major competitors (SAP of Germany and Oracle/PeopleSoft) would dominate this market.

The increased merger and acquisition activity in 2004 was not exclusive to the United States. In Europe, activity was beginning to pick-up. On February 25, 2004, Reuters reported increased activity within the European telecommunications sector.[22] After three years of relatively little activity and high rates of cash flow, companies were again looking towards mergers and acquisitions. With low levels of investment and a reluctance to return cash to shareholders, the logical investment options were in the areas of mergers and acquisitions. What does a company do with excess cash? Grow the company from within, which takes more time, or pursue the more expedient strategy for growth, which is to acquire other companies. France's Vodafone Group Plc, Dutch telecoms group KPN, and British-based mobile phone group MmO2 Plc have all been engaged in recent merger and acquisition activity. And there appears to be no end in sight.

WHAT CAN WE EXPECT IN THE NEAR FUTURE?

From the middle of 2003 and into the future, merger and acquisition activity was gaining momentum. Valuations of companies were improving and the cost of capital was low. The investor cautiousness of the early 2000s is slowly giving way to an eagerness to seek and invest in good opportunities.

---

[21] *New York Times* (02/24/04) Technology Section (Laurie J. Flynn) "PeopleSoft Urges Rejection of Oracle's Takeover Offer"
[22] http://www.reuters.com/newsArticle.jhtml;jsessionid=SKHBIIIMGW2HUCRBAEL FFA? type=topNews&storyID=4436096&pageNumber=0

The number of initial public offerings and mergers and acquisitions have increased. Merger and acquisition activity in the financial sector began to pick–up, and expectations for similar increased activity in the pharmaceutical industry are developing as research and development costs, along with marketing costs, continue to make it difficult to bring new drugs to the market.

Increased activity has also occurred in the airline, defense, media, and telecommunications sectors as companies look to expand existing market-share or enter new markets. The technology industry seems to be a particularly good candidate for increased merger and acquisition activity because after the downturn in the stock market in the early 2000s, many companies have improved their operating efficiency and increased cash holdings. This makes them more attractive to potential buyers. A few others have not made these changes, and unless they are able to turn their situation around, they risk becoming more attractive to liquidators who seek out companies in trouble and liquidate them for the value of their assets.

> *Those who do not remember the past are condemned to repeat it.*
> —*George Santanyana*

Mergers and acquisitions continue to be attractive to companies and investors in spite of statistical evidence that so many fail or underperform. Investors continue to pay more attention to the deal at hand than the history of other deals. An improving economy with continued low interest rates provides support for companies looking to leverage themselves and engage in mergers and acquisitions.

SUMMARY

Since 2003, the global economic environment has become more favorable to businesses and thus to mergers and acquisitions. Economic improvement is evident in many national and global business sectors. Consumers are spending more, interest rates continue to remain low, and business investment has picked up its pace. What does this mean in terms of merger and acquisition activity? Since mergers and acquisitions are a strategic tool used by businesses to expand their capabilities and market-share and current economic conditions remain conducive to business investment, odds are we will see an increase in merger and acquisition activity over the next few years.

As a security professional, it cannot be overstated, you must understand what is going on in the world as it relates to business and government activities in general, and in particular those events and trends that impact your company's markets and business. It is imperative that security professionals monitor these events and begin now to outline and develop plans to prepare for mergers and acquisitions affecting their companies. It is probably not a matter of if a merger or acquisition will take place involving the security professionals' companies, but only a matter of when.

Chapter 3

The Role of Security and the Security Manager in Mergers and Acquisitions

Every battle is won before it is ever fought. – Sun-tzu, The Art of War.
Quoted by Gordon Gekko in the movie Wall Street

INTRODUCTION

This chapter addresses why security is important to the process of mergers and acquisitions. We examine the most relevant security issues and concerns a merger and/or acquisition team encounters and why having a security professional as part of the team is essential to effectively resolving security issues, addressing security concerns, and applying appropriate security controls.

The security manager or their professional representative serves as a consultant to the merger and acquisition team, providing guidance and direction for all security matters. In essence, they are the merger or acquisition team's subject matter "expert" for all issues of security. In addition to the security consulting role, the security manager or professional also fulfills the role of a department or function manager responsible for directing and managing all security department-related activities in support of the team and the overall effort. The role of department or function heads is similar to the role of any other function lead on the merger and acquisition team. Each is responsible to ensure they manage all activities supporting the merger or acquisition related to their specific discipline and department; for example, the manager of finance ensures that all financial matters are properly handled by his or her organization just as the manager of facilities manages all relevant facilities issues.

Support from security for the merger or acquisition effort can be divided into two phases:

- Premerger support
- Postmerger support (see Figure 3.1)

Merger and Acquisition Phases and Major Process Steps

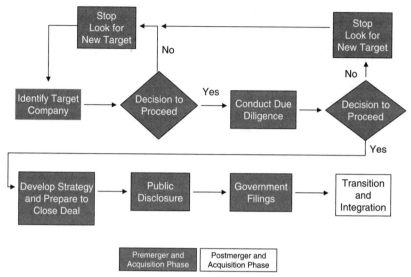

Figure 3.1   The phases and major steps of a merger or acquisition.

Furthermore, the contribution security makes to the entire effort can be further segmented into the following three categories:

- Protecting the effort itself: Security measures are applied to the merger or acquisition effort to ensure that it is properly protected. That includes the implementation of measures to protect the confidentiality of the effort and its people, information, and physical assets.
- Providing subject matter expertise: The security manager or professional serves as a member of the team and provides guidance, direction, and consultation on all security-related issues and concerns.
- Evaluating the security condition of the target company: The security manager is charged with assessing the security condition of the target company. Here the security manager conducts a security audit[1] of the target company's security program and overall security condition. That becomes part of the total team's assessment. Any issues identified are given consideration in terms of their effect on closing the deal.

---

[1] The term *security audit* as used here does not mean the same as an audit for compliance, as would be done by the auditing staff. In this context, it is an evaluation as to the asset protection measures in place; how they compare to that of the acquiring company; what must be done to bring them up to acquiring company asset protection standards; and what best practices they have in place and should be adopted by the acquiring company. In addition, the costs involved in this integration effort should be identified and added to the overall cost of the merger or acquisition.

Executing mergers and acquisitions usually requires a great amount of time and effort. Transactions can be costly and complex. Merger and acquisition teams engage in deals that shape the strategic direction of a company, some only slightly; others may cause a major change in the way a company operates. In any type of merger or acquisition, the acquiring company's security organization has an important role to play in this process. Security needs to be an active member of the merger and acquisition team from the start.[2] From the initial decision to pursue a target company, to the start of a due diligence effort, and right through the integration of the newly acquired or merged business, security has a role.

Merger and acquisition teams have a great deal of responsibility. The deals they make may bring great value to a company. If not executed properly, they could be a disaster. To be effective, the merger and acquisition team must be highly skilled in many disciplines. Furthermore, team members must work well together under stressful and sometimes adverse conditions. Mergers and acquisitions bring much external attention and interest to companies, and not all of it is positive. Highly experienced and skilled teams with proper cross-functional representation are best suited to manage this process. Furthermore, merger and acquisition (or divestiture) teams must operate within well-defined boundaries following established processes. These boundaries and processes must be institutionalized within a company charter.

Sample Charter for Executing Mergers, Acquisitions, and Divestitures

Our Company pursues mergers, acquisitions, and divestitures when such transactions will promote long-term growth in value for our shareholders. The Senior Executive for Business Strategy is responsible for providing strategic analysis and guidance for the development of long-range business strategies. When these strategies involve mergers, acquisitions, or divestitures, this position is responsible for the following actions:

- *Identify candidate target companies or business units for merger, acquisition, or divestiture*
- *Conduct initial analysis of each target's potential strategic and financial value to company*
- *Lead all due diligence activities ensuring the due diligence team identifies all issues and risks associated with any potential merger, acquisition, or divestiture.*
- *Provide valuation guidance for all mergers, acquisitions, and divestitures*
- *Make final assessment and recommendation for all potential mergers, acquisitions, and divestitures to the company CEO*

---

[2] http://www.csoonline.com/read/030103/mix.html CSO Magazine, March 2003

Mergers and acquisitions are complicated business transactions[3]. They become even more complicated when conducted internationally. In this post-September 11, 2001[4] world, issues given little or no consideration before the attack on the United States by international terrorists now must be considered. Conducting business in the Middle East became much more dangerous and problematic immediately after the events of September 11 and more so during the conflict in Iraq.

In a merger or acquisition, if the acquiring company is a U.S.- or European-based company, it must be concerned with laws, many of them recently enacted, prohibiting doing business in any way with other companies and countries that may be involved with sponsoring terrorism. Western companies are also faced with restrictions on sharing or transferring certain types of technologies, in particular, technologies with the potential for military application or technologies that can be used in the development or production of weapons of mass destruction.

At the very least, these restrictions create limitations on the exchange of information between an acquiring company and the target company. Limits on obtaining information may limit what one company can learn about the other. That in turn may affect the ability of the acquiring company to accurately value the target company. Knowing the extent of these restrictions beforehand will help to better understand what the union of the two companies will and will not create.

Process Steps for Executing Mergers, Acquisitions, and Divestitures
The transaction stages of any merger, acquisition, or divestiture occur in the following order:
1. *Identify the target for its strategic fit and financial impact to acquiring company based on a review of public data.*
2. *Make a recommendation to investigate when the results of the identification stage reveal a good strategic fit or other potential benefit to acquiring company.*
3. *Conduct a due diligence by establishing a team to determine the value of the target company. The team must review all aspects of*

---

[3] Determining the value of a company is a complicated process. To learn more about value, value-based management, and the process of valuation, the reader should consult other publications on valuation produced by companies involved in such matters.
[4] Reference to the post-September 11, 2001 world is made to highlight the change in global security conditions as a result of the acts of terror perpetrated on the United States. On this day, terrorists crashed airplanes into the World Trade Center in New York City and the Pentagon in Northern Virginia. More than 3000 people perished during these acts of terror, which were shortly followed by an American led "war on terrorism" and invasion of Iraq. This series of events created what many referred to as a "new normal" condition. This is to suggest that the safety and security of peoples all over the world will not be the same for years to come.

the target business and prepare a formal assessment including risk identification and the impact of all observations and findings on the value of the target. This assessment should be delivered to the company CEO or the company Board of Directors.

4. *Based on the findings, a recommendation to proceed or not to proceed is made by the due diligence team to the CEO and/or to the Board of Directors.*
5. *Define parameters of a negotiation and implementation strategy that will result in closing the deal and the signing of a contract with the target.*
6. *Public disclosure (press release or announcement) of the transaction is made. This disclosure does not include release of competitive sensitive information, only the disclosure of the transaction.*
7. *Government filings must be made, as various legal filings are required to implement and authorize the transaction. The legal department, with support from the due diligence team, has the responsibility to submit all filings*
8. *Conduct an orderly transition of the target into or out of the company. A divestiture must be spun off from the company and an acquisition must be integrated into the company.*

The acquiring company's mergers and acquisition team generally looks to the legal department to handle such matters. However, it has been our experience that often the legal staff doesn't have a good understanding of all the applicable security-related laws, regulations, and restrictions. This is especially true if one is dealing with a merger or acquisition between companies of different countries.

The security professional should not expect the legal staff to be the sole provider of such information to the team. The security professional assigned to the team should be knowledgeable in such matters and coordinate that information with the legal staff. After all, for security professionals to successfully assist with the merger or acquisition, they must have a detailed knowledge of the applicable laws, regulations, and such so that they can formulate the asset protection integration with the least amount of chaos—and there is usually some chaos that takes place with a merger or acquisition.

Laws and regulations bring with them close government oversight. This oversight can be used as a tool to help navigate successfully through the legal and regulatory requirements. However, laws and regulations are not the only concerns a merger or acquisition team must deal with. There are a plethora of considerations that must be addressed by the merger and acquisition team. It is up to the team to sort out all issues early in the effort and to ensure that a skilled and experienced team is in place to work them.

Having a cross-functional team with representatives from all critical disciplines along with a well-defined game plan increases the probability of success. The security staff is often overlooked when it comes to establishing a merger or acquisition team. If not invited to join the team, the security professional has an obligation to get on that team.

WHY SECURITY?

The role of security within a company is to protect people, information, and physical assets and to mitigate risks to the company assets.

> **Security:** *The American Heritage Dictionary defines security as: Freedom from risk or danger or something that gives or assures safety.*

These are some questions that are often asked about security's role in a merger or acquisition:[5]

- Why does a merger or acquisition need security support?
- Aren't mergers and acquisitions just ordinary business transactions?
- They seem to occur nearly every day, so what is so special about them that they require special security support, or any security support at all?
- What value does a security professional bring to a merger and acquisition team?

A security professional involved in a merger or acquisition must be able to answer these questions as part of convincing a mergers or acquisition team that security should be an integral member of the team. If invited on the team when the team is first formed, the security professional must still be able to answer the preceding questions as part of the security operations plan that is needed to ensure the successful merger and integration of the acquired or merged company.

---

[5] Throughout this chapter and this rest of this book we will address these and many more questions concerning the need for security in support of mergers and acquisitions. We intend not only to provide answers but to provide a framework of understanding of how mergers and acquisitions work and why security plays such an important role in the success of these business transactions. Furthermore, we will provide a model to be used as a guideline for security professionals to assist them in their effort to provide security support. Use of this model is not intended to be exclusive to the security professional. We expect it to be useful for any member of a merger and acquisition team in helping them better understand the complexity of the many issues associated with mergers and acquisitions. It will also help in understanding basic and unique security-related issues and the necessity of having a security professional as part of the team.

If the business relationship is one of a merger, generally a joint merger team is formed; however, employees of one or the other of the companies must take a lead position. Regardless of whether or not the security professional is in a security leadership role or just a support member of the security team, it is important to understand the security issues and the role of security to the project.

Getting Started and How Security Can Help

Mergers and acquisitions are extremely important matters and have a major impact on any company. In some cases, mergers and acquisitions are so large and encompassing that they drive a complete transformation of the companies coming together and essentially cause the creation of a new company. An action of this nature is not something to be taken lightly. Moreover, it does not successfully occur on its own. Much planning and effort are needed to make a merger or acquisition a successful event. Many business disciplines must be part of the planning process. To achieve maximum success, all affected business disciplines must become part of the process. Security is not an exception. A security manager or security professional staff member must be part of the team from the very beginning. This means that from the early planning stages, the merger or acquisition team needs to be thinking about security and must have the support and input of a security professional.

As alluded to earlier, security professionals should know how mergers and acquisitions get started. Company executives consciously engage in a strategy to expand or improve the business. There are many options available for them to consider for expanding or growing the business. Mergers and acquisitions are but one and are generally the fastest way to achieve growth. A company will often establish a business team to seek merger or acquisition opportunities. Within these teams is where the ideas for potential target companies germinate. Merger and acquisition teams generally include members with expertise in business strategy, finance and investments, and executive management. They should also include a security representative.

A large company may have the luxury of maintaining a full-time team of professionals dedicated to mergers and acquisitions. A small company or a company with less experience in mergers and acquisitions cannot afford to have a full-time team, so it forms an integrated process team, drawing from within the company to look for merger or acquisition opportunities. Usually a team consists of business professionals from within the company, led by financial experts or strategic planners, and with some support from outside expertise.

Involving outside expertise is always a good idea if for no other reason than bringing in an independent perspective. Someone who is sufficiently disassociated from the business to bring an independent view will help balance the team's thinking and complement its expertise. It is not uncommon for a merger and acquisition team to want a merger so badly that its own desires cloud its ability to see any negative aspects to making the deal. Using outside expertise may help prevent this from occurring. Furthermore, hiring a consultant when little or no internal expertise exists within the company may be a prudent course of action.

After the core merger and acquisition team is formed, it begins its work to identify potential target companies for capture. It is in these very early stages of the planning when the security representative to the mergers or acquisitions team should be relied on to assist. As part of the effort to identify suitable target companies, the team does preliminary work to learn more about potential target companies. It is precisely in these early stages where security can begin to offer much support. Generally, at this stage of the process, security can provide investigative or research assistance to help the team learn as much about the target company as possible. This support is much like conducting a preemployment background check on a potential employee. In addition, this initial step can use the same processes used for competitive intelligence collection.

The security manager can conduct a similar assessment for a target company. By searching court records, security can learn if the target company and/or its key executives have any history of criminality. Moreover, information about the reputation of the company may be learned through information brokers and public records. This information, if learned early enough, may help facilitate an early assessment and possibly early decisions. For example, learning that a potential target company has a conviction for corruption may influence how the value of the target company is assessed. If the information reveals problems of a more serious magnitude, an early decision may be made to scrap the effort, thereby reducing the likelihood of wasting future time and effort or from causing any embarrassment to the acquiring company and its reputation. Moreover, learning something similar about a key executive may trigger a more thorough assessment of the company to be acquired in an attempt to ferret out as much information as possible, thereby supporting the merger and acquisition team objective to make the best informed business decisions.

Security in the early stages of the effort involves more than the quest for quality background information on potential target companies. The role of security and the security manager reaches far beyond conducting investigations. The next sections describe other areas that require attention and support from security professionals.

Protecting the Effort Itself: Use of Operational Security Methods

Protecting the effort is where security begins. It is the first concern for the security manager and should also be a high priority for the merger and acquisition team leadership. If the merger or acquisition effort itself is not properly protected, it may be damaged or derailed.

Security is a protective discipline. When supporting a merger or acquisition effort, that responsibility does not change. Nearly all members of the merger and acquisition team are focused on making the deal. Each team member conducts an assessment of the target company working within his/her area of expertise. Collectively, they come together to create a final assessment. During this process very few, if any, team members focus on protecting the effort. The security manager must provide the leadership and expertise necessary to apply an appropriate degree of protection to the effort. The security manager is responsible for ensuring that proper security controls are in place, all team members understand what the controls are and how to work within them, and why they are important. An uninformed team will not consciously comply with security requirements. An ignorant or apathetic team will just ignore them.

Protecting the effort generally breaks down into three areas:

1. *Confidentiality of effort:* Protecting the confidentiality of the effort is paramount. When seeking to make a major strategic move such as acquiring another company, it is not wise to expose these intentions too early. Exposure of intentions too soon could alert competitors, causing them to react in such a way as to prevent this transaction from happening. That could mean they seek to acquire the target company themselves, thus making the desired acquisition that much harder. Furthermore, if the market has an indication that a deal is developing, the stock price of the target company could rise. If it rises high enough, the increase in value could kill the deal. It may cause the price to acquire the target company to rise beyond what the acquiring company is willing to, or capable of, paying.

Maintaining confidentiality of a merger or acquisition, in its early stages, may be the most critical element of the effort to protect, but it sure can be argued that it is the most difficult. It is not a natural action for a team used to sharing information with each other to effectively stay within those boundaries and not share information, albeit limited, with others outside the team. Moreover, team activities and behavior, when observed by knowledgeable people, can be very revealing. Confidentiality further breaks down into two major considerations:

- Confidentiality of the total effort: Knowledge that the effort exists may need to be kept from everyone outside the merger and acquisition team. Disclosure of this information may compromise or jeopardize the effort. For competitive reasons, it may be necessary to keep the existence of the effort unknown to all but the merger or acquisition team itself. At some point in time, all mergers and acquisitions become known, but that occurrence must be controlled, deliberate, and approved by executive management. It must not be accidental or happenstance. In the event a company is proceeding down the path of a hostile takeover action, at least in the early stages of the process, the acquiring company may not want the targeted company made aware of these plans. If the target company does become aware of plans to acquire them and it is not interested in being acquired, it may have sufficient time to develop a variety of defensive measures to prevent itself from being acquired. Hostile takeovers make for very good drama. Keeping a low profile for as long as possible can help prevent or mitigate this distraction.

- Confidentiality of the team's work must be maintained: Even if it is publicly known that an acquisition team from one company is pursing a targeted company, there are still things that must remain confidential. Specific strategies, plans, processes, analysis, and assessments must not be revealed to people outside the team without the expressed permission of team leadership, or another in the executive management chain. Unauthorized releases may compromise or harm the effort. At the very least, unauthorized releases may provide a competitor with information (intelligence) it did not possess and did not have to work to get. This information may even assist a competitor in a countermove, thus preventing the merger or acquisition or at least making it a more difficult transaction. An unauthorized release of information may allow a competitor to gain information of value at little or no cost to itself. This is never a good situation.

The security professional must work with the team leader, and both must accept and share responsibility for leading the protection of the entire effort. Accepting responsibility is part of the process of accountability. Team members play an important role in protecting the effort. Each must be made to understand the need for confidentiality. Each must adhere to approved practices and engage in appropriate behavior to ensure confidentiality. The security professional is responsible for developing and implementing processes and procedures used by all to protect the effort. Periodic testing of these processes and procedures is essential to ensure they continue to work well and serve as they were intended in the effort to protect.

2. *Protection of information:* In some ways, information is what the merger and acquisition is all about, notwithstanding the fact that teams' overall objectives are to find the best targets for mergers and acquisitions, and to successfully execute those mergers or acquisitions, thereby bringing the intended value to the company. To do so

effectively requires obtaining and evaluating information. Information is the lifeblood of any merger or acquisition effort. It is information that is sought, obtained, synthesized, analyzed, and acted upon. If the information gathered does not have integrity (true as opposed to false or inappropriately manipulated) and confidentiality and is not available when needed, it loses value. If there is a single critical component of the effort requiring protection, it must be information.

3. *Protection of the merger and acquisition team:* Merger and acquisition teams also may require protection. Not all work is accomplished within the confines of the company office building. Often the team must venture out to accomplish its work. If the target of the merger and acquisition team is a foreign company, some or all of the team will need to visit that company to perform critical elements of their analysis.

In a high-profile event, team members may require protection as they conduct their business outside the confines of the company office. Competitors, media and special interest groups may desire to learn more about the activity and get close to team members. These contacts must be controlled and not allowed to occur randomly. In addition, if information is known to the public, such teams may be the target of national zealots who oppose the foreign merger or acquisition. Terrorists may also attempt to gain maximum publicity by violent acts targeting the team. Effectively applying protective measures is the role of security, often in coordination with local law enforcement agencies.

Assessing the Security Condition of the Target Company

Assessing the security condition of the target company is of utmost importance. After all, it is all about protecting the company's assets.

• *Assess the security condition of the target company:* The most capable and prepared person within the acquiring company to assess the security condition of the target company is the security manager. In the effort to learn and know as much about the target company as possible, the services of the security manager are required. The security manager must be an equal member of the team to be an effective member of the team. With this tasking, the security manager is much like any other team member. A specific function within the target company must be evaluated as part of the overall team assessment.

Knowing about security vulnerabilities and related issues early enables the merger and acquisition team to consider these factors as it makes an assessment of the target company and assigns a value to it.

Unless severe security problems exist, security issues generally never break the merger or acquisition (deal). However, security problems or a substandard company security program can impact the value of the deal. Anything that may affect the value of the deal must be given serious consideration. Failure to do so is something less than a proper due-diligence effort.

Like any other member of the team, the security manager must conduct a security assessment that is as thorough an evaluation as possible. Recognizing that there will be limits on time and the availability of information, the security professional should have a set of measurement tools to use to sort and evaluate the collected information. Obviously, this must be accomplished to make sense of what is learned and to communicate that back to team members as a meaningful set of information useful to the overall assessment.

In every instance the functional team makes an evaluation of the current condition of each function within the target company. Moreover, each team seeks to understand the future condition of each function and anticipate potential issues or problems in terms of how those issues and problems could possibly affect the future capability of the company.

- *Help move the effort along:* Speed and thoroughness are necessary but competing objectives. Moving too quickly may lead to mistakes or missed information. Moving too slowly may be costly in terms of lost time. As is the case with all business transactions; "time is money." Moving too slowly will also allow time for a competitor to learn more about what the acquiring company is planning. The security manager can and must help the effort move along. As the team proceeds through the merger or acquisition process, without doubt, issues or problems will develop. Some of these issues and problems have security implications or require security support for resolution. Being able to react quickly to security problems and issues by implementing effective measures or solutions will help keep the effort moving along as quickly as possible.
- *Identify synergies:* Much of the merger or acquisition team's effort is spent seeking to identity potential synergies that can be exploited during the integration phase and can lead to cost reductions, process improvements, or increased productivity. Most of this activity will occur after a merger or acquisition is made. However, to the extent possible, identifying potential synergies before deal closure provides an integration team with an advantage. If you recall, synergies are achieved when two companies bring different strengths together, enabling them to improve or eliminate existing weaknesses and maximize on their strengths. Capitalizing on synergies is critical to achieving cost savings, cost reductions and cost avoidance. Moreover, synergies will be sought as part of the effort to eliminate redundan-

cies. In the postmerger or acquisition phase, all staff in all company functions and disciplines will be expected to examine their organizations, seeking opportunities for synergies. Security is no exception. How security does business in the target company must be examined. When the two companies come together, performance improvements will be expected. Best practices of either company should be considered for adoption and poor practices slated for reengineering or elimination.

Preparing for the Integration of the Newly Acquired Company into the Acquiring Company

The security professional must prepare for the integration of the newly acquired company into the acquiring company.

Identify Security Requirements for the New Company

What will be the security needs of the new company? The combination of two companies into a single larger company changes that company in many ways. Those changes should be anticipated and evaluated in terms of future security requirements. Some of the security needs of the newly created company may be driven by the security condition of the two companies coming together. Any security problems or vulnerabilities identified during the assessment phase will require attention during the integration phase. Understanding the impact of security problems and vulnerabilities early on will allow more time for planning and development of mitigation measures.

In some cases when two companies come together, it may not be practical to simply impose the security practices of the acquiring company on the new company. The structure and operations of the new company may be so different from either heritage company that the overall security needs and requirements for the newly combined company may now differ significantly. If this is the case, much work will be needed in assessing and understanding those needs and developing procedures and practices to support them.

Controlling Rumors

Rumors are not a good thing, but without doubt they will develop fast and quickly spread. It is often the case that rumors contain a sufficient amount of truth to be at the very least annoying and perhaps even harmful. Some rumors may be more false than true; others will be more true than false. In any event, they are still rumors. Rumors can be complicated. They may involve teams of people to make them happen. As information is exchanged, rumors develop and anxiety levels soar. Rumors grow and spread fastest when little is known about an activity. People have a tendency to fill a knowledge void with supposition and their own conclusions, no matter how fantastic these conclusions may seem.

Preventing rumors is impossible. Limiting and controlling them are possible. Frequent, structured, honest, and planned communications will cut down on the development and spreading of rumors. For the overall effort, this is a concern. Security is no exception. Within the security organizations, security managers must work to communicate openly, honestly, and frequently to ensure that the proper messages and information are communicated, not allowing for rumors or other forms of misinformation to develop. Rumors heighten the already high sense of anxiety employees have resulting from situations of uncertainty. Controlling rumors will help mitigate that tendency of anxiety. Communicating often, openly, and honestly will help keep employees informed and their anxiety level low. Using operational security methods will help mitigate such problems. The team's security manager may want to consider an operational security umbrella to cover the acquisition or merger and using compartmentation, plan for "rumor control." In fact, at the initial phase of any merger or acquisition, the security manager should provide the team with a briefing on how to use operational security methods as a tool to help maintain confidentiality of the proposed merger or acquisition.

Global or International Aspects

If the merger or acquisition effort involves companies from different countries, the role of security becomes more involved and demanding. International travel, laws, and regulations from multiple countries and cultural and language differences along with differing business practices make the task of protecting the effort, people, and information more complicated. Having an understanding of international business issues will be helpful. Having a security manager on the team with experience in international business, and security will be invaluable to the effort. When an acquisition team leader selects a security manager to support the team, the leader should keep in mind the importance of international business experience.

THE ROLE OF THE SECURITY MANAGER AND THE SECURITY ORGANIZATION IN SUPPORT OF MERGERS AND ACQUISITIONS

As alluded to earlier, the importance of security in support of a merger or acquisition can't be overemphasized. All mergers and acquisitions are faced with security issues and concerns. To properly handle them, security managers need to be involved. The extent of security involvement varies depending on the complexity and size of the total effort. Moreover, security issues and concerns vary according to the nature of the business, type of industry, and the maturity of the security programs. For example, security issues common to the banking industry differ from security issues common to the transportation industry.

Security and the security manager plays a supporting role. Like many other supporting organizations, security contributes to the overall success of the effort. Security is not the most critical component of a merger and acquisition team. The merger and acquisition team has a mission to:

- Identify potential targets for acquisition
- Assess those target companies
- Execute the merger or acquisition

The most critical function of any merger or acquisition team is to properly assess the value of a target company. That responsibility lies with the financial team. That is not to say that security is not an important element in preparing for and executing a merger or acquisition; therefore, it should not be ignored or relegated to a role of less significance. The paramount concern of the merger and acquisition team is to identify and properly value a target company.

The financial team focuses on determining the current financial condition of the target company. It also assesses its future earnings capabilities. With that information, a value is placed on the target company. This process is much like the actions of any serious investor when looking for an investment opportunity in any company. Investors seek the optimum deal. A deal that adds value to the acquiring company thus benefits its owners. When one company acquires (purchases) another company, that transaction is an investment. The role of the security manager is to do what is necessary to support the merger or acquisition team in its effort to accomplish this mission.

In any event, security plays an important role on the merger and acquisition team. The security team has a responsibility to mitigate risks and protect the interest of the company, its owners, and shareholders. In support of this obligation, security, as a member of the merger or acquisition team, helps the team make informed decisions and execute a successful transaction.

It is not always apparent to the merger or acquisition team leadership that security needs to be an active member. Nor is it always apparent in the early stages of the effort that the team will encounter situations where expert security support is essential to properly protect the effort and/or its related assets. This is particularly true with new or inexperienced teams.

Team leaders and team members with little to no experience in mergers and acquisitions may not recognize the importance of ensuring that security is an intricate part of the process. If this is the case, it is incumbent on the security manager to work with team leadership and help them understand the role security should play. Doing this early in the effort may help avert security problems from developing later on. Essentially, it may require the security manager to "sell" security to the team. It is important to sell security to team leadership based on real issues and the value security brings to the effort. Don't oversell with exaggerated claims of what security can or should accomplish. Be realistic. The credibility of the security manager and organization is at stake.

Selling security may be as simple as meeting with the team leadership, or all its members, and providing advice and counsel on relevant security issues and concerns along with creating an understanding of what the security organization can do to support the effort. In some instances, selling security may not be so easy and may require the development of a more formal business case characterizing to team leadership the precise value security brings to the effort. In developing the business case, the security professional should keep separate the protective role from the assessment role; thereby ensuring both are communicated and understood.

Team Consultant

Part of the role for security is to serve as the team's "in-house consultant," that is to say, serve as a subject matter expert and help the team learn as much as possible about the target company, particularly as it pertains to matters of security. There are many ways to learn about a target company. If the company is publicly held, much information may be obtained directly from the company itself through its investor relations organization. Moreover, in the United States, information can be obtained from the Securities Exchange Commission, stock market agencies, various publications, and many other sources. Learning and collecting information beyond what is available from these sources requires further investigative work. The gathering of competitive intelligence is a complex task the security manager can and should support.

Other Roles of the Security Manager

The role of consultant to the merger or acquisition team is only one of the important tasks of the security manager. The role of security is multifaceted and the security manager supports the effort in many ways.

Cost/Budgeting

Budgets and expenses must be managed. Every function is responsible for managing its department budget and its expenditures. Security is no exception. The security manager must plan for and manage the cost of security in support of the overall merger and acquisition effort. Additionally, the expected costs associated with providing security to the new company during the postacquisition period must be identified. The security manager must evaluate what resources will be needed to provide security to the company after the two companies merge.

During the premerger period most of the costs encountered by security are labor costs. To ensure that sufficient security expertise is supporting the merger and acquisition team, the security manager uses company security professionals or security consultants to do the necessary work.

During the postmerger period, the security manager focuses on what it costs to provide security to the new company. When two companies come together as one, the security statement of work must be changed. It must be adapted to meet the security needs of the combined companies. With a change in the security statement of work will come a change in the cost of security.

When it comes to spending money on security, one condition is certain: The cost of security for the new company will be expected (by company leadership) to amount to something less than the combined cost of security for the two companies when they were separate. The security manager will be expected to achieve cost savings when bringing two security organizations together. Company leadership will expect the security manager to find opportunities for the elimination of waste and redundancies and to capitalize on any and all potential synergies. Essentially, when it comes to combining two companies or two functions, management has an expectation that one plus one should not equal two. It should equal something less than two. It should never equal more than two.

The security manager must also remember the following:

- Some people will undoubtedly lose their jobs as part of an acquisition or merger and elimination of redundant processes and tasks. Telling people that they no longer have a job is not an enjoyable task. However, it must be done professionally and the sooner the better to eliminate the increased stress and loss of productivity suffered as a result of the merger or acquisition.
- Do not get talked into doing additional work without an increase in budget or a specific budget from which to draw funds to support the merger or acquisition. You will find that other managers will have additional budget available. Don't play the "dedicated, loyal company fool" by trying to do the additional work without additional budget.

Assess Impact to Other Organizations

Security cannot operate in a vacuum. Any analysis of security issues and concerns must consider the impact on the total effort, other functions, and the company as a whole. When assessing security issues, keep in mind the potential impact to affected organizations. For example, if a target company conducts business internationally with operations in high-risk countries, those operations should have in place contingency plans appropriately developed to mitigate those risks. If they do not have contingency plans in place, they may be operating at a higher degree of risk than is acceptable to the company. The extent of that risk varies depending on the size and value of the operation. The team, when made aware of these risks, must acknowledge them and either accept them or mitigate them. In addition, accepting the risks may lead to lowering the value assessment of the target company. Mitigating the risks may cause additional costs. Some organizations may be affected, as they may have to spend money later on to mitigate identified risk. They should know this as early as possible. Depending on the degree of risks and the cost of mitigation, the deal itself may be affected.

Communications

For security, communications is divided into three major categories:

- *Team communications:* Within the merger and acquisition team, communications are generally of a confidential nature. Information related to the merger or acquisition is communicated between team members and must stay within the confines of the team. None of this information is shared outside the team. It is the role of the security manager to define the parameters and requirements for protecting team communications. Clear communication guidelines and procedures must be established and shared with all team members.
- *Communications to employees of the target company:* As the merger and acquisition process evolves, it may be necessary for security to communicate information to employees of the target company or to all company employees. For example, if a change in a security procedure is necessary, that change must be communicated to all employees. A process should be established for all formal communications to ensure that all employees receive the necessary information in a timely manner. Since communications are very sensitive during a merger or acquisition, any communications processes developed must be coordinated with the team and especially the individual assigned responsibility for merger or

acquisition employee/company communications. Conflicting or improper communications must be avoided, as they are difficult to recover from. Because of the sensitive nature of a merger or acquisition, all outside communications should be through the communications focal point. This point cannot be stressed too heavily. Even if approval is granted for the security manager to communicate outside the team on such matters, this communication must be carefully evaluated by the security manager, as any adverse impact caused by such communication will be blamed on the security manager whether or not the blame is valid.

- *Communications within the security community:* Security management must effectively communicate with all members of the security team. These communications should occur regularly and be as thorough as possible. Within this context security communications take two forms: (1) communicating security-related issues and actions to security employees to ensure that everyone is working toward the same plan and the same objectives and (2) communicating to the security team in their capacity as a company employee.

Security professionals and staff are employees, too. Security management must communicate to security employees to keep them as informed as practical concerning the changes occurring within the company. Security employees, like all other employees, experience high levels of anxiety during periods of uncertainty. To keep this anxiety at a minimum, regular and frequent communications are essential.

Ethics

Behaving ethically should not be something employees and management have to be reminded to do; however, this is often the case. Newspapers and business journals are filled with stories of companies and their employees engaging in unethical behavior. Unethical behavior almost always has negative ramifications and will end up costing any company more than the perceived gain. During a merger and acquisition effort, much trust is placed on the merger and acquisition team. Sensitive information, plans, and strategies are shared with team members. Team information is often confidential and requires proper handling and use. In some cases, the handling of information is governed by legal or regulatory requirements. Using any of this information in a manner not sanctioned by the team or company is inappropriate. Misuse in terms of government regulation or law may be punishable with criminal sanctions (e.g., you may be fined and also go to prison!).

Security personnel have the same obligations as all team members—to behave ethically. Furthermore, security personnel are often entrusted with sensitive information beyond that of the average team member. As protectors of information, security professionals should perform their duties to the highest standard of behavior, setting an example for all.

Planning

In any business endeavor, planning is essential. Planning allows a team to think through the activity and identify actions and issues. As actions and issues are identified, they can be carefully considered for alternative actions and implementation. The process of planning causes a team to consider all aspects of the endeavor, good and bad. The process of planning brings the team to a common level of understanding as to what must be accomplished and how it is to be accomplished. The product of planning is the creation of a written plan. The plan itself is the documented result of planning and the metrics by which goals and objectives are measured against. It can be argued that the true value of the plan is the process of planning. For the plan to be most effective, it must be communicated to the team, shared by the team, and, perhaps most important, agreed to by all team members.

An experienced merger or acquisition team will have a plan. That plan should cover everything from the process of identifying target companies to closing the deal and all actions that lie between. A portion of the total plan should be dedicated to security. As a subset of the total effort, a security plan must be developed. The security plan should address security actions and issues for all phases of the effort as a subplan of the overall merger or acquisition plan. The security plan should also include the actions and procedures needed to keep the effort confidential, an operational security (OPSEC) plan. The security plan is obviously most useful when communicated and made available to all of the team members.

SECURITY SUPPORT: PREMERGER AND POSTMERGER OR ACQUISITION

A merger or acquisition can be divided into two major phases: premerger and postmerger. Each phase is made up of different activities and therefore requires different types of support. In the early stages, the security organization should focus on protecting the effort and the team and participating as a team member in assessing the condition of the target company. After the merger or acquisition, the role of security changes. With the initial phase of the effort complete, security shifts to focusing on the protection requirements for the new company. The security manager is also responsible for supporting the integration of the newly acquired business into the existing company. Like every other functional lead, the security manager is responsible for integrating the two security organizations together to form a new security organization. If the acquired company is a large business, integrating them into the acquiring company is no small task. The larger the company, the more complicated and involved the integration effort.

Premerger or Acquisition

During the premerger or acquisition phase, the role of security is primarily fact-finding and protective:

- *Preliminary background investigations:* Learn as much as possible about the target company and its leadership. All knowledge gained early will have value in later phases. The more the merger and acquisition team can learn about the target company the greater the possibility of good business decisions being made.

> **Due diligence:** *Such a measure of prudence, activity or assiduity, as is properly to be expected from, and ordinarily exercised by, a reasonable and prudent man under the circumstances; not measured by any absolute standard but depending on the relative facts of the special case . . .*[6]

- *Due diligence:* During the due diligence phase of the effort, the merger and acquisition team has an opportunity and an obligation to take a more in-depth look at the target company. This examination is still limited. How extensive it becomes may require an agreement by both companies. Nevertheless, it will be an opportunity to learn more about the target company than is available from open sources. The time frame for the due diligence is limited but should be sufficient to allow for obtaining enough information about the company so that when this information is combined with data gathered from other sources as well as open sources, chances of making the correct decisions are enhanced. It is during this phase that the team leadership identifies and considers all problems and concerns. The problems are evaluated and a decision is made to proceed with the merger or acquisition or abort the effort.
- *Operations security:* Operations, or operational security (OPSEC), refers to the measures and controls applied to the effort to ensure that the day-to-day activities of the team are protected to the extent appropriate. The security manager is responsible for leading this

---

[6] *Black's Law Dictionary*, DeLuxe Fourth Edition, 1974.

effort and for developing and implementing the necessary protective measures. Protective measures vary with each phase of the effort, as each phase differs in its need for control. For example, the initial discussion concerning the team's intentions to acquire a target company and the background assessments of that company and its executives generally need to occur under very tight controls. Preventing knowledge of the discussions from becoming public could have competitive and legal implications. For example, if publicly traded companies are involved, information suggesting the possibility of a merger or acquisition could have an impact on the stock price of one or both companies. Consider when Comcast announced its intentions to acquire Disney. The stock price of both companies was immediately affected, with Comcast stock dropping and Disney stock rising. Moreover, much of the information pertaining to proposed mergers and acquisitions is subject to control by government regulations, so companies are obligated to control the release of information.

Day One of the Merger or Acquisition

Actions taken before a merger or acquisition, as already mentioned, are limited for many reasons. Until the acquisition is complete, the acquiring company does not own the target company and therefore does not have the authority or right to do anything that will change or alter the target company. Once the target company is acquired, however, the new owner has complete authority to fully examine all aspects of the acquired company and make whatever changes are necessary. What does this mean to the security manager and the security organization? The security manager is now free to fully examine and assess the security program of the newly acquired company and begin to address issues and make changes. Having been part of the due diligence assessment, the security manager should already have a basic understanding of the acquired company's security program and a good idea of any security problems that exist. Moving forward from this baseline of knowledge, a more detailed assessment should be planned.

Postmerger or Acquisition

In the postacquisition period, the premerger and acquisition work would have been accomplished, including the preliminary background assessment. Furthermore, the due diligence phase can now be expanded into a complete analysis of the security condition of the newly acquired company. Since during the premerger phase there are limits on the amount of information available for analysis, the total assessment cannot be completed until after the merger or acquisition occurs. It is during the post-merger or acquisition period when all data are made available.

The expanded assessment should include a complete threat and vulnerability analysis. Keep in mind that the expanded assessment must be accomplished on the acquired company as it operated in its pre-merger or acquisition environment. Understanding how the acquired company functioned before the merger will be useful when leading the acquired company through the integration phase in becoming part of the new company. Will the security issues of the acquired company impact the new company? If so, how and what needs to be done to mitigate those issues?

Once the postmerger period begins, most of the effort will shift from assessment to integration. Integrating the two companies together requires an integration of the two security organizations. The integration effort is always the most problematic phase of any merger or acquisition. It is often neglected and poorly planned. From the beginning, so much attention is focused on making the merger or acquisition happen and closing the deal—what some refer to as the "sexy part of the effort." The postmerger integration is much less "sexy" and takes much longer to accomplish. A successful integration requires a well-defined end state, as well as a clear and communicated plan to get there.

Changing the Culture of the Organization

In an ideal state, when two organizations merge, a new and desired culture is developed. A desired culture should reflect the values and expectations of the new organization's leadership. This does not happen on its own. Changing an organization's culture requires much work with clear and concise communications expectations. If left unattended, a new culture will develop but it will not be the desired culture. It is possible that the culture of each of the two separate companies will continue to exist in conflict if they are not driven to change. The result will be a dysfunctional condition, with clashes in cultural behavior inhibiting the development of a new efficient and effective organization—the opposite of what the company leadership and owners need and expect.

To achieve a desired culture, the expectations and values of the new company must be communicated clearly, consistently, and often. Behavior that is consistent with the stated expectations and values of the newly formed company must be rewarded. This is as true for the individual functions that make up the entire company as it is for the company as a whole.

Within the security organization, the security manager has the responsibility to bring the two organizations together working toward a common purpose of achieving stated expectations. The security manager must ensure that this is accomplished in a manner that is consistent with the stated values of the company. This is no easy task and achieving success requires the use of integration tools such as the following:

- *Security council:* Establishing a security council can be an effective tool in large companies with large security organizations. A security council is really nothing more than a forum to bring together those charged with implementing and managing the company security program to ensure they work toward a common approach. In essence, it is a forum for the organization's security leadership to come together and work toward the same objectives. A security council gives all of security management a seat at the table. It is a tool of inclusiveness. When two companies come together, each of the similar functions will operate somewhat alike but possibly not the same. Expectations and objectives will differ as each entity holds on to what it knows and what it values. Merging into a single entity will require changing what each knows, the values, and the expectations. Accomplishing this integration will not occur naturally. It has to be designed to happen. Each organization must understand and "buy-in" to a single common vision and set of expectations. Getting there will require developing trusting relationships within a framework of common expectations and using common tools, including common processes and the institution of common policies and procedures. Reinforcing this behavior should be the implementation of common measures and rewards. A security council should be a chartered body established for the primary purpose of being the deliberative body for security's functional issues when the function is large and disparate. The membership should include the organization's senior functional (security) management along with members from other disciplines with a major stake in the security program. This council can also be used as a forum to develop strategies and processes to ensure that commonality is achieved and redundancies are eliminated.
- *Policy and procedures:* Long- and short-term policy changes (not intended to cover every area, but at least the critical areas) serve as an interim operating guidance until long-term objectives are defined. Policies and procedures are considered the company-created rules. They are a declaration of how the business intends to operate. They define the operational parameters. Every company must have a set of company security policies and procedures. They establish the rules within which everyone, including security professionals, are expected to operate. When properly designed, they are a very powerful tool for influencing performance and behavior.
- *Service agreements:* These agreements establish boundaries for continuation of services until more permanent measures can be

taken. They are particularly useful when only a business unit of a company and not an entire company is acquired. They are also useful during a divestiture when a portion of a company is sold but not the entire company. For many reasons, it may be necessary for the divested business unit to remain linked to the divesting parent until provisions can be made for a complete separation. For example, if a divested business unit shares a facility with elements of the divesting company, it may be necessary for the acquiring company to lease back facility space from the seller to keep the newly acquired business unit operational. It may also be necessary for a period of time for the acquiring company to buy back services until the separation is complete. These services may include security services. When service agreements are established they should meet the following conditions:

1. They must be established for a short period of time. As short as possible is best. Continuing the relationship for any length of time will be problematic. Keeping it as short as possible will reduce the likelihood of problems.
2. The type of service provided must be well defined. Leave no ambiguity in the agreement.
3. Service agreements must be part of the sale contract.
4. All security issues must be clearly stated to prevent failures or misunderstandings from occurring in the future.

Service agreements may be a necessary tool and can be a useful tool. Because they are part of the delay in separating the business unit from its parent company, they should be used sparingly.

- *Cost of security:* Cost is always an issue. Within most companies, security is a cost center and not a revenue center. Unless the company is in the business of selling security products and services, security does not usually generate revenue. Like other supporting functions, the security organization exists to fulfill a protective and compliance role. Company assets protection, driven by laws, regulations, and the need to mitigate risks, are the reason security organizations are formed. Moreover, to protect their own interest, most companies establish a set of rules (policies and procedures) to provide a protective framework for employees to operate within. This costs money.

When a merger or acquisition occurs, executive management and ownership have an expectation that value will be created with the union of the two companies. One way to increase that value is to reduce costs. Capitalizing on synergies and eliminating redundancies are common means of reducing costs. Every function within the company will be expected to make a contribution. Security is no exception. There are other potential issues of concern:

- *Disgruntled employees:* Every merger or acquisition brings with it at least one disgruntled employee. Of course there is usually more than one but at the very least there will be one. Human nature is such that someone will not be happy with the deal. Even when owners and management are quite pleased with the transaction, recognizing it to be an important and valued-added event, someone will not be happy. Disgruntled employees can be disruptive. At the very least, they can be difficult to work with and thus create a level of tension within the organization that is enough to disrupt the normal work process. When employees are unhappy about a merger or acquisition, they usually don't keep this to themselves. Some passively resist change and are not supportive of the effort to integrate into the new acquiring company. In some cases, disgruntled employees can be very disruptive. Angry employees are not pleasant to be around. Their negative behavior and attitude may create an environment where unresolved conflict develops and even thrives. This is not a condition conducive to good employee morale, teamwork, and sustained high levels of productivity. In extreme cases, disgruntled employees may act out and even attempt to "sabotage" the integration process. Recognizing disgruntled employees and taking preemptive corrective action are the responsibilities of disgruntled employees' immediate management. Dealing with disgruntled employees may also require the assistance of the human resources organization and security. In dealing with a disgruntled employee, the security manager usually does not need to get involved unless employee behavior or actions create a disruptive or hostile work environment. Should an incident of workplace violence occur, the security manager should be immediately engaged as part of a threat assessment team or incident response management process. Disruptive employees and incidents of work place violence must be handled swiftly and decisively.
- *Working and doing business with governments:* Foreign mergers and acquisitions can be more complex than mergers and acquisitions occurring within the same country. Many factors contribute to the complexity of a merger or acquisition. Pursuing a foreign company greatly complicates the transaction. Success requires an ability to work within the legal, political, and cultural structures of the target company's country. Every country has a different set of governing principles for business activity affecting mergers and acquisitions. Within some countries, the laws and regulations are

friendly toward mergers and acquisitions; in other countries, the laws and regulations are so complex and onerous that they make executing mergers or acquisitions nearly impossible. In other countries only specific industries are afforded protection with antimerger and acquisition regulations. Generally, those industries or sectors are considered national assets and provide a economic power or advantage to the host country. Understanding these considerations; as well as the society and culture of the foreign country, is essential in the earliest stages of a merger or acquisition. Knowing about these issues in the early stages of the effort may prevent a major loss of time and money.

- *Classified government work:* Merging with or acquiring a company that does national security (e.g., classified government work) creates another set of issues. Where classified government contracts are involved, strict regulatory and legal requirements drive how those companies must conduct business. If an acquiring company seeks a target company from another country and that company is engaged in classified government contracts from its host country, the acquisition may or may not be permitted. At the very least, if permitted, layers of separation will be necessary, ensuring the national security interests of the host country are protected. In essence a "firewall" must be installed to ensure that the acquiring company is separated from the target company's host country protected information. These controls are complicated but can be accomplished. For example, if a British company chooses to pursue the acquisition of a U.S. company doing classified work for the United States Department of Defense, the British company must obtain approval for the acquisition from the U.S. Department of Defense and other interested government agencies. Once these approvals are obtained, conditions must be established that ensure that classified information from the host country (United States) is protected from unauthorized release and exposure to non-U.S. citizens. This could even require separation and protection of information from the entire British company. In accordance with U.S. Department of Defense regulatory requirements, formal controls and separations must be established to ensure these separations.[7] If the merger or acquisition occurs between two U.S. companies, both involved in classified government programs, the approval process is much easier, as fewer, if any additional controls, are required. The U.S. Government may require an integration plan along with operational waivers allowing the acquired company to

---

[7] For specific information see U. S. Government regulation promulgated in the *National Industrial Security Program Operating Manual* (DoD 5220.22-M).

continue to operate in its currently approved mode, at least until formal requests for change are submitted to the appropriate government agency.

WHAT SHOULD A SECURITY MANAGER BE ON THE ALERT FOR WHEN FIRST GETTING INVOLVED IN A MERGER OR ACQUISITION EFFORT?

As stated earlier, the security manager is a critical member of the merger and acquisition team, but that may not be recognized or understood by the team leadership. This is often the situation if the team is an inexperienced team. As a security manager, you must expect to spend time with the team leadership to convince them of the value a security manager or team can bring to a merger or acquisition.

All mergers and acquisitions are not the same. The size and nature of the transaction will drive the complexity of the issues. Unless a security manager is highly experienced with mergers and acquisitions, one condition is certain: more time will be spent supporting the effort than was planned. If the security manager is not experienced with mergers or acquisitions and sufficient security expertise is not available within the company, do not hesitate to seek outside support.

Sometimes, things go wrong even with "the best laid plans." Keep Murphy's Law in mind at all times: If something can go wrong, it will. When it does, immediate attention is necessary. Act swiftly to address and solve problems. Not all problems must be solved right away. Some do and must be quickly recognized. Solving them promptly will improve the team's ability to quickly and properly move through the effort in conducting their assessment.

During the premerger and acquisition phase, the team may have limited access to information. The details of the inner workings of the company will not be fully revealed or understood until the postmerger and acquisition period. At that time, the security manager and the entire team should expect that sufficient information will be available to the team to allow them to value the target company and determine if there are any major security issues. Less obviously, issues will not surface early. Usually these issues develop during the postmerger and acquisition period when the integration of the acquired company into the acquiring company occurs.

Remember why companies engage in mergers and acquisitions. They are done for strategic reasons and always with the intent to add value to the acquiring or newly formed company. Much of the newly created value lies in the skills and capabilities of the employees and management team from the newly acquired company. It is a natural reaction for the acquiring company to want to keep the most skilled employees from the acquired company. It will not be a simple process or natural reaction to follow through.

With few exceptions, skilled newly acquired employees will not be kept at the expense of employees from the acquiring company. Not all employees are let go. Most are often retained, as they are needed to perform the work and produce the products that made the company they work for such an attractive acquisition target in the first place. Almost always, some will have to go. Some companies will conduct a competitive bidding process in an attempt to identify the most skilled people from both companies, place them in critical positions, and release those considered to have less value or to be less skilled. Other companies will focus on eliminating redundant jobs and redundant people with little or no consideration of talent.

What does this mean to the security manager or security professional? If you are with the acquired company and are directly supporting a business unit or contract, you are likely to be left in place. Odds are your services will still be needed. If you are a security manager or professional working at the corporate headquarters, start looking for work. One of the first organizations eliminated in any acquisition is the acquired company's corporate headquarters structure. Immediately upon acquisition, a second corporate headquarters becomes a redundant and costly burden. Swift elimination is the cure.

MAKE OR BUY: SHOULD A SECURITY MANAGER OUTSOURCE WORK TO CONSULTANTS OR KEEP ALL WORK IN-HOUSE?

Like every other business function, security is faced with budgetary constraints. Operating within a budget and fielding the most efficient and effective organization is a difficult task. Security departments are staffed with employees possessing the necessary experience and expertise to accomplish the organization's statement of work. They are generally not staffed with reserve resources they can deploy to special assignments as needed. The condition is usually to the contrary. Security departments are staffed at some minimal level without excess resources to divert to efforts as large and important as a merger or acquisition. Furthermore, since mergers and acquisitions occur so infrequently, the likelihood of having employees experienced with them is low. Therefore, when a merger or acquisition occurs, the security manager must make a decision to pursue one of the following courses of action:

- Add to the security staff by recruiting skilled personnel experienced with mergers and acquisitions.
- Allow current staff to take on the challenge of working security issues for the effort, possibly leaving other work to be completed at a later date.
- Hire an outside expert—a consultant—to provide guidance and direction to the security staff to support the effort, or possibly hire the consultant to do the work.

Essentially, a decision to make the service or buy the service must be made. That is to say, provide security support from within the organization using company security professionals or seek the support of external experts and purchase their service. Mergers and acquisitions can be complicated. None are simple; they all vary in size and degree of complexity. All require security support to some degree. If a security manager has never been involved in a merger or acquisition, getting outside help from an experienced consultant is a prudent course of action.

If Assistance Is Needed, Get It

If a security manager or the security team is not experienced with mergers and acquisitions, it is a good idea to solicit help. Help can be obtained from many sources, including from within the merger and acquisition team or within the company. Team members experienced with mergers and acquisitions are good resources for identifying potential sources for assistance. It is foolish to proceed without capable support regardless of where that support comes from.

An inexperienced merger and acquisition team may not understand the need for outside security assistance, or, because of budgetary constraints, the team may not authorize external support. In this situation, the security manager will have to rely on the best effort of the security team and security professionals. There are low-cost options available to a security manager where support may be obtained. These options may not be the best choice, but they can be useful by offering guidance to help navigate through the merger and acquisition process. The following are potential sources for assistance:

- For premerger support, experts within the company may be a valuable source. During the postmerger period, experts within the acquired company may be useful.
- The security manager's personal network of security experts and colleagues: A security manager can consult colleagues who may have experience with mergers and acquisitions, "picking their brains" and learning from their experiences. Until a merger or acquisition is made known, this should only be done in a limited way never revealing anything about the target company.
- Consult the available literature including journals, articles, and books. There are publications devoted entirely to mergers and acquisitions that may be useful. Large libraries and on-line book sellers are good sources.
- Professional associations are another potentially valuable source for information. The American Society for Industrial Security

maintains a listing of currently available security publications that may be helpful.

- Companies offering security services usually have an experienced investigative capability to include experience with due diligence efforts. Some of the larger security consultant firms and service providers may have a wide range of experience with mergers and acquisitions. There are also law firms with this expertise. They may be expensive but will possess the necessary skills to provide quality support. Their expense must be weighed against their value. After all, "doing it right the first time" with experienced professionals may in the long run be a more effective and efficient way of merging companies together.

One problem of seeking assistance from outside of the company is that it expands the number of people with knowledge of the effort. It also requires releasing sensitive company information to persons not part of the company. This concern can be simply addressed. Support can be obtained without exposing or compromising the confidentiality of the program. Use of trusted sources who sign nondisclosure agreements will greatly reduce the risk of compromising information. A good security practice is to have all team members, including security personnel from within and outside of the company, sign nondisclosure agreements. It serves as a reminder to all participants of the importance of protecting sensitive information. Furthermore, should someone deliberately misuse information, having a signed nondisclosure agreement will assist with any necessary action for recourse.

SUMMARY

Whether it is an acquisition of an entire company (total assets), a product line, or two equal companies merging together to form a stronger and more capable company, there will be a requirement for security support and a role for the security manager. The security effort may be as simple as providing guidance and basic security support to the merger or acquisition team, or it could be as extensive as creating a full-time security team to support the effort.

Recognizing the need for security support is not always the case with merger or acquisition team leaders. A security manager may have to "sell" security to an inexperienced team. Moreover, a security manager may have to go outside the company to obtain necessary expertise if it is not available within the company.

Section II

Premerger and Preacquisition Support

This section addresses the role of security in the premerger and preacquisition phase. From the time a decision is made by company executives to pursue a merger or acquisition until the day it is officially accomplished, security must play a prominent role in support of the effort. Issues such as ensuring the effort itself is not compromised (discovered by those who do not have a need to know) to participating in assessing the condition of the target company require the support of the security organization.

Perhaps its most important task is to provide directions to the mergers or acquisitions team as to why and how to protect the overall effort. What the team does, how it operates, the information it possesses, and the merger and acquisition team members all require some level of security support. During the early stages of the effort, security support is the most critical, particularly for maintaining confidentiality.

Security is also necessary to support of the competitive intelligence process. Here security plays multiple roles. Information is collected as part of the process to develop competitive intelligence. Security contributes to the gathering of data as a source of potentially useful information. Security also works to ensure defensive competitive intelligence measures are in place, thus limiting what unauthorized persons may learn about competitive strategies.

Finally, the security manager is a member of the due diligence team. As the team works to develop an assessment of the target company, the security manager makes a contribution by assessing the security condition of the target company in particular, looking for any security issues significant enough to adversely impact the deal.

Chapter 4

Gathering Information and Producing Competitive Intelligence

Knowledge is power. – Sir Francis Bacon[1]

INTRODUCTION

This chapter focuses on the process of collecting information and using it to produce competitive intelligence. The type of information collected is information that has potential value in the processes of making business decisions about mergers, acquisitions, or divestitures. The information collected is analyzed with the intent of producing a usable product. That usable product is referred to as business intelligence, competitive intelligence, or corporate intelligence.

Competitive intelligence has value. The extent of that value depends on its timely and relevant application and use. Having competitive intelligence is of little value if it is not used properly or in a timely manner. Competitive intelligence is used to assist planners, managers, and executives in preparing to make good strategic decisions involving mergers, acquisitions, or divestitures plans.

Competitive intelligence has value in many areas of the business; however, it is vital to the successful decision-making processes of mergers and acquisitions. Competitive intelligence can be produced through the gathering of information from a variety of sources. These sources and their collection are discussed along with the process for developing useful intelligence. Furthermore, the types and usage of competitive intelligence are examined.

---

[1] Sir Francis Bacon (1561–1626), *Religious Meditations, of Heresies,* 1597.

Intelligence, n. 5. information received or imparted; news. 6. a. secret information esp. about an enemy or potential enemy. b. the gathering or distribution of such information. c. the evaluated conclusions drawn from such information. d. an organization engaged in gathering such information: military intelligence.[2]

COMPETITIVE INTELLIGENCE

Within the context of this book we use the term *competitive intelligence*. However, we sometimes refer to it as *business intelligence* or *corporate intelligence*, and in this book, the terms are used interchangeably. In the "real world" these terms refer to the same process or product and are used as a matter of preference as opposed to a matter of distinction. Essentially, corporate intelligence, business intelligence, and competitive intelligence refer to the same product.

Regardless of what it is called, competitive intelligence is produced and used to provide a company with a competitive advantage within the marketplace. *Produced* is the key point. Intelligence does not just happen. It has to be produced, but there is nothing mystifying about competitive intelligence. Like anything else of value, it takes skill and hard work to create. Producing competitive intelligence is not unlike producing many other products. It involves a defined process, disciplined and skilled workers, careful analysis, and proper application or implementation. It is as much an art as it is a science. The value of competitive intelligence depends on where, when, how, and under what conditions it is used.

In a very basic way, competitive intelligence is produced and used every day. People collect or gather relevant business information, analyze that information within some defined context, making that information more useful as conclusions are developed or the information is refined in such a way as to have more significant meaning. That refined product is then applied or used to make a more informed decision, develop a better plan, or some other value-added purpose.

Competitive intelligence is more than just information or data. Collecting information, even massive amounts of information, does not create competitive intelligence. Volume is not the key. Relevant information analyzed within the context of specific needs can lead to the creation of intelligence. Information and data may have value as intelligence without further analysis. Data may be useful as intelligence just as it was acquired. Generally, that is not the case. For most information or data to be useful as intelligence, it must be analyzed and applied within the context

---

[2] *Random House Webster's College Dictionary* (New York: Random House, Inc., 2000).

of what is known to help better understand what is unknown. For effective analysis, the task needs to be performed by a skilled analyst or someone, at the very least, with subject matter expertise. Any data or information collected is most valuable when it is transformed through skillful analysis into results that are useful.

Why is competitive intelligence valuable? Competitive intelligence is a tool to help leaders, executives, managers, and practitioners better understand their operating environment, marketplace, and competitors. Having competitive intelligence can be useful in positioning any company to quickly react to challenges and changes within the marketplace.

When the informal or routine process just described is engineered in a more systematic and disciplined way, a useful corporate or competitive intelligence process is born. This process, if effectively implemented, contributes to the body of knowledge available for company managers and executives to use to make better business decisions. In business, knowledge gained about competitors and the marketplace is an essential ingredient in the quest for any company to become more competitive. Having an in-depth knowledge of competitors and the marketplace may provide a company with a competitive edge.

The old adage "knowledge is power" is true. Knowing more about the marketplace and your competitors within that marketplace can provide a competitive edge. In some cases, having this knowledge may be the only advantage a company has. To be successful within any market a company must differentiate itself from its competitors. It must produce a better product, provide a better service, sell at a lower price, or be the lower cost producer. Use of quality intelligence can help a company develop an advantage in any or all of these areas. Keep in mind we said *help* a company develop an advantage in any or all of these areas. Knowledge only provides an advantage if it is properly used.

Good intelligence contributes to the overall body of knowledge. Knowing and understanding competition and the marketplace are essential for becoming a successful company. Without such knowledge and understanding, a company may have a short period of success but will not sustain this success over the long haul. Knowledge of competition and the marketplace is particularly important to the process of long-range strategic planning. It is also important to the process of mergers and acquisitions.

> *Competitive, adj. 1. of, pertaining to, involving, or decided by competition. 2. well suited for competition: a competitive price. 3. having a strong desire to compete or succeed.*[3]

---

[3] *Random House Webster's College Dictionary* (New York: Random House, Inc., 2000).

What Is Information?

In this age of electronic and digital information, people and businesses are inundated with data. More than any other time in human history, information is abundantly available to more people, businesses, governments, and various institutions. So much information exists, and the task of managing it so complex that new disciplines such as knowledge management have evolved. Knowledge management, a relatively new discipline, seeks to better manage the body of knowledge contained within a company or organization and its people. Knowledge management is used to help a company manage what it knows and who knows what.

With so much information available, it is difficult to determine what information has value and what information does not have value. Moreover, with so much information available, valuable information gets lost within the sheer volume of it all. For practical purposes, if information is needed but not available when it is needed, it may as well be lost.

In the April 2000, second edition of its College Dictionary, Random House Webster defines information as knowledge communicated or received concerning a particular fact or circumstance. Continuing on information is further defined as knowledge gained through study, communication, research, etc.: data

---

Information in and of itself has value; however, it may or may not be intelligence. Facts and figures by themselves may only be interesting, but when facts are combined with other data, placed within a specific context, and analyzed with a purpose, the value of that information may increase. That information may become useful competitive intelligence.

Information alone, if it is not analyzed within a specific context and applied to a condition or situation, may not reach its full value or potential. Information acquired or supplied about something or somebody, when transformed through analysis, may produce a more useful product. That product may contribute to the body of knowledge or provide an answer to a question heretofore unanswered. If that occurs, that product has value. That product is intelligence. In a business context, that product is business intelligence or competitive intelligence. In business, the more known about a particular subject, issue, or problem, the better are the chances for making good decisions.

How Does Someone Get Information?

Information does not just fall into one's lap. Well, actually it may very well fall into one's lap considering how ubiquitous it is, but generally information, particularly useful information, does not. Information needs to be acquired and developed. Collecting information is both simple and complex. Gathering information from public sources such as newspapers and journals requires only the purchase or borrowing of a copy, then searching through the publication looking for useful information. This is a time-consuming but simple process. Moreover, much of the information available may be vague or general and not specific enough to meet one's needs.

To obtain more specific or more narrowly focused information, the use of less prevalent sources is usually required. There are sources available that are highly skilled at gathering and collecting large amounts of information and data. These sources generally focus on a narrow range of subjects for which they have an interest or expertise. For example, if looking for data on product reliability, it may be useful or necessary to find a source that compiles such data.

When seeking information, one should have an idea of the type of information that is needed. Since so much information is available, determining the type of information needed and then matching it to sources that may be able to provide that type of information is the simple and efficient approach. For example, when gathering information about a company listed on the New York Stock Exchange, a good place to start is with a stockbroker or the Security and Exchange Commission. Both possess, or have access to, much information about companies listed on the stock exchange.

When seeking business-related information, there are two places to begin the quest. The first is internal—right inside your own company. The second is external—any source outside of your company, and there are many.

Internal Sources (Sources Within Your Company)

Within any company, there are many potential sources for acquiring business information.

- *Company Library:* Many large or medium-size companies maintain a small, internal library where business-relevant publications are acquired and kept. This is usually a convenient place to start when looking for basic business information. Company libraries usually contain current business publications and journals. A librarian may even be available to assist in searches for specific sources or information.
- *Other employees:* Any company with more than one employee has people who may possess, or have access to, useful business information. Talk to them. Often employees know more about a competitor or a particular market than they do about their own company. Engage the

wider organization. Within any company are employees with different experiences, viewpoints, and perspectives. If asked, they are usually willing to share what they know. Much of what you need to know about competitors or other companies and markets may already exist within your own organization. Information about competition and markets is important to many employees in the company. Consequently, they have much information for their own use to share. One word of caution, some employees may have knowledge of sensitive proprietary information from their past employers. Providing that information may be at the very least unethical and at most illegal. When interviewing employees, they should be cautioned not to provide any information of a proprietary nature belonging to other corporations for whom they had worked. When in doubt, the interviewer and/or interviewee should check with their company's legal staff.

Company employees must become part of an information-gathering network. A competitive intelligence organization or process can't be effective operating in isolation. Knowledge and learning grow from interaction with others. It is important and valuable to work with different internal communities who share objectives, knowledge, learning, and experience. The security professional should develop internal information sources and, to the extent possible, integrate them into an information network to help create a robust learning environment.

> *Another word of caution: this is not to say a "spy" network should be established. That should be made clear to the employees during their interviews, and the purpose for gathering the information should be explained to them to the extent possible. Gathering information and producing competitive intelligence are done ONLY using legitimate means. It is a business process and must be accomplished legally and ethically. Dispelling false impressions that this process equates to "spying" is as critical as operating within well-defined and appropriate boundaries.*

Creating an information-gathering network needs to be accomplished without the burden of an administrative structure. The process for producing competitive intelligence needs to be structured, but the networks feeding information into the process must be unencumbered by constraints of a formal structure. A skilled manager of the competitive intelligence organization should be able to manage an information-gathering network in an informal and unstructured way and yet ensure that it operates within the ethical framework of the company's values.

For the greatest value, an internal information network must be developed from within the entire company and not limited to just those disciplines familiar with, or experienced in, the competitive intelligence process. The security professional or other appropriate member of the mergers or acquisitions team should reach beyond the traditional organizations of strategic planners or merger and acquisition specialists. These networks ought to include disciplines such as the following:

- *Business development:* The business development organization possesses business information and is a large user of competitive intelligence. Charged with the responsibility for developing new business for the company, business development professionals spend much of their time learning about their marketplace and competitors. Successfully developing new business requires an understanding of how the market works and what the competition in that marketplace has to offer. Knowing the strengths, weaknesses, and intentions of competitors can provide an advantage. This is particularly true in mature markets where competition is at its highest levels and there is little that differentiates one company from another. Business development is both a user of competitive intelligence and a great source for business information and business intelligence.
- *Executive management:* They are key users of competitive intelligence. As they lead the enterprise and plan its strategic direction, access to competitive intelligence will contribute to their overall understanding of the marketplace. Executives are excellent sources for providing business information and competitive intelligence. They regularly interact with executives from competitor companies. They do this directly or through associations, friends, and colleagues. In that process, they learn and observe. What they learn and observe often has competitive value. To be useful, that information needs to be shared within the company. In some way, executive management must be connected to the information gathering networks and the competitive intelligence process.
- *Information management:* These employees can be an important contributor to the competitive intelligence process. In particular, they provide information systems support and can provide information on computer systems and other high technology developments and practices.
- *Knowledge management:* Companies today are developing and using knowledge management programs to help them "know what they know." A knowledge management program may be a useful place to obtain information, particularly when looking for technology-related information. Many knowledge management programs begin with a focus on capturing technology capabilities and the skills of individual workers. Employees within your own company, particularly those with unique capabilities and knowledge, are

often a good source for acquiring new competitive information. Employees with advanced or unique knowledge of technology and technological developments often know much about what their colleagues are doing at other companies. They may know what other companies are doing, are capable of, and know people at those companies who may possess useful information.

- *Legal:* The company's legal staff should be a permanent member of the internal information network and the competitive intelligence process. Legal staff should also serve as an advisor to the competitive intelligence team in order to: (1) provide legal guidance to the team and help develop legal, ethical, and value operational guidelines for the team members to follow; (2) review team/program operation practices for legal issues and concerns; (3) raise confidence of executive management as legal members give the team legitimacy; management is more likely to accept higher levels of risk, if they know legal is part of the process or at least supporting the process; (4) provide direct legal counsel if necessary. If lawyers are part of the team they will have a better understanding of how the team operates and how the competitive intelligence processes works; this knowledge and understanding provides lawyers with a better framework for understanding issues within the proper context and providing good legal advice; (5) assist in the analysis of information by working with assessment teams and providing a legal perspective of competitive issues; legal departments and lawyers also have competitive intelligence needs; as they deal with complex legal issue or actual legal cases involving such activities as counterfeiting, trademark and patent infringements, and support for matters of litigation, they too benefit from knowing more about these issues within a competitive context; and (6) share information they learn; as part of the legal system, lawyers are regularly exposed to information with potential intelligence value.

- *Security:* Because security professionals spend much time and effort protecting company information, they are familiar with methods used to collect such information. Sharing those methods with competitive intelligence teams is one way in which security professionals can contribute to the process. Security professionals are particularly useful in developing defensive measures used to combat competitive intelligence collection efforts against their own company. Since security is usually the "owner" of the company information protection program, it should be conducting training and awareness sessions for key, if not all, employees. During these sessions, defensive measures for protecting sensitive information can be emphasized. This training serves two purposes:

  - First, it helps employees become more aware of external efforts to collect information from them. Employees should understand that they may be targeted by outsiders seeking competitive information from them. Defensive training should sensitize employees to the pitfalls of sharing company-sensitive information with people who don't have a need to know.

- Second, training may make employees more aware of how they can obtain information from others, which may have potential competitive value. If properly implemented, an information protection program with an emphasis on employee awareness serves both the offensive and defensive mechanism. Again, a word of caution is needed here. The training must include how the employees can help the information-gathering process and therefore the merger and acquisition team. Furthermore, emphasis must be placed on ethical and legal conduct.

- *Marketing and sales (including field sales offices):* These professionals are huge users of intelligence and benefit directly from receiving it. They are also close to customers, as they interact with them daily. This interaction makes them potentially useful sources for business information and competitive intelligence.

- *Merger or acquisition teams:* These teams use, develop, and have access to business information. Some of this information has value as competitive intelligence or is useful in developing competitive intelligence. When conducting assessment of potential target companies, merger and acquisition teams spend much of their time analyzing competitors and their marketplace. Merger and acquisition teams work closely with strategic planning organizations and often are embedded within them. In the process of gathering information and developing intelligence for their own use, they acquire or develop information and intelligence that may be useful to others.

- *Human Resources:* Human resource professionals know people. They work closely with people and organizations, and possess information related to pools of talent. They can be useful to a competitive intelligence team in identifying potential sources for information.

- *Purchasing organizations:* Purchasing agents gather information about competitors and the marketplace through their day-to-day contact with suppliers. Through suppliers, they may learn of purchases or actions taken by competitors that, when coupled with other information, could reveal tactical or strategic initiatives. Having a purchasing professional as part of an internal information network often proves useful.

- *Outside sources:* In addition to the many available and useful internal sources for business information and intelligence, there are some outside sources that may be as useful as internal sources and nearly as convenient. Business colleagues working in the same business sector and attending the same trade shows (particularly if interested in learning about new entrants into the business) are often available to engage in discussions about the marketplace and the competition. Although they may not necessarily share information about their own company activities, they may share information they have learned about mutual competitors. Generally, the time you have to spend with them is limited, so know what you are looking for before you engage them in related conversations.

Employee participation in internal information networks and communities supporting the competitive intelligence process can be just as valuable to the individual employee as it is to the company. It is important to demonstrate to employees why they should participate and how they benefit from participation in these networks. Based on company policy and company culture, they should be encouraged to participate for their own good and the good of the company. Employees should understand how they are adding value to the competitive intelligence process. They also need to know that they get something in return for their support and participation.

Once they are connected to internal information networks, it is important to keep them connected. One useful way to do this is to share successes with them. When an employee makes a contribution to the competitive intelligence process and that contribution results in a success, let them know it. Show them how information they provided led to a business-related success. When appropriate, let them know that senior management is aware of their contribution. Such information will allow the employees to feel more connected to senior management. That should help keep them motivated to stay involved. Some of the benefits to employees for participating in information networks are:

- Participation in the intelligence network helps them develop a better understanding of what is happening in the organization.
- Participation alerts them to others who may be working in this area.
- Participation alerts them to other projects that are being worked and if any are duplicative.
- Participation may make them aware of available resources including the most important resource, money.
- They may learn where the competitive intelligence team gets its competitive information, thereby developing new sources for themselves.
- They can learn about the kind of business information that is collected and analyzed.
- They can learn about associations and conferences and which team members may or may not be attending various meetings and conferences.

- They will be able to learn how to develop a source of information that may be uniquely useful to them with their own job.
- The will learn how they can expand their individual network for their own benefit and the benefit of the company.
- Again a word of caution: Such employees must understand the goal and the ethical and legal methods of gathering information. Furthermore, such action should be used only when required and only by employees who fully understand how to operate within well-defined legal and ethical parameters established by the company's legal staff.

External Sources Outside the Company

Additional external sources that may be of value to an acquisition or merger team are as follows:

- *Associations:* Professional associations are useful sources for information. To obtain information from them may require association membership. Generally, a membership fee is required to participate. In turn, relevant industry information is available to its members. Limited company-related information may also be available.
- *Information brokers:* These brokers are individuals, organizations, or companies that collect and sell information. They may specialize in specific types of information (e.g., financial, political). They have many sources for the information they gather, sort, and make available to their customers for a price.
- *Service providers:* Companies that conduct investigations and perform due diligence work are also information service providers. The information that they provide is gathered from many sources to include assessments made of specific organizations through their investigation process.
- *Public sources:* These sources are available to anyone and are essentially free or at very low cost. Public libraries, news media, and the Internet all possess and make available a wide variety of business, economic, political, legal, and cultural information, which may be useful in learning about another company, business, market segment, or nation's economy.

> *Public information essentially refers to all information you can legally and ethically identify, locate, and then access.*

- *Job applicants:* Job applicants are another potential source for gathering information that could be useful in developing intelligence.

Obtaining relevant information is best accomplished during the job interview process. During this process, a candidate is often willing to share information about what they have been working on in order to demonstrate their capabilities and potential value to a prospective employer. During the interview, candidates will do their best to sell their services, and in some cases that means sharing more information than they should. An important part of selling oneself to a prospective employer is to convince them you are the best person for the job. One way to accomplish this is to use examples of one's role in the development of a new technology or new product. Again, caution should be exercised, and interviewees should be instructed by the interviewers that trade secrets and other proprietary types of information of former or current companies is not being solicited or wanted.

Who Collects Information?

Anyone can gather and collect information. In fact, almost everyone does. People regularly collect and use information from multiple sources. Employees use information as part of accomplishing their daily work and making routine business decisions. Information is gathered as part of improving the knowledge and understanding of individuals and organizations as they conduct daily business. To collect information in a more organized and deliberate manner for specific objectives and results, such as for a successful merger or acquisition, requires a more formal structure. Effective use of information requires disciplined collection, analysis, distribution, and application.

As part of a systematic approach to collecting information for competitive reasons, the process must be well defined. Establishing a competitive intelligence capability needs to be well thought out, with well-defined objectives and operating rules clearly stated. Furthermore, executive management support is essential for the following reasons:

- *Credibility and recognition:* A merger or acquisition competitive intelligence process and team, to be successful, must have credibility with the people who receive and use their product. Knowing that the organization has the full support of executive management is the foundation for credibility. Ultimately, executive management is the recipient and benefactor of products produced by a competitive intelligence organization. The product (competitive intelligence) is used to shape the short- and long-range business plans of the company. If plans, supported by competitive intelligence, are implemented successfully, executive management benefits, as does the entire company and its stakeholders.

- *Resource commitment:* Executive management makes the decision to commit or not to commit resources to the merger or acquisition competitive intelligence-producing process. For management to commit resources, it must be convinced that there will be a return on the investment. In the short term, limited results may be acceptable. In the long term, quantifiable results are the measure of success and what will be demanded. It is doubtful that management will continue to commit resources to a losing proposition.
- *Accountability:* The success or lack of success of a competitive intelligence effort ultimately rests with management. If a competitive intelligence effort is successful in producing intelligence that effectively supports and shapes the short- and long-term (tactical and strategic) objectives of the company, management will be pleased and reap the benefits. If it is not successful, management will be unsatisfied and will probably make changes to the process before actually eliminating it altogether—although one never knows what management will do! A danger lies with the tendency to "throw the baby out with the bath water." That is to say, if the competitive intelligence process is not producing results, management's reaction should be to change the process, not to eliminate the process. A properly implemented competitive intelligence-producing process can add value to a company's merger or acquisition effort.

A successful competitive intelligence process will be highly prized within any company, regardless of whether it is initiated for a specific merger or acquisition or as a general business function. However, there is one area of danger for which management must maintain a constant vigil. Perhaps the biggest threat to the continuation and success of a competitive process is how it operates internally. If the process is successful but the team members conduct themselves outside the boundaries of acceptable ethical and professional behavior, the process will lose credibility and at best will be tainted and at worst lead to its own destruction. Conducting business outside the boundaries of acceptable operating standards can have serious consequences to the company, as alluded to earlier, from damaged reputations to loss of credibility and, in some cases, litigation.

Establishing responsibilities for implementing the competitive intelligence process as part of a merger or acquisition effort is essential. Ideally, the task of producing competitive intelligence should not be an extra duty assigned to someone or some department, but must be a key subset of the entire merger or acquisition project. In the real world, however, it sometimes is handled as an extra duty assignment. The competitive intelligence process is too important to the company's merger or acquisition strategies and projects to be delegated to just anyone and far too important a process to be left alone without the benefits that come with a team or organization structure. Large companies with more resources are generally better able to dedicate adequate resources to the company-wide competitive intelligence process, or the more narrowly focused competitive intelligence subprocess supporting a specific merger or acquisition project.

Smaller organizations usually don't have sufficient resources to dedicate to the competitive intelligence process. In these companies, it is more likely that the competitive intelligence process will be an extra duty assignment and not a primary responsibility of one of the merger or acquisition team members. In any event, and regardless of the size of the company, management makes the decision to build or not build a competitive intelligence merger or acquisition subprocess, supporting it with a formal organization structure. That decision, whether intended or by omission, will have a lasting impact on the company's success with all mergers or acquisitions.

An effective competitive intelligence process requires a disciplined approach. Without the support of an organization structure and established, well-defined processes, maximum effectiveness will not be achieved. Without an organization structure, essential merger or acquisition competitive intelligence will not be produced and delivered in a timely and systematic manner. The competitive intelligence process will be subject to the ever-changing demands of the merger or acquisition project team members' daily needs and getting attention only when it is a priority and lacking attention when it is not a priority. Unless the competitive intelligence process has a highly energetic and capable champion, the ebb and flow of the merger or acquisition project team's other processes will derail it. An organization with the responsibility or charter to manage the process should be formed.

For future consideration and after the competitive intelligence-producing process has proven to have value for merger and acquisitions, executive management should consider the greater value of establishing a permanent competitive intelligence organization. If it is deemed appropriate, the processes must be institutionalized to the extent it becomes an accepted business process and part of the company culture (Figure 4.1).

Once the formal merger or acquisition competitive intelligence process is established, it needs leadership and skilled management. Leadership should come from the highest levels of the company. Executive management should establish the vision and direction for the competitive intelligence process. Management of the day-to-day operation should be led by someone who:

- Is a professional or expert in the field of competitive intelligence
- Knows how to collect information
- Understands the merger and acquisition process
- Knows how to develop information into competitive intelligence for a merger or acquisition

Competitive Intelligence Process

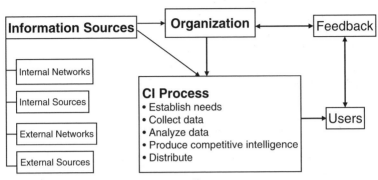

Figure 4.1   Sample of a competitive intelligence process.

Furthermore, management must understand the potential uses for competitive intelligence. Ideally, management should be someone who understands the real and potential value of gathering competitive intelligence for any merger or acquisition. The manager of the competitive intelligence process must be someone who can work with the varied interests, requirements, and intelligence needs of different organizations. Keep in mind that the uses of competitive intelligence produced for mergers and acquisitions can vary extensively, depending on the needs of its project team members.

The type of intelligence needed by an information systems merger or acquisition team member differs from the type of intelligence needed by a finance organization team member. That is not to say they can't find value in the same information, although the degree of value may differ. It is to say that each merger or acquisition team member has specific, unique interests and needs. Those needs have to be addressed to achieve maximum value from competitive intelligence for all the merger or acquisition team members.

A mature manager with proven effective management skills is required to successfully manage a merger or acquisition competitive intelligence collection process. The manager must have enough skill to keep the effort to develop intelligence consistent with the goals and objectives of all the project team members. The manager must be someone who can manage the process and use meaningful metrics to continually evaluate the performance and success of the intelligence collection process. These are some of the important characteristics that a competitive intelligence process manager should possess:

- Passion for the topic
- Networking skills

- Leadership ability
- Subject matter knowledge
- An ability to see the larger picture
- Excellent facilitation skills
- Access to executive management
- Knowledge of the industry, competitors, and own company
- Active in associations and the greater business sector

How to Transform Information into Competitive Intelligence

Developing or producing competitive intelligence to support a merger or acquisition team should be accomplished within a systematic process. It should not be a massive effort to collect huge amounts of information, hoping for the best as the information is sorted and evaluated. The process for developing useful, competitive intelligence should, at a minimum, follow the seven steps below (see Table 4-1).

Table 4-1 Checklist for the Competitive Intelligence Process	
Process Steps	Process Actions
Establish Needs	• Who needs intelligence? • What information is needed? • Prioritize needs
Collect Information	• Develop research strategy • Identify sources • Collect information • Review information to ensure you have what is needed.
Analyze Information	• Ensure data is relevant to needs • Analyze data • Draw conclusions • Conduct supplemental data collection if necessary • Review analysis in context with other known information
Produce Intelligence	• Package intelligence to meet user expectations and needs • Protect intelligence: release only to those with a need to know
Distribute to Users	• Deliver intelligence in a timely fashion
Apply Intelligence	• Integrate intelligence into decision-making process • Use in context with other relevant intelligence • Protect the intelligence
Receive Feedback	• Was the intelligence supplied useful? • Was it delivered in a timely and relevant fashion? • Have user needs changed?

1. *Establish needs:* What must be known? What questions need to be answered? How will the results be used? Who needs the intelligence? These questions must be asked at the beginning of the information-gathering process. Answers to these questions will help focus time and energy on specific types and categories of information. Proceeding without answering these questions first will lead to wasted time and effort.

2. *Collect information or data:* Once intelligence needs have been identified and separated into specific categories or types of information, the process of gathering information can begin. The next step is to identify the specific sources for information. For example, if the question that needs to be answered pertains to the size of a competitor's share of a market segment, then sources where that information is expected to be found obviously should be tapped.

3. *Analyze information or data:* The information collected must be analyzed within the context of the questions that need to be answered and in concert with other available relevant information. In other words, the new information must be analyzed along with what is already known within the context of the questions asked.

4. *Produce intelligence:* The product of the analysis should be refined or more useful, new information produced. At the very least, the product of analysis should contribute to increasing the body of knowledge in the areas in which further understanding was sought. As additional information is acquired and analyzed, it, too, should contribute to enhancing the total body of knowledge. For a merger or acquisition team, the information must be relevant to the specific project to have maximum value.

5. *Distribute intelligence to users:* Competitive intelligence must be shared in a timely manner with merger and acquisition team members. Competitive intelligence, under an operational security umbrella, is to be protected, yet shared with the appropriate project team members. It should be kept from those who have no need to know and only shared with those who do have a need to know. Regardless of how valuable new competitive intelligence is, unless it is placed in the right hands in a timely fashion, its value may be diminished or totally degraded.

6. *Apply intelligence:* Merger or acquisition project team members who receive competitive intelligence must act on what they learn. Having additional knowledge about a competitor or market can create an advantage for any company. Having additional knowledge related to specific competitive issues or situations leads to an opportunity for a competitive edge during discussion, planning, and negotiations for any merger or acquisition. Using that knowledge (competitive intelligence) is where the ultimate value is

added. Unapplied knowledge is not very useful and, in fact, may cause the company to acquire or merge with another company when it shouldn't. In addition, the acquiring or merging company may pay more than it should for a company. The results of such a bad decision based on failing to acquire quality competitive intelligence, apply that knowledge to the merger or acquisition, or using faulty or bad information are obvious.

7. *Feedback:* Get regular feedback from all merger or acquisition project team members. Are they being supplied with the intelligence they need? What is the quality of the product they are provided? Has there been a change in their interest and needs? What additional intelligence do they need? These and other questions should be asked of the team members and regular feedback encouraged. Ensuring the quality of the product and its continual improvement should be fundamental goals for any merger or acquisition competitive intelligence-producing process.

Who Else Uses Competitive Intelligence Information?

As discussed previously, the merger or acquisition team members must have reliable competitive intelligence to successfully support the goals and objectives of their merger or acquisition. However, that same competitive intelligence may be useful, in fact needed, and used by many people and disciplines within a company. The extent to which it is used varies from organization to organization.

Leaders, executives, managers, professionals, and other business practitioners all may have a need for competitive intelligence. Their needs will vary depending on their mission and objectives. Nevertheless, to a greater or lesser extent, most organizations can benefit from competitive intelligence. A marketing department may benefit from having a better understanding of competitors' marketing strategy, whereas a product development organization may benefit by learning the technology limits or direction of competitors. This knowledge may allow them to react in such a way as to pursue an alternative strategy or seek to fill a gap within their own capabilities or within a particular product line.

How Do You Know Whether the Competitive Intelligence Produced and Applied Has Value?

Knowing the value of competitive intelligence is essential yet difficult to accomplish. If the cost to produce competitive intelligence exceeds the value or gain from its use, was it worth the time and money to produce? Can the merger or acquisition project team justify an investment in a competitive intelligence process, organization, personnel, or program if the gain from the intelligence produced is marginal or unknown?

The competitive intelligence process must be measured. Was the intelligence produced useful to merger or acquisition team members? Did it enhance the decision process of the merger or acquisition team members? Was it delivered in a timely manner? How did the competitive intelligence add value to successfully meeting the objectives of the merger or acquisition project team? Ideally, the measure of effectiveness or value should connect to the successful merger or acquisition, or decision not to acquire or merge with another company. It also should connect, therefore, to the "bottom line" of the company.

Effectively measuring the value of competitive intelligence is not an easy task. However, neither is producing the competitive intelligence itself, but it should be done. Measurement is the only objective way to assess the value of competitive intelligence as it is used to contribute to the success of the merger or acquisition project team. After a successful merger or acquisition or when explaining the decision not to merge or acquire another company, metrics are an effective way to help communicate that information. In addition, such success backed by metrics can be used to help motivate employees. Metrics are best used after the merger or acquisition takes place as part of a postmerger or postacquisition evaluation (e.g., a lesson-learned process that can be helpful with future, similar projects).

> *In 1994, NutraSweet's CEO publicly valued competitive intelligence to NutraSweet at $50M. That figure was based on a combination of revenues gained and revenues that were "not lost" to competition.*[4]

TWO TYPES OF COMPETITIVE INTELLIGENCE

Competitive intelligence is developed for use in many ways and in support of many of the merger or acquisition team goals. In general, competitive intelligence information can be divided into two major types:

- Tactical competitive intelligence
- Strategic competitive intelligence

---

[4] John J. McGonagle and Carolyn M. Vella, *Competitive Intelligence* (Westport, Connecticut: Quorum Books, 2002).

Tactical Competitive Intelligence

Tactical implies short term. There is a short term between the delivery of intelligence and the ensuing action. Tactical competitive intelligence is easier to measure, as results are more immediate and can be linked back to the merger or acquisition project team's decisions. Tactical competitive intelligence addresses immediate questions and issues and needs a prompt ensuing action. Tactical competitive intelligence ties more directly to an action, and its value, or lack of value, is more apparent.

Tactical competitive intelligence more aptly applies to information required in the short term, that can be collected and produced in the short term, and therefore is more immediately useful to the merger or acquisition project team members, as they operate under the always present time constraints in any merger or acquisition effort.

Strategic Competitive Intelligence

Strategic implies a longer term. There is a much longer term between the delivery of intelligence and the ensuing action. Strategic competitive intelligence is highly analytical and future oriented. It is often used for the development of contingency plans more so than it is used for concrete decisions. Strategic intelligence is not just a report or a forecast; it should generate dialogue and cause leadership and management to discuss and debate issues and questions of strategic importance. In this process, strategic competitive intelligence is used to develop strategic thinking and strategic options.

One of the primary uses for strategic competitive intelligence is as part of the strategic long-range business plans. Long-range business plans address such areas as the type of business a company wants to be in, whether to grow that business organically or through the merger or acquisition process, and how they plan to do that. In other words, identify what types of companies they are looking for, a list of likely candidates, and a time frame within which they are to be pursued.

Measuring the effectiveness of strategic competitive intelligence should be closely linked to the strategic business plan of the company. The linking of the results produced by strategic competitive intelligence information collection may not be as readily apparent as a result of the extended time passed between application and results and the broader (less specific) nature of the information.

Strategic competitive intelligence should be used to help the company shape its growth strategy and thus its merger and acquisition strategy. Strategic competitive intelligence should be a product that provides executives with knowledge about the marketplace within which they operate, as well as their strongest competition. Knowing the marketplace and one's competition is essential to effectively shape any merger and acquisition strategy.

The analysis process for developing strategic competitive intelligence must have a point of view focusing on what is possible and not what has happened in the past. Strategic intelligence, to be useful, should be convincing and conclusions drawn should be connected to the facts such that the decision made whether to merge with or acquire a company becomes obvious.

Offensive and Defensive Competitive Intelligence

Competitive intelligence can be divided into two other basic categories, other than tactical and strategic, as noted previously. The two other basic categories are offensive competitive intelligence and defensive competitive intelligence.

- *Offensive competitive intelligence* is the category of intelligence that has been the subject of most of this chapter. Offensive intelligence encompasses the total effort to collect information and develop competitive useful intelligence. Competitive intelligence is the kind of competitive knowledge that can be used to create a competitive edge. An offensive strategy seeks to capitalize on competitive weaknesses within a market segment or to take advantage of a weakness of a specific competitor.
- *Defensive competitive intelligence*, unlike offensive competitive intelligence, is not a process for producing useful competitive intelligence. Actually, it is quite the contrary. Defensive competitive intelligence is used to defend against others who want to collect competitive intelligence from, or about, your company, thereby producing their own offensive competitive intelligence and using it to their competitive advantage. Defensive competitive intelligence is not the domain or responsibility of the traditional competitive intelligence collection organizations but usually lies within the purview of the security organization. As the entity charged with protecting company physical assets, information, and people, security has the responsibility to protect the company from efforts by others to gather information for which they have no need to know. Defensive competitive intelligence information collection is really a component of the information security program. The defensive competitive intelligence strategy is designed to protect against the intelligence-producing efforts of competitors. It is the countering of a threat, and in today's global information age, it is a real threat.[5]

---

[5] For more information on this topic, the reader should obtain a copy of the book, *Netspionage: The Global Threat to Information*, also co-authored by Dr. Gerald L. Kovacich and published by Butterworth-Heinemann, 2000, ISBN: 0-7506-7257-9

TARGET- AND TECHNOLOGY-FOCUSED COMPETITIVE INTELLIGENCE

Two more narrowly focused approaches to developing competitive intelligence that are useful to merger and acquisition teams are used when a company is pursuing a specific merger or acquisition strategy.

Target-Focused Competitive Intelligence

Targed-focused competitive intelligence is limited to an assessment of a few specific competitors that may be potential candidates for acquisition. With a target-focused process, a competitive intelligence process that may be located within a business organization of a company will focus on understanding as much as it can about a limited number of competitors. The objective is to develop an expanded understanding and knowledge base of the competition. Learning as much as possible about these few competitors and their strengths, weaknesses, opportunities, and threats can help a company make a more informed decision whether or not to pursue a merger or acquisition. Specific areas of focus should include an examination of the following capabilities:

- Current and future products and services
- Current technologies supporting products and services
- Current market activities
- Current and future business strategies
- Current and future competitors

A target-focused competitive intelligence collection process can be viewed from either a strategic or tactical point of view, based on the time factors involved.

Technology-Focused Competitive Intelligence

Technology-focused competitive intelligence collection is useful for companies seeking to acquire new technologies or other companies on the leading edge of developing new technologies or companies possessing desired technological capabilities. This focus is important in industries where technology developments and breakthroughs provide those companies with a competitive edge and where the organization's strategic focus is on technology. The primary emphasis is to exploit opportunities resulting from technical and scientific change and developments. Like a target-focused competitive intelligence collection process to be used as part of a company's merger or acquisition, plans can be viewed from either a strategic or tactical point of view, based on the time factors involved.

PROFESSIONALISM AND ETHICS

Professionalism and ethics are not just ideals worthy of pursuit. In today's business environment, both must be engrained in the culture of any company. Being an ethical company is essential to survival, never mind a requirement to flourish. During the early years of this new millennium, too many companies suffered from failures in professional and ethical behavior. In some instances, companies imploded because they engaged in unethical and even criminal business practices. With companies such as Enron and Arthur Anderson serving as "poster companies" for unethical practices, the last few years produced many examples of how not to run a business. Furthermore, their actions led to government responses with development of new regulatory and legislative controls.

Sarbanes-Oxley legislation was enacted by the U.S. Congress as a means of implementing stringent accountability measures within U.S. companies. With an emphasis on financial and accounting controls, Sarbanes-Oxley seeks to hold the most senior executives from publicly held companies accountable for their decisions, actions, and performance.

For the competitive intelligence professional, especially one engaged in a company's merger or acquisition project, adhering to high ethical and legal standards must be a way of life. In a discipline where opportunities to cross the boundaries of ethical and acceptable business practices often present themselves, company employees (and that includes all levels of management!), as well as the entire merger and acquisition project team, must not succumb to any temptations to conduct themselves in other than the most ethical manner.

Credibility is an essential component of success for the entire company and the entire merger or acquisition team. Once credibility is damaged, the recovery process may take years, if it occurs at all. The consequences of a transgression in ethics may be so severe as to permanently damage the individual and company. Unethical behavior is never worth the perceived or expected gains and can result in the failure of a merger or acquisition, the benefits of which may have been enjoyed by consumers, stockholders, and employees alike.

Even in the performance of routine merger and acquisition tasks, the importance of ethical behavior is critical. The company and project team must always be objective. How information is analyzed and presented can be manipulated to support many positions. All team members and all company employees must avoid "spinning" information. Intelligence must be presented based on what it tells you and not what you want it to tell you.

Ethical standards and operating within acceptable business practices is so important that the most prominent professional association for competitive intelligence professionals, The Society for Competitive Intelligence Professionals (SCIP), prominently maintains a code of ethics. Visiting their web site one will find the following[6]:

The Society for Competitive Intelligence Professionals Code of Ethics

- *To continually strive to increase the recognition and respect of the profession.*
- *To comply with all applicable laws, domestic and international.*
- *To accurately disclose all relevant information, including one's identity and organization, prior to all interviews.*
- *To respect all requests for confidentiality of information.*
- *To avoid conflicts of interest in fulfilling one's duties.*
- *To provide honest and realistic recommendations and conclusions in the execution of one's duties.*
- *To promote this code of ethics within one's company, with third-party contractors and within the entire profession.*
- *To faithfully adhere to and abide by one's company policies, objectives, and guidelines.*

SUMMARY

When a company chooses a strategy for growth and expansion through mergers or acquisitions in lieu of internal or organic growth, they will need a competitive intelligence capability to support that strategy. Executing successful mergers or acquisitions does not occur by chance. Much research and analysis must occur to properly target and acquire companies that help achieve strategic objectives and goals.

Useful competitive intelligence is an invaluable tool to any merger or acquisition team. Merger or acquisition teams are expected to make the best deals possible. They are expected to identify target companies offering the greatest potential to support strategic growth and expansion objectives. This can't be successfully accomplished without learning as much as possible about target companies. A competitive intelligence process will support this goal. Any company seriously engaged in the strategic pursuit of mergers and acquisitions will require a competitive intelligence capability.

Mergers and acquisitions can also be a source for developing new intelligence. During the postmerger and acquisition period and into the

---

[6] See http://www.scip.org/ci/ethics.asp

integration effort of bringing two companies together, there is an opportunity to develop new intelligence. The employees of a newly acquired company bring with them their knowledge of the industry, competitors, and company that can be unique and should be exploited. A competitive intelligence organization should move swiftly to work with the newly acquired employees, taking advantage of this valuable source of social capital by bringing them into information networks and communities supporting the information-gathering process.

New employees bring different perspectives, experiences, and information to the company that can be useful in developing new competitive intelligence. Because information has a perishable lifecycle, moving swiftly is essential. If the newly acquired company has a competitive intelligence team, keep them. They may have already developed an internal information-gathering structure that can be immediately exploited for development of new competitive intelligence. To the extent possible, don't allow that resource to go away unused. As noted earlier, any information requested and/or received from employees of a former company must meet the stringent legal and ethical conduct tests.

The role of security in support of a competitive intelligence process may be limited or may be extensive. At the very least, security is one source of many available to feed information into the competitive intelligence-producing process. Security also leads the defensive competitive intelligence effort for the company as the function charged with the responsibility for protecting company-owned information.

Competitive intelligence is an important tool for executives and business managers. Competitive intelligence contributes to the body of knowledge available for decision makers, helping them to make better business decisions. Producing competitive intelligence is not "magic" or "rocket science." Following a well-defined, systematic, and disciplined process can successfully produce useful competitive intelligence that will lead to a successful merger or acquisition.

Competitive intelligence has value in many areas of business. Merger and acquisition teams benefit from competitive intelligence about the marketplace, competitors, and companies targeted for merger or acquisition. Remember that security plays an important role in the competitive intelligence process, particularly in developing and implementing defensive competitive intelligence measures.

Chapter 5

Why Premerger and Acquisition Security Support?

We have met the enemy and he is us. – Walt Kelly (the words of Pogo, 1971)

INTRODUCTION

This chapter discusses the importance of protecting the effort, that is, protecting the activities of the merger and acquisition team from the time when they come together as a team until the merger or acquisition is actually completed. In this section, we examine what needs to be protected, how to protect it, and from whom it must be protected.

Since mergers and acquisitions are not daily occurrences, companies don't have organizations in place dedicated to working them. Instead, companies put together teams, usually an integrated process team, that brings together the necessary expertise, skills, and disciplines to effectively execute a successful merger or acquisition. When these teams are formed, as previously alluded to, security must be part of the team, from the earliest point possible. Merger and acquisition teams often move quickly. Early in the effort they engage in activities requiring security support. To reduce risks and mitigate vulnerabilities, security planning and support begins here, including efforts to develop an operational security plan (OPSEC).

It is important to protect the activities of a merger and acquisition team throughout the entire effort. It is particularly important to protect the very early stages. Planning for mergers and acquisitions usually occurs in secrecy. Tight controls are placed on the team and those few outsiders preparing for the transaction. Because a merger or acquisition is a strategic business action undertaken to improve the competitiveness of a company, its revelation to those without a need to know could have serious consequences. Exposure may even kill the deal. If a competitor were to learn of company "A's" desire to merge with or acquire company "B," thereby, making company "A" much stronger and more competitive, that competitor may take actions to prevent the deal from occurring. They may even go so far as to attempt to acquire company "B" themselves.

PROTECTING THE EFFORT

Anyone not part of the merger or acquisition team should be considered an outsider. An outsider may be another company employee, a competitor, the media, or anyone not officially part of the team. How does someone become an official member of a merger and acquisition team? Team leadership must make that decision. The team leader will generally be decided by the chief executive officer (CEO) or even by company charter. If the team leader determines a person (or persons) should be involved because they can make a material contribution to the effort, then the team leader coordinates with applicable level(s) of management to get an employee with the required expertise assigned to the team. Thus, a need to know is established for that new team member. Caution must be taken not to divulge more than is necessary when coordinating with management to get an employee with specific expertise assigned to the team. It is imperative that the less others know about the merger or acquisition project, the better it is for maintaining operation security.

Once a person is selected by the team leader to be part of the merger and acquisition team, he or she needs to be made aware of responsibilities as a team member, including security responsibilities. All team members have specific functional responsibilities; they also have individual security responsibilities. These obligations should be communicated to team members through the security manager or security representative. The security manager should be the one to brief team members as to their specific security. This should be supported with a signed written acknowledgment to this effect. This written acknowledgment should be in the form of a nondisclosure agreement. Putting the team's member on a binding document reinforces his or her personal obligations. It also gives security and the legal department a tool to use in litigation in the event that becomes necessary. Figure 5.1 is a sample nondisclosure agreement.

Because of the need for a merger and acquisition team to operate under tight controls and not allow persons without a need to know access to its activities, the operational condition will cause the team to be somewhat isolated. In terms of protecting the merger or acquisition effort, it is much like an "us against the world" approach.

The World Is a Dangerous Place

Mergers and acquisitions occur with great frequency in the United States. Over the last decade they are occurring more frequently in Europe and Asia

To: Merger, Acquisitions and Divestiture Team Member
Subject: Confidentiality Agreement
From: Project Team Leader

You have been asked to participate in the confidential review of project _____. By signing this document, you agree that you understand the terms and obligations described in this document that are imposed upon you as a member of the team.

As a member of the review team, you will receive or have access to project sensitive information in a variety of forms, including spoken and visual presentations, written materials, facility tours, and question and answer sessions. "Information" is defined as any and all data provided to Company X, or its agents, concerning or relating to the project (regardless of the form of communication, whether written, oral, electronic, graphic or otherwise), and includes those notes, analyses, compilations, studies, interpretations, diagrams, charts and other documents prepared by Company X employees, agents, or representatives which are based upon, reflect, or contain any such information.

This project will also involve the disclosure of Company X sensitive information to actual or potential competitors. The information and materials generated by or provided by you may be competition sensitive and must not be disclosed outside the project or used for any purpose other than this evaluation. No copies or reproductions of the project information in whole, or in part, are to be made without the express authorization of the Company X Law Department.

You are not to disclose the fact that the evaluation is ongoing, or disclose any information or opinion regarding the evaluation. Any inquiry on the subject should be answered with the statement, "It is Company policy not to respond to any question of this nature," or by referring the requester to the Team Leader. Any inquiry from outside Company X, or that seems unusual, should be reported to the Team Leader immediately.

Upon notice from the Team Leader, all copies of project documents and information are to be returned to the Team Leader. All materials generated by you or others based on any project information and in your possession are to be returned or destroyed.

Be advised that United States federal securities laws and Company X policies prohibit the purchase or sale of securities on the basis of material non-public information and prohibit the communication of such material non-public information to any other person. You should consider the information to be material and non-public for the purposes of these laws and policies.

Please sign below and return a copy of this agreement to the Team Leader. Your signature constitutes your agreement to be bound by these provisions.

Read, Understood, and Agreed:
By (signature): _____ Date: _____

Figure 5.1 Sample nondisclosure agreement to be used for a merger or acquisition team project.

(see Chapter 2). Before September 11, 2001, security issues associated with mergers and acquisitions focused on protecting the effort mostly for competitive reasons. Today and in the future (with no real end in sight) another major security consideration must be acknowledged. The world is rapidly becoming a more dangerous place. This is particularly true for Western companies doing business in Asia, the Middle East, and Africa. In April 2004, the U.S. Department of State released its report on patterns of global terrorism characterizing the global threat to U.S. citizens and U.S. interests. Some of the highlights of the statistics include the following:

- There were 190 international terrorist attacks in 2003, based on the U.S. definition of a terrorist attack.
- 307 people were killed in the attacks; of those, 35 were U.S. citizens.
- 1,593 people were wounded in the attacks.
- Both the highest number of attacks and the highest casualty rates occurred in Asia; 70 attacks resulted in 159 deaths and 951 injuries.
- 16 U.S. citizens were killed as a result of Palestinian attacks in Israel.
- Nine U.S. citizens were killed in the May 12 attacks on expatriate housing in Riyadh, Saudi Arabia.

Although these statistics only include attacks on U.S. interests, the threat to all Westerners and Western interests is expanding. This is particularly true in predominantly Islamic countries. What does all this mean to a company seeking to merge with or acquire another company? It is a warning, both loud and clear, that if doing business in certain parts of the world, there are more issues to be concerned about than just protecting information from competitors and foreign governments.

Terrorism is a real and present concern. Terrorists target U.S. and others' interests. These interests may be institutions of government, symbolic institutions, or economic institutions. Economic institutions include U.S. and primarily Western companies. The suicide car bombing at the J.W. Marriott hotel on August 5, 2003[1] in Jakarta, Indonesia, is a strong reminder of the vulnerability of such Western targets. This particular hotel was regularly used by Western business people. The hotel was an intended target and not a coincidental victim.

Understanding that the world is a dangerous place is particularly important to companies doing international business. According to *Fortune* magazine, the United States leads the world with the largest number of global companies having 189 of them in the top 500. These 189 U.S. companies account for 39% of the total revenue generated by all 500 Global Companies on this list[2] (Table 5-1).

---

[1] See http://www.cnn.com/2003/WORLD/asiapcf/southeast/08/19/indonesia.arrests.names/
[2] See http://www.fortune.com/fortune/global500/articles/0,15114,662294,00.html?cnn=yes

Table 5-1 Listing by Country of the Fortune 2004 Global 500		
Country	No. of Companies	Revenue ($ Billions)
United States	189	5,841
Japan	82	2,181
France	37	1,246
Britain	35	1,079
Germany	34	1,363
China	15	358
Canada	13	185
Netherlands	12	388
Switzerland	12	382
South Korea	11	266
Italy	8	300
Spain	7	162
Australia	7	107
Sweden	6	96
Finland	4	71
India	4	60
Russia	3	62
Britain/Netherlands	2	250
Norway	2	60
Denmark	2	35
Brazil	1	63
Belgium/Netherlands	1	57
Mexico	1	49
Venezuela	1	46
Malaysia	1	26
Singapore	1	15
Taiwan	1	14
Ireland	1	12
Thailand	1	12

Of the top 500 global companies, more that 75% are from Western countries. Understanding world security conditions, particularly in countries with strong anti-Western sentiments, is essential for the safety of personnel and success of the enterprise. Therefore, any mergers and acquisitions must consider protecting mergers and acquisition team members traveling overseas. Also, the increased cost of security at the potentially newly acquired company must be considered as part of the merger or acquisition, especially if there is little or no security program for that overseas company because there is no threat against these native workers or business. All that changes if the company becomes part of a U.S. or other nation's company that is on a terrorist's target list.

Competitors

First and foremost, a company must protect its merger or acquisition intentions from its competitors. Competitors are the most interested in the strategic actions of your company. It is they who are affected by your success and they who may gain (at least in market share) from your failures. Competitors pay close attention to what their competitors do. They gather information about competitors and produce competitive intelligence information to help them better understand their competitor's intentions and to better compete with them. When they learn about their competitors actions, capabilities, and successes, they react. Competitors will adjust their own strategy to stay competitive. In some cases, they will do anything necessary to stay competitive. Depending on the type of business, there may be few or many competitors. These competitors may be domestic or international. They may be large or small. They will always watch what others are doing, just as their competitors watch what they do.

International Competitors

Who are your international competitors? Are they just other businesses operating in the same global marketplace? Could they be foreign governments? Could they be foreign companies and foreign governments working together for their collective advantage?

International competitors are no different than domestic competitors whether they are another business, company, or corporation competing head-to-head in the marketplace. However, when a company operates in a foreign environment (outside the boundaries of its own country), its competitors include foreign governments. The global business environment is a competitive and even hostile place. The United States, Europe, and East Asia have the most developed economies in the world and the most competitive businesses. Other countries, and even other governments, would like this to change to their advantage. Foreign governments, in support of their own economic and business interests, often provide support to their own companies. For example, Airbus, the European producer of commercial aircraft, receives support in the form of subsidies from its European owners (Germany, France, Spain, and the United Kingdom). Some believe this support gives Airbus a competitive edge, since the U.S government does not provide similar subsidies to the U.S. company, Boeing, Airbus' only global competitor.

In other cases, the form of support provided to companies by their host governments includes engaging in activities that range from creation of tariffs and other barriers to subtle, or not so subtle, forms of economic espionage. Make no mistake about this. Competitive espionage by foreign countries and companies is a real threat. Thus, in 1996, the U.S. Congress passed the Economic Espionage Act.[3] The U.S. Congress intended to enact a body of laws designed to protect the economic interest of the U.S. and American companies against foreign interests and foreign governments.

Domestic Competitors

Domestic competitors operate in the same marketplace and are based in the same country. Every industry segment has competition. In the U.S. automotive industry, General Motors competes with Ford. In the computer products industry, Dell competes with Gateway, IBM, etc. However, this competition has gradually changed over the years; for example, previously foreign automobile manufacturers exported their automobiles to a foreign country. Now, many of these foreign manufacturers have opened manufacturing plants in the foreign nations or merged with other automobile manufacturers, thus, in many ways making them a "domestic competitor."

One must remember, however, that these companies are still headquartered and controlled by a foreign company in a foreign nation. Therefore, for our purposes, they are still considered a foreign competitor. Over the years, there has been a blurring between what is a foreign company and what is a national company; for example, operating in the U.S., is Toyota USA a foreign or domestic corporation?

> *There have been many rumors, some verified and others not verified, of governments supporting their country's businesses by planting listening devices in business class sections of aircraft and in hotels rooms frequented by international business travelers. One other, more sophisticated, example is a business traveler in a foreign country who may use the hotel room's telephone line to send and receive business emails. Obviously, the emails will discuss business such as a merger or acquisition, the reason why the business traveler is in a particular foreign country. The emails may be sent through a special computer (i.e., server) in the hotel or other location where the emails are all captured by the server for the local nation's foreign intelligence agents before being sent on their way. Also, there is the possibility that the emails can be changed or even not sent as methods of providing an advantage to foreign nation's companies.*

Regardless as to how you look at it, now or in the not-too-distant future, competition can be considered 100% global; therefore, all competitors can be viewed as "global" and not exclusively foreign or domestic because a competitor will usually be competing globally against other competitors who are also global. Another example is the on-line seller of books

---

[3] See http://www.cybercrime.gov/EEAleghist.htm

and other items, Amazon.com. Although it is a U.S.-based company, it sells products and competes on a global scale against on-line sellers from around the world, both foreign and domestic.

Competition is good for consumers and ultimately good for the companies involved, as competition inspires innovation. Competition also creates a demanding and difficult marketplace. For example, many companies are engaged in the production and sales of specific types of products. Therefore, each works to maintain a competitive edge over the others. It is difficult to achieve growth within a marketplace where there may only be one primary customer (e.g., a government agency) and the companies are subject to nonmarket conditions. That is to say, politics plays a major role in government spending on some products.

Consequently, to achieve revenue and earnings growth, it is necessary either to take market-share away from a competitor or to engage in mergers and acquisitions. To successfully take market-share from a competitor usually requires performing better than a competitor. It may also require developing strategies that provide a competitive edge. This is not accomplished in a vacuum. It requires learning and knowing as much as possible about a competitor including their long-term business strategies for growth such as plans for mergers and acquisitions.

Employees

Employees are one of a company's greatest assets and biggest challenge. (Some may argue that computer systems and the information that they display, process, store, and transmit are today's companies' greatest assets. After all, employees usually can easily be replaced, but information and computers cannot.) Regardless, for the sake of discussion here, employees make companies what they are. It is employees who possess and use their knowledge and skills to make their company successful and provide that company with a competitive edge. Naturally, many other important factors are necessary to create successful companies; however, no company achieves success without employees. So why would employees, being the "greatest asset" of a company, also be the biggest challenge?

Unintentional Harmful Behavior

Employees don't work in a vacuum. For most of what employees do, operating in an open environment is the normal practice as opposed to operating within secrecy. In successful companies, employees collaborate with each other working with and as members of teams to accomplish their tasks and achieve success. Employees build networks for sharing information and for getting work done. Their natural tendency is to seek, share, and learn. They gather and share information that will help them be successful.

Keeping information confidential or protected often counters this tendency. Unless employees fully understand the need to keep certain sensitive information confidential, it is likely that information will be shared and not afforded the level of protection necessary to prevent those with no need-to-know from gaining access. Expanding the number of people who have knowledge of sensitive information also increases the probability of someone without a need-to-know learning that sensitive information. This condition presents a problem for security in protecting company information and in particular, protecting information about very closely-held projects such as mergers and acquisitions.

Employees, through casual and unintended actions, also may help competitors obtain information through discussions with friends and associates. People like to talk about what they do particularly with other people who have an appreciation of the importance of the work being done.

To combat this tendency, security must have in place an effective information protection program. But, that by itself is not enough. What is needed is a common behavior, or a company culture, where employees understand the need to protect sensitive information and their effort to do so is as natural as performing other business related actions.

Deliberate Bad Behavior

Deliberate bad behavior is the exception and not the rule. Most employees do not engage in deliberately harmful behavior; however, some employees do. When an employee, for whatever reason, deliberately releases sensitive information to persons without a need to know, the consequences can be damaging to any company. In the late 1990s, Boeing employees (some formerly Lockheed Martin employees) plotted to obtain trade secrets from Lockheed Martin to help Boeing win rocket contracts. The consequences to Boeing for these actions included the loss of seven existing rocket contracts, a ban on bidding for future Air Force rocket launches, and having to face a civil lawsuit from Lockheed Martin alleging corporate espionage.[4] The consequences for this transgression were severe. Because the incidents were discovered and they involved government contracts, there was national press coverage of the incident, making the general public aware of the matter. The Boeing experience causes one to ask just how many other situations exist where corporate espionage is committed and no one is the wiser?

Merger and acquisition teams, faced with the need to protect information, can take some preventive actions that will be helpful in reducing the likelihood of a "bad" employee becoming a member of the team:

- Ensure that members of the team are hand-picked for their skills and discretion.

---

[4] See http://www.nlpc.org/view.asp?action=viewArticle&aid=16

- All team members must sign nondisclosure agreements. (This will not stop dishonest employees from unauthorized release of merger or acquisition information, but it will make it easier to prosecute them later.)
- Security must brief all team members on their protective responsibilities.
- When the effort is complete, all team members must be advised of their continuing responsibility (if any) to protect information.

News Media

Releasing information to the news media is never appropriate without the expressed approval from appropriately designated company executives. Release of information concerning a merger or acquisition to anyone outside the merger and acquisition team must be approved by the team leadership. Releasing information to the media should also have the approval of the company CEO and, in some cases, the company Board of Directors.

Once information is released to the news media, all company control of that information is lost. Therefore, all news media releases must be intentional, well thought out and planned, and preferably created by the company's public relations professionals who know how to deal with the news media.

SHOULD THE EXISTENCE OF A MERGER AND ACQUISITION TEAM BE ACKNOWLEDGED WITHIN THE COMPANY AND/OR OUTSIDE THE COMPANY?

To prevent competitors from learning about the company's intentions, knowledge of the effort must be limited to those persons who have a need to know. In other words, only those people with a need to know should know that the activity exists. If someone is not part of, or directly supporting, the merger and acquisition team, he or she should not know that the effort exists. Operating under this condition limits the probability of compromise. If the effort is compromised and competitors learn of the company intentions to merge with or acquire another company, the competitor may be able to take counteractions that could prevent the company from making a successful transaction.

To successfully limit knowledge of a merger or acquisition effort, particularly in its early stages and up until a deliberate decision is made to publicly reveal the effort's existence, requires implementing well-thought-out security controls. Successfully limiting exposure of the effort requires protection of team communications, controlling all information and protecting access to all relevant materials from unauthorized persons. It may even be necessary to develop a cover story for the team so that their actions do not arouse suspicion or the unwanted attention of those who have no need to know. If their actions do arouse suspicion, a well-crafted cover story will help reduce the likelihood of revealing the company's true intentions. Keeping those who may benefit from a failed effort or from having advance knowledge of the company's intentions is obviously a good and even essential practice.

Once it is decided to publicize the company's intentions to pursue a merger or acquisition, then the limits on who may know of the effort may decrease or disappear in its entirety, depending on the company's reasons for releasing specific information. For example, when Comcast made known its intentions to pursue the acquisition of Disney, it did so at a time when it was to the advantage of Comcast. Once intentions were revealed, there was no longer a need to control knowledge of the effort. However, all other aspects of the effort still required protection. Public knowledge of intentions to pursue a merger or acquisition is not the same as knowing the specific details and plans. Sensitive information must continue to be protected; as necessary, protection must also be provided to team members.

INFORMATION PROTECTION

Information is the lifeblood of any company operating in the Global Information Age we now live and work in. Protecting information is not just a good thing to do. It is essential and must be considered a critical business process. Protecting information is a reality of doing business. Every company must have a plan in place to identify its sensitive information and protect it. In today's global information-dependent marketplace, not having a plan in place to protect information borders on irresponsible behavior and is clearly not the way to run a business.

As is obvious by now, information is the lifeblood of any merger and acquisition. In terms of protecting information for a merger or acquisition, how that is done should be consistent with the company's overall plan to protect information. Protecting information for a merger or acquisition is really a highly focused subprocess of protecting company information. To provide a framework for protecting information, we first look at why every company should have a plan for protecting information and how that plan should work. From there the unique and specific elements and concerns for protecting information within a merger or acquisition effort are discussed.

Merger or Acquisition Information Protection (Plan or Program)

Information has value. The protection of information in the age of electronic and digital information is more important than ever before. The loss or theft of information critical to a corporation's products, methods, or processes may be devastating. In this age of global competition, the importance of having in place a comprehensive program for information protection is critical and cannot be overstated.

> *In the April 2000, second edition of its College Dictionary, Random House Webster defines information as knowledge communicated or received concerning a particular fact or circumstance. Continuing on information is further defined as knowledge gained through study, communication, research, etc.: data - Today, most data resides on electronic information systems (computers)*

Three Basic Categories of Information

Although there are no generally accepted standard categories of information, information can logically be placed into three overall categories: personal, private information; business information; and national security (both classified and unclassified) information.

- *Personal, private information:* This type of information is usually about an individual. Protecting it is an individual preference and concern, but it is also a concern for governments and businesses. A person may want to keep private such information about themselves as their age, weight, address, cellular phone number, salary, and their likes and dislikes. At the same time, many nation-states have laws that protect information under some type of "privacy act." In businesses and government agencies, it is both a matter of policy, regulation, and/or law to safeguard certain information about an employee such as age, health information, address, salary, etc. In most cases, this type of information would not apply to a mergers or acquisition project.
- *Business information:* Information created, gathered, owned, and used by businesses also requires protection based on its value. The degree of protection required is dependent on the value of the information during a specific time period. That is to say, some information is perishable; after a certain time period, its value lessens. This type of information obviously would most definitely apply to a mergers or acquisition project.
- *National security information:* This information is determined by a government agency to be sensitive and requiring protection. The degree of sensitivity and protection varies with the type of information. National security information should be protected from compromise that would allow an adversary to develop a countermeasure, compete in building like systems, or delaying operational use of a sys-

tem. Within the United States, national security information is divided into two categories: classified and unclassified. In most cases, this type of information would not apply to a mergers or acquisition project.

Generally, the types of information that have value to the business and that must be considered as part of any merger or acquisition, and that requires protection includes: all forms and types of financial, scientific, technical, economic, or engineering information including, but not limited to data, plans, tools, mechanisms, compounds, formulas, designs, prototypes, processes, procedures, programs, codes, or commercial strategies, whether tangible or intangible, and whether stored, compiled or memorialized physically, electronically, graphically, photographically, or in writing.

Examples of information requiring protection may include research, proposals, plans, strategies (short and long term), manufacturing processes, pricing, and product. Generally, companies categorize this type of information using some sort of a scale of importance. The following is an example of such a scale:

- Company Internal Use Only
- Company Private
- Company Sensitive
- Company Proprietary
- Company Trade Secret

All companies handle sensitive business information and sensitive personal information. Few companies handle national security information. For those that do, each country maintains strict and specific regulations and guidelines directing the rules for handling and processing such information.

Determining the Value of Merger or Acquisition Information

If merger or acquisition information, such as competitive intelligence, has value, it must be protected; protection is expensive. The consequences of not properly classifying information as part of a mergers or acquisition project could lead to overprotection, which is costly, or underprotection, which could lead to the loss of that information, thus the competitive advantage and profits.

- Protect only information that requires protection
- Protect information only in a manner necessary based on the value of information
- Protect information only for the period required

To determine the value of information, one should first understand:

- What is meant by information
- What is meant by value of information
- How to properly categorize and classify the information

> *Value is defined in Random House Webster's College Dictionary (April 2000) as ". . . the worth of a thing in money or goods at a certain time; market price . . . ; that quality of a thing according to which it is thought of as being more or less desirable, useful, important, etc. . . . ."*

One might ask, "Does all the information related to a corporate merger or acquisition have value?" If you were asked that question, how would you answer it? The follow-up question might be, "What information does *not* have value to the merger or acquisition?" Is it information that the project team determines has no value? When the originator of the information says so? Who determines whether information has value to a merger or acquisition project team?

These are questions that one must ask before identifying information that must be protected as part of a merger or acquisition project. The holder of the information may be a member of the project team or called on by the project team to determine the value of the information as it would relate to a merger or acquisition. As you can see, the number of people who become involved in a merger or acquisition project continues to expand. Therefore, it may be important to establish various categories of merger or acquisition information that can be protected at different levels, depending on the need-to-know criteria. For example, there may be "limited-use information" for those who are called on to answer a specific question or complete a one-time, short-term task that would help the project team. There may be another classification for information that all the team members must know, and one or more other classifications in-between. One word of caution, such classifications should be logical and limited in number so as not to be more of a burden than an asset to those involved in the merger or acquisition.

Each person places a value on information in his or her possession. That information, which is necessary to successfully complete his or her work on the merger or acquisition project team, is valuable to that person; however, it may not be valuable to anyone else on the team. For example, if you were an accountant, the accounts payable records of the company being considered for acquisition or merger may be important, and, without them, you could not do your job on the project team. For the person analyzing the manufacturing capabilities of the potential corporation being acquired, however, the information has little, if any, value.

Some believe that the originator determines the value of the information. In many cases this is true, but that individual does not determine the value of information in a vacuum. He or she categorizes or classifies the information, usually according to the guidelines established by the employer or company. An important fact to remember is that all information is time-dependent; thus, its value changes over time. For example, date and time of the landing on Normandy Beach by the Allied forces during World War II was very valuable information and classified at the highest levels. After the invasion began, however, the information was no longer classified for obvious reasons—the Germans knew it.

When members of the merger or acquisition project team determine the value of information, they should also determine what it costs to produce that information. Also to be considered is the cost in terms of damages caused to the corporation because it was released outside protected channels. Remember, increased revenue and reducing the costs of doing business across the newly formed company are at the heart of the merger or acquisition. Therefore, all costs must always be considered when analyzing a potential merger or acquisition. As previously mentioned, many mergers and acquisitions never realize their expected savings and revenue increases because they did not properly consider all the relevant costs associated with the transaction.

Additional consideration must be given to the cost of maintaining and protecting that information. How these processes are combined determines the value of the information. Again, don't forget to factor in the time element.

There are two basic assumptions to consider in determining the value of information:

- All information costs some type of resource(s) to produce (e.g., money, hours, use of equipment)
- Not all information can cause damage if released outside protected channels.

If information costs to produce (and all information does) and no damage is done if released, you must consider, "Does it still have value?" If it costs to produce the information, but it cannot cause damage if it is released outside protected channels, then why protect it? The time factor is a key element in determining the value of information that cannot be overemphasized.

Business Information Types and Examples

This section provides some examples of the various common classifications used in business that can also be applied to mergers and acquisition information.

Types of Corporation Internal Use Only Information

- Not generally known outside the corporation
- Not generally known through product inspection
- Possibly useful to a competitor
- Provides some business advantage over competitors
- Examples: Corporation telephone book, corporation policies and procedures, corporation organizational charts

Types of Corporation Proprietary or Private Information

- Technical or financial aspects of the corporation
- Indicates corporation's future direction
- Describes portions of the corporation business
- Provides a competitive edge
- Identifies personal information of employees
- Examples: Personnel medical records, salary information, cost data, short-term marketing plans, dates for unannounced events

Types of Corporation-Sensitive Information

- Provides significant competitive advantage
- Could cause serious damage to the corporation
- Reveals long-term corporation strategic direction
- Examples: Critical corporation technologies, critical engineering processes, critical cost data, competitive intelligence data and assessments, strategic plans, merger and acquisition plans

Questions to Ask When Determining Value

When determining the value of your information, you should, as a minimum, ask the following questions:

- How much does it cost to produce?
- How much does it cost to replace?
- What would happen if I no longer had that information?
- What would happen if my closest competitor had that information?
- Is protection of the information required by law? If so, how much protection is required? If so, what are the consequences of not protecting it?

Case Study: A Process for Determining Information Value

The following is a short, simple example to help demonstrate a process for determining the value of some company information:

A department wants additional information to support its merger or acquisition activities. A new software application is purchased to provide that information. The collection of this information is determined to be $1,000 (personnel time, documentation, input, and a proportion of hardware and software costs). Use of the information costs was $50 (processing, error checking, mailing it to users, etc.) per month. The use of this information causes an efficiency improvement of $2,000 per year. If the information is used for five years, the value analysis would indicate:

Costs:

Cost amortized over five years = 1000/5 = $200

Cost of yearly utilization = $50 × 12 = $600

Yearly cost = $800

Information Value:

Quantifiable factors: = $2000 per year

Nonquantifiable factors: improved productivity, greater accuracy, better database

Total value = $2000 + nonquantifiable factors

Example Process for Determining Information Value

$800 yearly cost < $2000 + nonquantifiable benefits.

Results: Cost < Total Value.

The preceding example is one way to approach assigning a value to information. In most companies, analytical tools are seldom used to determine the value of information. Usually experience, past practices, benchmarking, current policy, and even antidotal examples are used to help categorize information and assign some sort of value. Whatever works best for your company is the process that should be used. Achieving a useful and efficient process may require some trial and error.

INFORMATION ASSURANCE

Information assurance refers to the protection provided to merger or acquisition information after it has been categorized, classified, or valued in accordance with company guidelines on the sensitivity of company information and is then placed on information systems. Information assurance is a subset of information protection. Information security includes all information regardless of form (paper, idea, electronic, etc.). Information assurance focuses on the protection of information that resides on, is processed on, displayed on, and transmitted by information systems. It is an integral protection concept that must be integrated into a successful mergers and acquisition information protection project.

Information assurance is predicated on the fundamental philosophy that information relative to a merger or acquisition, which the team has identified as sensitive, is not to be released outside the project team. Moreover, the information systems (usually computers) themselves must also be protected in order to fully protect sensitive mergers or acquisition information they store, process, transmit, and display. Information must be protected from *destruction, degradation, manipulation, and exploitation* by unauthorized and even authorized persons. Keep in mind, the biggest threat to this information comes from within an organization. For a variety of reasons, from employee carelessness to disgruntled workers, there is an ever-present threat to the merger or acquisition-sensitive information, making the need to protect it critical and the task of protecting it difficult and demanding. Part of the difficulty with achieving this protection is that one day a party may be collaborating on the project and will need access to the sensitive information, and the next day that party may no longer have a need–to know. This risk is doubled when the two companies collaborate on the merger or acquisition from the start.

A Government Perspective on Information Assurance

In 1996, the U.S. Department of Defense defined information assurance as: "actions taken that protect and defend information and information systems by ensuring their availability, integrity, authentication, confidentiality and non-repudiation." This includes providing for restoration of information systems by incorporating protection, detection, and reaction capabilities.

Information security and information assurance are concerned with both intentional and unintentional threats. Information assurance also addresses areas not considered by information security, such as perception management. Information assurance can be considered at three levels: physical, information infrastructure, and perceptual.[5]

Information assurance includes the following:

- IA Authentication: Security measure designed to establish the validity of a transmission, message, or originator, or a means of verifying an individual's authorization to receive specific categories of information (National Telecommunications Information Systems Security Instructions (NSTISSI) 4009).
- IA Availability: Timely, reliable access to data and information services for authorized users (NSTISSI 4009).

---

[5] Reprinted by permission of Springer Verlag Publishing, from their book, *Information Assurance: Surviving in the Information Environment,* September 2001.

- IA Confidentiality: Assurance that information is not disclosed to unauthorized persons, processes, or devices (NSTISSI 4009).
- IA Integrity: Protection against unauthorized modification or destruction of information (NSTISSI 4009).
- IA Non-repudiation: Assurance that the sender of data is provided with proof of delivery and the recipient is provided with proof of the sender's identity, so that neither can later deny receipt or dispatch.

PROTECTING INFORMATION DURING A MERGER OR ACQUISITION EFFORT

As mentioned previously, the task of protecting information related to a merger or acquisition is a subset of the overall task of protecting company information. Protecting information created, used, and disseminated during a merger and acquisition is a more narrowly focused and concentrated effort. However, because of the nature of a merger or acquisition—that is, confidentiality and even secrecy are necessary—the effort to protect can be more demanding. Generally, most information associated with a merger or acquisition is sensitive, particularly during the early stage of the effort when information about the existence of the effort requires protection.

During a merger or acquisition, the task of protecting information from those who do not have a need to know is difficult at best. To begin with, the natural tendency of team members is to share information as part of getting the job done. Sharing information is also a part of demonstrating one's success. A mature team can usually overcome this tendency, but an inexperienced team may have difficulty. Those who have access to this information include finance specialists, technical experts, process experts, management experts, executives, lawyers, and even corporate board members—anyone who is identified as having the expertise to assist in a merger or acquisition for the company (Figure 5.2).

CEOs need to share information with shareholders and the investment community at large to demonstrate they are doing all they can to increase the value of company stock. Protecting merger and acquisition-related information is the responsibility of all team members and participants. The charge for having procedures and practices in place to facilitate information protection lies with the merger or acquisition team's leader and the security organization.

- *Unintended release:* This type of release can occur in many ways. More often than not it is caused by carelessness on the part of overworked employees or employees not fully understanding their obligations to protect sensitive information and not fully understanding the degree of sensitivity of that same information. When employees are provided with well-defined guidelines on the

Merger and Acquisition Team Supporting a Large Transaction

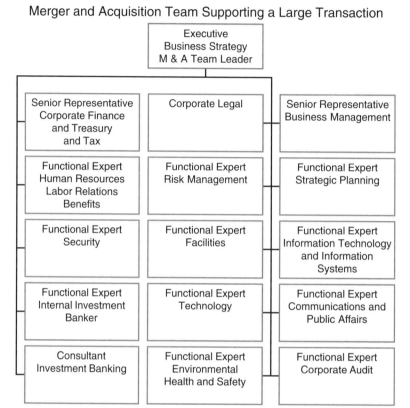

Figure 5.2 Merger and acquisition team supporting a large transaction.

sensitivity of information and how to handle that same information, they better understand their obligations.

- *Unauthorized release:* An unauthorized release is more difficult to control and may stem from an employee or team member fully aware of their obligations to protect information. The release is deliberate for reasons not necessarily to the benefit of the merger and acquisition team or the company. Ensuring that all employees and team members fully understand the consequences of releasing information without authorization is essential. This can be accomplished by having a written policy prohibiting unauthorized release, ensuring the rules of an authorized release are clearly communicated, and having each team member sign nondisclosure agreements that include clearly stated consequences for failure to fulfill individual obligations to protect information. Most important, it is essential to advise those involved that all leaks will be fully investigated and members who violate the policy can be prosecuted to the full extent of the law. If such a violation does take place, the company should follow through with what it says it will do: investigate *and* prosecute the individual(s) involved, either criminally, civilly, or both.

Information designated for release by authorized persons is generally not a concern. However, when released in conjunction with other information, it may become a concern. All information released must be coordinated and approved by team leadership, security, and public affairs.

- *Protection from competitive intelligence efforts:* Protecting information from being collected through legitimate means requires policies, procedures, and protocols to be in place that clearly establish mergers or acquisition information sensitivity and handling methods. It also requires training team member so that they are aware of how they may contribute to this process and what actions they may use to mitigate collection efforts or at least not support them or make them easier. Protecting information from being collected through illegitimate means is a different ball game. As much as possible, such processes should follow the normal company processes for the protection of sensitive company information. The primary difference is to compartmentalize that information in a strict need-to-know working environment.

  One of the illegitimate means of obtaining information is the use of electronic listening devices. It is not unheard of for a competitor to listen in on the communications transmissions of another company. This may be an illegal practice, but it does occur. One way to prevent it from occurring is to use electronic countermeasures to find or defeat devices used for this purpose. More than likely, security managers will not possess the equipment and training to effectively use electronic countermeasures on their own. The good news is that there are many local and national companies that have the capability, equipment, and expertise to do this for them. When starting up a merger or acquisition effort, particularly when doing so off company property or at a location not afforded constant security controls, it is best to conduct an electronic countermeasures sweep before the start of activities. After the sweep, the area must be secured and access tightly controlled.

  The collection of information by competitors through illegitimate means can be facilitated if a company does not properly protect all of its electronic information systems, particularly, stand-alone and portable systems such as laptop computers, cellular telephones, PDAs, and the like. When these systems are used in support of a merger and acquisition, protecting them may be more critical than it is within the daily work environment. In the fast-paced merger and acquisition environment, computers and other such devices are widely used by team personnel and executives to accomplish their business and objectives. When these items are used outside the normal controlled areas, where merger and acquisitions are often worked, their use becomes more problematic. Protecting information systems and devices from improper use, unauthorized access, and theft is a challenge. Often there is so much activity and movement of people that it is easy to lose control of information systems.

The security manager must develop a mergers or acquisition information systems protection plan. All persons who will use or possess these systems must be made to understand proper use, storage, and protection of these systems and the information they contain. Records should be maintained of all such equipment used and an inventory conducted before and after the actual effort. Any loss or improper use of equipment and systems should be immediately reported to ensure appropriate actions can take place to mitigate the loss. These systems should be sealed to prevent tampering (e.g., the installation of a listening device).

The use of cellular phones must be limited and controlled. Actually no telephones but encrypted phones should be used to discuss mergers or acquisition information that requires protection. Furthermore, the project team should be cautioned not to try to use their own "code words" or "talk-around" methods to try to discuss sensitive information about mergers or acquisitions on any communications devices.

- *Document control:* Much of the material handled in support of a merger or acquisition is routine business information. However, if the team's intentions are to keep the effort unknown, then nothing is routine. Any information that could reveal the existence of the effort, if exposed, must be protected. This includes simple items such as telephone notes and routine correspondence containing information revealing the efforts existence.

  Procedures for the project team's control of information in document or written form should be developed and implemented for use by all. Any procedures used should be as similar and consistent to normal company protective practices as possible. However, in some environments, this may not be possible, so procedures specific to the effort need to be established and implemented. All personnel involved with the effort should be aware of these procedures and must follow them. And by all means, information should be destroyed only by shredding, using the best shredders available—those that shred the material into the smallest pieces—or by burning the documents in their entirety. Such burnings must at least be witnessed by a project team member if team members do not themselves burn the documents.

To ensure that team members are aware of the need to protect sensitive project information, documents should have as a permanent project cover sheet. The cover sheet should contain basic handling and protection information that is visible and therefore readily available to anyone who handles the document (Figure 5.3).

When U.S. government officials were held hostage in Iran, terrorists were able to painstakingly, but successfully, reconstruct shredded documents. When millions if not billions of dollars or equivalent funds are at stake, the incentive to gain unauthorized access to merger or acquisition information by reconstructing shredded documents may be too difficult to resist.

OPERATIONS SECURITY

As alluded to earlier, mergers or acquisitions projects require an OPSEC philosophy, methodology, and plan. OPSEC is an analytical process used to deny any adversary the ability to obtain information concerning intentions and capabilities, in this case a company planning a merger or acquisition. OPSEC does not replace other forms of security; it is a form of security in and of itself. Operations security requires team members to be cognizant of their daily routine and behavior and to understand what that behavior may reveal. Every team member must understand what others can learn by observing their daily actions.

Routine actions that can be linked to other activities may enable others to draw conclusions about a larger picture. For example, assume a CEO of company "A" is interested in acquiring company "B." Normally, the two companies do not conduct business with each other; therefore, there is little to no interaction between the two CEOs. What may be learned if a competitor observes the CEO of company "A" making frequent visits to company "B" and its CEO? How useful will that bit of information be if associated with an announced strategy made by company "A" of future intentions to grow its business through mergers and acquisitions? Remember also that it may not be a competitor who learns of a potential acquisition or merger. It may be someone from the news media or a stockbroker, especially those who specialize in monitoring certain companies and/or certain business sectors. These individuals are always on the lookout for something out of the ordinary happening at companies or company executives acting in other than a routine manner.

For example, will the executive management of a firm or others in the company spend weekends at their offices when that is normally not the case? Will they be working later than usual, traveling to places they do not normally travel to? These are but two of the many changes in routine that news media, competitors, stockbrokers, and others may look for. News reporters in the United States who covered the military often say they knew when some military action was to take place by combining the latest

Sample Cover Sheet for a Project Sensitive Document

Company _____ Sensitive Information
Due Diligence Project _____

*The information contained in this document requires a
higher degree of protection or standard of care.
Protect in accordance with company standards for protecting the most
sensitive company information*

*Designation Criteria
for determining the sensitivity of project data*

Project information and data is sensitive if it does any of the following

- Provides Company _____ with a competitive edge
- Reveals the existence of project _____
- Its unrestricted, outside disclosure may cause harm or damage to Company _____ or to the target company
- The project information relates to or describes some aspects of the target company's business that is not generally known outside the target company (i.e. non-public information)
- The project information indicates strategic or operational direction over a period of time that is not otherwise known outside the company
- The project information is important to the technical or financial aspects of a specific product or the business as a whole and is not generally known outside the company

Designation authority of this document
Originator

Storage of this document
Keep in a lockable container, office

Transmissions of this document
- Express Mail
- Fax – Must be encrypted

Retention/Destruction

*DO NOT RETAIN OR DESTROY
Return to Originator upon completion of Project*

Figure 5.3 Sample document cover sheet.

incidents around the world where U.S. military action was possible with the late working hours of the Pentagon staff who ordered many pizzas from local establishments. It seems that when there was a crisis where U.S. troops may have been sent or some other U.S. military action taken, the Pentagon's staff worked late, and when they did so, they ordered many pizzas.

These independent actions that can be linked to other actions, activities, or events are referred to as *indicators*. Indicators are what an adversary or competitor looks for when trying to learn more about a company. Indicators are useful in developing competitive intelligence. When associated with planning and operation processes for a merger or acquisition, indicators must be identified, controlled, and protected.

Indicators are nothing more than actions or patterns of behavior that people take and that may reveal something important or sensitive when associated with other information or actions. Indicators may be seemingly innocuous actions, but, when coupled with other actions or information, they reveal much more collectively than independently. What conclusion would you draw if you were to witness a significant increase in the frequency of visits to your company headquarters by an investment banking team? By itself, it may not mean much; associated with an increase in visits from attorneys working for a firm specializing in mergers and acquisitions, it may reveal quite a bit.

Competitive intelligence gatherers are trained to look for indicators. They watch for actions and indicators that may be revealing and associate them with other known facts to develop conclusions about intentions and motives. When merger and acquisition team members don't pay close attention to their own actions, they make it easier for others to observe and learn from them. Merger and acquisition team members must understand the importance of keeping a low profile and not calling attention to themselves. Team members should ask themselves the following questions anytime they venture outside their secure confines:

- What could others learn if they observed my actions?
- What could others learn if they obtained information I routinely have in my position?
- What could others learn if they had a copy of my schedule, contact list, or other seemingly innocuous routine information?
- What could others learn if they could hear the conversations I have on my cell phone?

Good operations security can be achieved only if all team members understand what others may be interested in and how their own behavior may help others gain information about sensitive merger or acquisition operations. Team members must act to prevent information from being revealed through their actions. Effective operations security can be achieved but only with the willing cooperation of an aware mergers or acquisition project team. (See Figure 5.4 for an example of a project OPSEC plan.)

Sample Operation Security (OPSEC) Guidelines for Project XXX

Operations Security Guidelines for Project XXX

Purpose

This plan provides guidance and establishes security requirements for the protection of project XXX. The existence of project XXX and all related information must be protected in accordance with the guidelines and requirements contained within this document.

General

Company XXX will enter into a "Confidential Agreement" with a target company for the purpose of engaging in discussions on the potential for a merger or acquisition. As part of these discussions, Company XXX will conduct a due diligence of the target company in order to assess the value of the target.

Once the agreement is signed, all Company XXX executives, employees, and agents must adhere to non-disclosure obligations set forth in the signed agreement. Consequently, it is essential that Company XXX strictly control its review of the target company. These restrictions apply to all phases of the project and will remain in full effect until written authorization or direction is provided to the contrary.

Once the "Confidential Agreement" is signed by all involved parties, the exchange of information[1] will begin. A due diligence team, composed of functional experts, will be assembled to visit the target company. The specific purpose of the due diligence is to conduct an assessment of the target company and identify major areas of liability, as well as areas where substantial investments will be required after purchasing. Access to project sensitive information will be in a variety of forms, including spoken and visual presentations, written materials, facility tours, and question and answer sessions.

During the due diligence, project leaders are assigned to coordinate access briefings as well as manage information that is collected, received, copied, or disseminated during the due diligence. Concerns or questions not specifically covered within this plan are to be directed to the project lead and the team security lead.

---

[1] Any data provided to Company XXX employees, agents, or representatives that reflects or contains any such information relating to the project. That data may be written, oral or electronic and graphic communications as well as notes, analysis, compilations, studies, interpretations, diagrams, charts, and other documents.

Figure 5.4 Example of a project operational security (OPSEC) plan.

Legal Requirements

U.S. Securities laws (and Company XXX policies) prohibit the purchase or sale of securities on the basis of material non-public information and prohibit the communication of such material non-public information to any other person. Information received during the project is to be considered material and non-public for the purposes of these laws and policies. Any person who fails to comply with the following may be subject to liability under the federal securities laws and/or disciplinary action by the company:

- Until this project has concluded, project members MAY NOT trade in Company XXX securities without written authorization.
- Project members MAY NOT trade in securities of the target company, or of the company or group of which the subject forms a part until advised in writing that the project is complete and all information received is no longer non-public.

Protecting the Project

Code Names: The Vice President of Strategy will assign a code name to the project (merger, acquisition, or divestiture). This is done to protect the project's specific purpose from being exposed to persons outside of the project team and from revealing the identity of the target company or business unit.

The code name assigned to this project will be: _____

Project Cover Story: During the due diligence effort it may be necessary to use a cover story to ensure existence of the project is not revealed to anyone outside of the project team. A cover story will aid in disguising the true nature of the project and offers authorized team members a means of explaining their actions without revealing the true nature of their task. Persons who have not been briefed/assigned to the project are considered to be persons without a need to know. All persons without a need to know are to be kept outside of the project area and information about the project must not be shared with them. This list of persons may include company employees and managers and extends to all types of people who may exhibit curiosity about the project (e.g., hotel employees, travel agents, etc.)

The cover story for this project is:

_____

Disclosure

Due diligence members must read and sign a non-disclosure agreement acknowledging acceptance of responsibilities and obligations to protect all project-related information and materials. Moreover, release of project information or project material is absolutely forbidden without expressed consent of the project leader and security representative.

Figure 5.4, cont'd

Information obtained before, during, and after the project must not be disclosed to any person or persons who are not briefed to the project, to include co-workers, family, and friends. Prior to disclosing project information to any authorized individual, their status as a project team member must be verified through the team security representative. It is important to note that due diligence/project team membership often changes. *DO NOT* assume an individual briefed to a previous project has access to the current project. Individuals briefed to this project must adhere to the following requirements:

- DO NOT disclose the identity of the buyer or seller or any information or opinion regarding the evaluation of the target. Moreover, do not disclose the existence of an ongoing evaluation.
- DO NOT answer any questions regarding the project. Any and all external inquiries should be answered with the statement *"It is Company policy not to respond to any questions of this nature,"* or by referring the requester to the Vice President of Business Strategy or the team security representative.
- DO NOT use information and materials generated for any purpose other than for evaluation of the target company. Information obtained may be competition sensitive and must not be used for any purpose other than for the authorized due diligence evaluation. Team members must be alert to the competitive nature of the information provided.
- DO report any and all inquiries made from outside the authorized project team to the team security representative or the team leader immediately.
- DO report any known or suspected breach of the Confidentiality Agreement to the team security representative or the team leader.

Document Control

All project-related documents are to be strictly controlled. This includes documents in both hard copy and electronic form. At the onset of the project an administrator will be assigned to monitor and control all creation, distribution, reproduction, and disposition of all documents. A document-tracking process will be established unique to this project and all documents will be accounted for. All team members will be held responsible for the safeguarding and accountability of all documents and materials they receive, originate, and/or reproduce during the entire duration of the project.

Storage: In Company XXX facilities all documents and information in any form must be properly safeguarded. Hard copy documents are to be stored in locked containers when not in use. Electronic documents are to be stored on information systems which are password protected.

Away from company facilities, documents and project information must be keep in the possession or control of a team member at all times. If left in a vehicle, that vehicle must be locked and the material stored in the vehicle trunk. While in a hotel, if available, a room safe should be used for maximum

Figure 5.4, cont'd

protection. In unpredicted situations, common sense coupled with good security practices should ensure the protection of information from unauthorized disclosure.

Reproduction: No copies or reproductions of the project information in whole, or in part, are to be made without the express authorization of the team leader, the Company XXX legal department, or the team security representative.

Transmissions: All electronic transmission (email, fax, voice, etc.) must be encrypted using company approved commercial encryption. For specific information please see your team security representative. Electronic information is to be transmitted only to properly authorized team members. Team membership can be validated through the team security manager.

Destruction: All destruction of project documents and material must be coordinated with the document administrator and the team security leader. Under no circumstances is any team member to take the initiative and destroy material without proper coordination.

Retention of material postmerger, acquisition, or divestiture: Under no circumstances will project-related information, documents, or material be retained by team members without the expressed approval of the team leader, document administrator, or the team security representative.

TRAVEL

All project-related travel must be approved by the team leader, and be accomplished in such a manner so as to not disclose team member's objectives and intentions or to associate the team member and the Company XXX relationship with the target company. In essence a very low profile must be maintained. Some important guidelines follow:

Transportation security
- Do not call attention to yourself and the relationship between Company XXX and the target company.
- Prevent disclosure of information on airplanes by ensuring that documents and information exposed do not contain company names and/or confidential project information.
- When talking with other passengers, avoid revealing personal or company information. Be polite, but be careful. The person sitting next to you may be a competitor!
- Never place project material in your checked luggage or check computer equipment that contains project material.
- DO NOT use laminated business cards on your luggage and avoid putting the Company XXX name or any logos on your luggage.
- Never leave your bags unattended.
- Never ever leave computers or personal digital devises with storage capability unattended.

Figure 5.4, cont'd

Reservations: When making travel arrangements team members must ensure all travel is consistent with routine department business travel and not out of the usual routine. Avoid using administrative support from other departments for travel arrangements unless the individual is project briefed.

Hotels: Use only hotels approved by the team leader or team security representative. Large groups of team members should avoid staying at the same hotel.

Rental Cars: While participants are discouraged from obtaining individual rental cars, enough cars should be available to transport project members to and from the target site. Coordinate car rental requirements with your team leader to limit the number of cars rented from a particular rental company.

Meeting Rooms: Meetings in which project-related material is presented or discussed should be held in a controlled environment. If this is not possible, due to group size or location of meetings, arrangements should be made with the host to ensure privacy is maintained during the meeting. Furthermore, the person responsible for arranging/leading the meeting must determine that all attendees are properly briefed to the project. If appropriate, a walk through of the room should be conducted to ensure the room is not equipped with recording or listening devices.

PROJECT CLOSE

Upon close-out of the project each team member will be required to complete a "Certificate of Return and/or Destruction" for all documents held in their possession. Each team member must read, sign, and return the certificate to the document administrator or the team security representative immediately following completion of the due diligence or upon notification by the team leader.

Figure 5.4, cont'd

PROTECTING MERGER AND ACQUISITION EXECUTIVES AND TEAM PERSONNEL

More often than not, merger and acquisition team members require some level of executive protection during the period they are actively working a merger or acquisition. This includes the premerger and acquisition period and the postmerger and acquisition period. Executive protection is a security discipline or process developed and used to provide protection to high-profile company executives as they go about their daily business and routine life actions. Generally, merger and acquisition teams are not made up of senior company executives; however, some senior company executives are usually involved with merger and acquisition teams as members and advisors. Because merger and acquisition teams are staffed with some senior executives, mid-level company managers and specialists, and outside consultants, and because they engage in highly sensitive activities, some level of protection (similar to executive protection) is required. Today, because of terrorist threats, it may be necessary to provide some form of protection to all merger and acquisition team members, especially those traveling to a foreign nation, particularly in the Middle East. In essence, merger and acquisition teams need some type of personnel protection program because of the nature of their work, where they may be traveling to, the type of people involved, and the severe consequences to the company if the effort is compromised.

From a competitive perspective, there is always a threat to merger and acquisition teams. Competitors will always be interested in learning of their plans and actions. There are also other threats to a merger and acquisitions team. Since merger and acquisition teams often venture into unknown or unfamiliar areas (particularly when engaged in international business activities), they experience the threats normally faced by business-people and high-profile executives venturing into the global marketplace. These threats, real and potential, vary during the premerger or acquisition and postmerger and acquisition stages, as does the level of support required. What will not vary is the value gained from providing protection to the team.

The type and degree of personnel protection support required vary depending on many factors. Protection is not necessary in all situations. The need for personnel protection will be situational, depending on what is being done, where, when, and by whom.

Protecting a team or any members of the team requires the application of reasonable protective measures to mitigate the risk to personnel, strengthen vulnerabilities, and avoid threats. Providing personnel protection for a merger and acquisition team is a proactive effort, not a reactive effort. Although there are reactive elements, proaction is the only way of effectively providing protection. Proaction is a preventive approach and calls for much advance preparation; in situations where reaction is necessary, it occurs automatically.

Extending protection to members of the merger and acquisition team should be approached as an expansion of the existing executive protection program and, in some cases, an extension of a special events protection process. The first step in building a personnel protection program for the merger and acquisition team is to get to know those who will require protection. Not all team members will engage in high-profile actions or be high-profile people. All are not critical to the effort and all will not be placed in situations of increased threat. Establishing criticality to the effort is not to say that any particular team member is not important to the effort. Rather, only a critical few are so important as to warrant additional protection. Remember, in some parts of the world, it is not a terrorist threat that one may have to worry about, but the threat of kidnapping for ransom.

How are those requiring additional protection identified? Team leadership and security must work together to determine the criticality of the executive or team member to the effort and assess the threat to them. One way of thinking about criticality to the effort is to ask the question, "What would be the impact to the team if a specific executive or team member was suddenly not available?" Loss of expertise, loss of leadership, or even exposure of the effort should all be considered in the assessment. How this assessment is made varies from company to company, as each company has different levels of tolerance for risk and different perceptions of threats. Nevertheless, the importance of using some methodology to establish the type and expanse of additional protection provided to the team cannot be overstated.

The personnel protection effort begins when it becomes necessary for executives or team members to leave the confines of the company facility, an already secure area, and travel to a location where they are more vulnerable to an identified or potential threat. Recognizing this protection effort to be primarily a proactive preventive effort, it must begin with the development of a plan. The effort to protect personnel begins with advance planning activities and ends only with a safe and uneventful (in terms of security) return of personnel. It must include all of the steps in between, from departure, movement, stops, arrival, and a safe return. Therefore, it should be included in the overall mergers or acquisition security plan along with the information security and OPSEC plans.

The ultimate purpose of a personnel protection program is to protect key members of the merger and acquisition team and to eliminate or significantly reduce the possibility of disruption to the business. The loss of a key executive or team member critical to the effort can have a serious and adverse impact on the effort and even the company. A protection effort helps reduce the overall risks to the business.

Eliminating risk is neither possible nor practical. Reducing or managing risks is both. A personnel protection program is much like earthquake insurance. If you don't have it when you need it, the consequences may be disastrous; however, to have it, proactive steps must be taken to get it. Moreover, there are costs involved. Like earthquake insurance, executive protection is not free, but it does not have to be expensive or cost prohibitive. A cost-effective and efficient executive protection program can be established. It requires developing an understanding of the threats, risks, vulnerabilities, and needs of the company and its executives. In some cases, an extensive program may be required. In other situations, very little effort may be necessary. Thus far, one can see that many unforeseen— unforeseen by executive management at least—costs are beginning to accumulate when it comes to a merger or acquisition. The same may hold true for team members other than security

Such unforeseen costs often come as a shock to executive management. Therefore, it behooves the security professional to have an up-to-date plan of action in the event a merger or acquisition is considered. Such a plan should include all the premerger or acquisition and postmerger or acquisition costs.

A protection program should be designed to facilitate team members working and moving about safely and efficiently. They can't be locked up. Their ability to move around and work freely is essential to their performance. Facilitating this mobility in a safe and secure manner is the objective of an effective protection program. In essence, the protected persons are being made into a "hard target," that is, a target that is difficult to reach and damage but still effective in conducting everyday business. Achieving this goal in such a way as not to inhibit the team member's ability to conduct business is what makes the difference between an effective project and an ineffective project. Too much protection, or improperly applied protection, will inhibit the ability of the team member to perform and will lead to resistance on their part. This resistance could be as strong as to resist any protection at all. On the other hand, not enough protection leaves the team member vulnerable, with a false sense of security and the company at risk. As with so many other aspects of the business, balancing cost and benefit effectively will produce positive results.

Determining the type of threats to executives and merger or acquisition team members and identifying the specific risks are essential and fundamental to providing effective protection. Threats and risks vary widely, but some are quite common to most executives. Here is a list of potential threats and the likelihood of their occurrence:

- *Harassment:* This is one of the more common threats a team member, particularly a very visible executive, may face. If the merger or acquisition is unfriendly, disgruntled employees, shareholders unhappy with stock performance, and people who determine it to be their mission in life to harass a business executive can cause problems. Most harassers are just a nuisance and can be effectively handled. Few represent a threat of violence, but violence cannot be casually dismissed.

- *Kidnapping:* As stated earlier, this is a serious threat in many parts of the world. However, since most mergers and acquisitions occur in North America, the risk to merger and acquisition teams is low. If the merger or acquisition were to occur outside North America, such as in South American countries, the risk would be much higher. Kidnapping in South America has become a cottage industry. According to the Ackerman Group, International Security Consultants,[6] in 2001, Colombia alone reported 3,072 cases of

---

[6] See http://www.ackermangroup.com

kidnapping. These kidnappings range from the "express kidnapping," which is relatively unsophisticated, lasts only for a few hours or days, and includes a trip or trips to an ATM, to very sophisticated, well-planned kidnappings that target specific wealthy executives, politicians, high-profile persons, and, in some cases, travelers.

The "good news" is that even such severe risks can be managed. Kidnapping and ransom insurance can be obtained to help the company reduce its risks. There are several providers of kidnap/ransom and extortion insurance that can be purchased to insure the safety of employees and protect company assets. Along with these policies come the crisis management and negotiation services of international business risk consultancy companies. If a kidnapping, ransom, or extortion situation does occur, the importance of utilizing the services of companies that have expertise in this area cannot be overstated. Of course the best way to deal with kidnapping, ransom, or extortion is to prevent it in the first place. This is easier said than done, but preventive steps can be taken to help mitigate the risks.

- *Street violence:* Crime and street violence can be a problem in most any country in the world. Although no area is completely safe, the risk of becoming a victim of crime or street violence is greater in areas with high crime rates. High-profile people, people who appear vulnerable, and people traveling in unfamiliar areas with high crime rates are most at risk. They give the appearance of being a good target. Proper planning to avoid high crime areas will contribute greatly to preventing an occurrence of crime or violence.
- *Medical emergency:* Medical emergencies are a potential threat. They do occur and are influenced by many factors such as age, lifestyle, and personal habits. Each factor may contribute to increasing the likelihood of a medical emergency. Reducing the probability of an incident will best occur if the persons protected are aware of their own high-risk actions and make an effort to change that behavior. In the event of a medical emergency, having a personnel protection specialist who is trained in basic emergency medical techniques may prove invaluable.
- *The unexpected event:* It is not possible to plan, or be prepared for, every conceivable threat. With limited resources and the need for executives to be mobile, just reducing the overall risks and countering the threats is the primary objective. Thorough preparation and planning are the best course of action to reduce the probability of an unexpected occurrence. Careful planning to counter the most likely threat will reduce the risk. When an event does occur, prior training and preparation will enable the protection specialists to properly react.

Not all members of the team will be receptive to personnel protection support. Some will not agree with security threat assessments and stated risks; others will see themselves as quite capable of taking care of themselves. It is important that security work with each team member to ensure that everyone understands all real and potential threats and increase in risks when protection is rejected. Moreover, when protection is being provided to a team, it is important for all members to cooperate, as their failure to do so may put the team at higher risk. In either case, the company should consider investing in an insurance policy to cover the identified employee(s) as an added precaution against loss or kidnapping.

An important part of understanding the threat to the team or any of its members is to identify anyone who would want to harm them. This is much easier to do within the context of an established personnel protection program where those being protected are well known to those providing the protection and have been subject to risk and vulnerability assessments. Identifying any threat to a merger and acquisition team beyond threats and vulnerabilities associated with geography and political condition is much more difficult. For example, if company "A" is attempting to acquire company "B," there will be much company "A" will not know about company "B" stakeholders. Are they in favor of the acquisition? Are there outside interest groups, such as trade unions, that may be opposed to a takeover? If so, how will they react to the acquiring company's intention and to the merger and acquisition team? These questions should be considered when trying to assess the threat. Here are other questions security must ask or consider when attempting to establish the existence of any threat:

- Why would someone want to harm the team or any of its members?
- Who would want to harm the team or any of its members?
- Are there any known persons who have expressed a hostile reaction to the attempted acquisition?
- Do team members engage in any activities that make them a target?
- What organizations, political figures, or government figures are the company associated with that may cause others to react negatively, making the team a target?
- What team members, if any, are at risk and are vulnerable?
- What team members would cause the greatest harm to the company if rendered unavailable to the team and company?

This assessment should be undertaken purely as a business decision. Protection is not a "perk." It is a security process used to reduce a business risk. (See Figure 5.5 for more information about protective service operations for merger or acquisition team members.)

Additional Executive Protection Measures for Use During a Merger or Acquisition Project:

1.1   Know the personnel being protected

It is essential for those who protect (protectors) to know as much as possible about those being protected. In the event of an emergency or crisis, quick and informed decisions can be best made from a useful knowledge base. There will also be times when knowledge of the protected personnel will be useful in routine situations and in the process of facilitating movement. For example: during a medical emergency being able to communicate to emergency medical personnel specific health information and history may be life saving. The following is a listing of the types of information that should be made part of the protection biographical file on all personnel being provided additional protection. The executive's biographical file should include the following:

- Basic medical history
- Physical description and characteristics that should include a photo, voice recording, fingerprints, handwriting sample, and if possible, a DNA sample
- Listing of all family doctors
- Location of home
- A listing of all phone numbers
- A vehicle profile for all vehicles owned
- A description of personal habits (for example, likes to play golf every Sunday morning)
- A listing of emergency contacts with phone numbers, addresses, and description of each person
- A description of outside activities, hobbies, and interests
- If weapons are owned, a listing of each and the location should be made

1.2   The protector

What type of person is required to perform personnel protection duties? What characteristics must they possess? What skills must they have? Is being skilled and trustworthy sufficient for a personnel protection professional? Keep in mind, someone's well being, and even their life, may depend upon this person. Like every profession, certain skills and characteristics are necessary for the professional to be effective. Below is a list of characteristics and traits a personnel protection specialist must possess.

- <u>Trustworthiness:</u> This is perhaps the most essential trait a personnel protection specialist can have since the person being protected will not be comfortable, or even cooperative, with someone they don't trust.

Figure 5.5 Information about protective service operations for merger or acquisition team members.

- Integrity, discretion, loyalty, and honesty: These are all traits that help build the confidence of the protected and the trust between the protected and the protector. A trusting relationship will facilitate honest communications which sometimes may be difficult but necessary. A lack of trust will inhibit the protector's ability to perform. They may be shut out of situations which are personal in nature yet still require support. For example, if the protected does not trust the protector, letting them into their home or other personal and sensitive areas may not be allowed.
- Fit mentally and physically: There may be times where physical strength and agility is needed to get out of difficult situations or provide aid to the protected. A fit protector is better able to deliver in a crisis. Being fit also helps a protector deal with long hours and grueling travel schedules which many executives regularly keep.
- Low profile: Blending in to the environment so that attention is not called to either the protector or the protected. This trait may also help preclude embarrassing situations.

Organized: Knowing what to do, what tools are needed, and how to do it requires organization skills. Facilitating the smooth and uninterrupted movement of an executive requires good planning and organizing. A disorganized protector will make mistakes.

- Professionalism: Knowing the job, being able to perform, and maintaining an honest professional (not intimate) relationship with the protected enhances the level of protection provided. A good protection professional does not allow distractions to develop, be they personal or situational.
- Preparation: Planning, rehearsing with the use of "what if" scenarios, and learning from each experience enables the protector to be prepared for most any contingency.

Keep in mind that in most cases, full time personnel protection personnel are not required. Whatever the need, skilled executive protection specialists can be obtained. Many corporations require protection services only on a part-time or periodic basis; therefore, they should seek the services of one of the many qualified companies that provide this expertise. These companies employ skilled and capable protection specialists and can effectively fulfill requirements on an as-needed basis. Moreover, outsourcing will help minimize costs since using a service provider is generally less expensive than maintaining an experienced staff.

One draw back to using any out-sourced provider of personnel protection services is they lack familiarity with the persons they will be charged with protecting and the business operating environment. Furthermore, they also lack an understanding and awareness of situations that come from working a protection detail for a particular person or team of key personnel over an extended period of time. This weakness can be balanced to some degree. The security manager can provide contract support with as much of the essential information needed to provide proper protection. Information such as threats, risks, vulnerabilities, and other relevant mission data will help the

Figure 5.5, cont'd

unfamiliar protector develop a familiarity and working understanding of the personnel to be protected and situation.

In addition, this new protection will seem unusual and may alert those watching to a change in the company and remember, any change is looked at in detail as to its meaning.

1.3   Advance work

Advance work allows the personnel protection specialists to thoroughly plan and prepare for an event or activity. For example, if a team member requires protection at an unfamiliar or new venue, the protection specialists needs to develop a base of knowledge about that location. In essence, do some intelligence gathering. The best way to accomplish this is for the protector to do it him or herself and go there. Intelligence is best when gathered first hand. In that way, nothing gets lost in the transition or translation. Walk, drive, or run, start to finish, through the trip. Visit the site and learn as much as possible about its layout and peculiarities. Establish support and assistance contacts and do as much advance work as possible.

Advance work helps the protector be better-informed, thus reducing the level of risk. Advance preparation helps reduce exposure, facilitate ease of movement, establish safe areas to include contiguous safety, and identify significant issues. Below is a checklist of things to consider and address as part of an advance assessment:

Getting there:
- Where is the venue?
- How will the protected personnel get there (mode of travel and route)?
- What will they be doing while they are there?
- How many locations will they visit?
- Who will they be with?

Once they are there:
- Is anyone in the area considered a threat?
- Is there a threat to similar people (other business executives)?
- What type of information about the protected personnel is available and accessible?
- What is going on at the location, today and tomorrow?
- Who will be there? Any other high-profile persons?
- What type of assistance is available?

Conduct a site survey to identify issues, routes, and layout of the following:
- Meeting location
- Hotels, resorts, and restaurants
- Private residences
- Convention center
- Emergency facilities
- Airports

Figure 5.5, cont'd

Identify all concerns and issues:
- Is there anything out of the ordinary to be concerned with?

Departure:
- What is the return route (direct and fast)?
- Establish alternates routes

Emergency Services:
- Where are the nearest medical facilities?
- Will medical personnel be available on site where the protected personnel will be visiting?

Once the advance effort is complete, review findings and share them with only those people who have a need-to-know. Brief the protected personnel involved so they are familiar with all plans and issues.

1.4 Transportation

How team members move from location to location is always a concern. Team personnel use many different modes of travel. Aircraft, automobile, watercraft, and even travel on foot are used. Generally, most travel is accomplished on the road in a sedan. Ideally, the sedan being used should have the following characteristics:

- Low profile – not flashy so that it will attract attention
- Full size – to provide sufficient bulk for crash protection
- Large engine – to enable quick acceleration and getaway ability
- Comfortable and safe – to protect personnel and provide enough room for up to four persons (driver, one or two protected personnel, and one or two protection specialists)
- Trained driver

Vehicle movements present ordinary risks associated with traffic conditions. These risks are unrelated to personnel protection issues but, when combined with them, the overall risks of vehicle travel elevate and warrant the use of skilled drivers. Drivers trained in defensive and evasive driving techniques should be used. This type of training is available in many locations from skilled providers and for a reasonable cost.

In today's global environment, air travel is both routine and essential. Merger and acquisition team members regularly travel via commercial carrier and even private aircraft. The great advantage of air travel is time. It allows personnel to reach distant locations at great speeds, very safely. The disadvantage of air travel is its cost, particularly for private aircraft. Commercial aircraft are the primary target of terrorists and hijackers. When possible, the protected personnel should travel by private aircraft.

Traveling via aircraft is generally safer than road travel. Not withstanding the events of September 11, 2001, the probability of injury or death due to a

Figure 5.5, cont'd

plane crash is less than the probability of injury or death due to an automobile accident. However, there are issues with air travel that a protection specialist should be concerned with. One issue is that of many members of the team traveling together. Even though the probability of occurrence is low, in the event of an air vehicle crash, if several team members are flying together, all could be injured or killed. The impact to the team and company could be devastating.

Loss of such key people who possess knowledge of company operations and management and technical expertise may be impossible to replace in sufficient time to allow the business to recover in a highly competitive global marketplace. A protection specialist must work to ensure key personnel travel separately or in small groups. Never should they all travel aboard the same air vehicle.

Another issue is that of providing security to private or company aircraft. Commercial air carriers generally provide adequate protection to aircraft, limiting just who has access and what that access is for. Security for private aircraft varies greatly. Beyond the basic requirements mandated by the Federal Aviation Administration[i] (FAA), physical security and access control varies among private aircraft owners. When key personnel use private aircraft, the protection specialist must ensure proper physical security and access controls are in place. Working with the flight crew and airport personnel, adequate procedures can be developed that will meet all security needs without inhibiting aircraft operations.

1.5   Office and home

In the workplace, much of the protection key personnel need is already built into the physical work environment. Their office is generally located within a physically secure building or facility. Only a few additional measures are needed above and beyond basic protection measures already in place. For example, in the event an intruder or unwanted person breached the layers of security, and reached the office area where the merger and acquisition team is working, the ability to lock down that office area is critical. Careful thought and consideration are necessary when planning for a location for the merger and acquisition team to work. Convenience, functionality, and comfort are important. Security is equally important.

Protecting key personnel outside of the work environment may or may not be necessary. If it is, it is generally more complicated. Usually, team members, unless they are very senior and high-profile company executives, will not require protection in their home. However, when a determination is made that home protection is necessary to reduce the probability of harm or incident, than an assessment of the home must be conducted.

Applying protective security measures for the home is no different than applying protective measures to the office, with one exception. That exception is with the issue of privacy. A home is a very private place.

---

[i] See http://www.faa.gov/

Figure 5.5, cont'd

Few people openly accept the intrusive application of home security measures. Regardless of how seemingly unobtrusive a security professional views home security measures, the personnel being protected and having their home modified with these measures usually holds a different view. The security professional must proceed patiently and acting as an advisor. The touch of a teacher and gentle powers of persuasion will be very useful here.

Security layers are applied to create a defense-in-depth environment. Layers of security controls are put in place to reduce the potential exposure and vulnerability of the protected person and their home and family. The use of basic physical security measures such as barriers, locks, alarms, video surveillance, package and mail delivery screening, fire prevention measures, emergency response, and first aid must be considered. Tools such x-ray scanners and duress alarms should be part of the protection system. Furthermore, particular attention must be directed at visitors to the home, both invited and uninvited.

As with any effort to apply security controls, the first activity in securing a home is to conduct a site physical survey. A threat assessment should also be made. To do this effectively, all members of the key person's family should be interviewed, as they may be able to provide useful information in establishing any level of threats. A completed survey will provide a base-line assessment from which additional and necessary controls can be developed and implemented.

1.6 Mail and packages

Often the easiest way to reach key personnel is through the mail. Large amounts of business materials are sent each day. Key personnel receive more mail than they can effectively handle. Generally, they have persons on staff who will screen all mail, routing to them only that mail they actually need or want to see. The most significant threat common to mail is the risk associated with suspicious packages:

Suspicious packages: Although rare, packages or letters containing bombs, chemicals, or biological hazards have been directed at key personnel. One only need recall the series of anthrax letters sent to U.S. government personnel[ii] and others shortly after the events of September 11, 2001. Effective screening measures can be established with the use of x-ray scanners and other equipment. Moreover, personnel can be trained to recognize potentially dangerous packages, screening them out and seeking assistance from law enforcement personnel. The extent these procedures are employed should be consistent with a risk assessment of threats and vulnerabilities.

[ii] See http://www.wired.com/news/politics/0%2C1283%2C47649%2C00.html

Figure 5.5, cont'd

HOSTILE TAKEOVERS AND PROXY FIGHTS

Hostile takeovers make for good press. CEOs battling it out with each other in the press sells. During the last 20 years, hostile takeovers have become an accepted practice.[7]

Hostile takeovers can raise the profile of companies and their CEOs. A company attempting a hostile takeover of a publicly held company must engage in a very public solicitation of shareholders, making a premium offer for stock above the prevailing market price. Time is a factor, as federal securities laws limit the time available to execute the deal. Companies need to move quickly to execute the transaction.

Proxy fights are another form of taking control of a company. An activist shareholder works to have his or her own candidates elected to the company board, thus taking control of the company through its board of directors. Proxy fights generally take a long time to complete. They also require much work and significant costs. Remember the discussion about competitive intelligence collection? In a proxy fight, such information is "worth its weight in gold."

What does all of this mean in terms of security? Executing a merger or acquisition is not an easy task. Add to that the following conditions, and the potential for some form of hostile act committed against the company or one of its executive's increases.

- Premium price means the deal will likely create financial pressures.
- The time to complete the deal is limited.
- Anxiety is high among the target company executives, employees, and shareholders.
- There is a greater level of attention from the press.

Any security manager attempting to provide protection for a merger and acquisition team working on a hostile takeover or proxy fight would be wise to engage skilled security support immediately. If the necessary expertise does not exist within the company, the security professional must go outside to a skilled provider and purchase those services. Events will unfold rapidly. Being prepared, even overprepared, may well be worth the expense.

SUMMARY

As soon as a company begins planning to implement a strategy for a merger or acquisition, the company security manager must become involved. Security must have a permanent place on any merger or acquisition team.

---

[7] See http://www.MergerForum.com

Early in the effort, plans need to be developed and implemented for protecting the effort.

The first challenge is keeping the effort confidential; from there it grows more difficult. Information and team personnel require protection. The pace of the effort is fast, with no time to waste and little time to test procedures and processes. Having skilled and experienced security support is an advantage. Since mergers and acquisitions don't occur often, experienced security personnel may not be available within the company. It may be necessary to seek outside expertise.

Chapter 6

Security's Role in the Due Diligence Assessment

As you make your bed, so you must lie on it. – Saying

INTRODUCTION

The security professional must understand the concept of due diligence. Furthermore, security must be part of the due diligence process and a member of the due diligence team. Like all other functional organizations and process owners, security has an obligation to assess the security condition and capabilities of the company targeted for merger or acquisition.

WHAT IS DUE DILIGENCE?

In short, due diligence is an effort to find out if the company you may merge with or acquire meets your expectations and needs (e.g., product quality, financial stability, and potential growth capabilities). When accomplished as part of a merger or acquisition, due diligence is an effort to learn as much about a target company as possible in order to make an informed business decision as to whether to acquire or merge with the target company. Conducting a due diligence of a prospective company targeted for merger or acquisition is not an option. It is a necessity and an obligation. Executives from the acquiring company have an obligation, to their own company, employees, and stockholders to ensure they execute business deals that will benefit the organization they manage and lead. Failure to "do the homework" and conduct a proper due diligence is a breech of their obligations.

> One version of Random House Webster's dictionary provided the following definitions:[1] Due: *1. owed or owing; 2. owing or observed as a moral and natural right; 3. rightful; proper; fitting:* Diligence: *1. constant and earnest effort to accomplish what is undertaken.*

---

[1] Random House, *Webster's College Dictionary*; April 2000; Random House, New York

In a practical sense, a due diligence is an effort to develop as deep an understanding about a target company as possible. Is what you think you are getting really the case? Is the target company a good fit with the acquiring company? It may be a wonderful and capable company, but will it fit into the acquiring company's business strategy?

A due diligence is more than just making sure a company's numbers add up before a takeover. There are considerations that reach beyond financial statements and contractual agreements. They may even be critical to achieving a successful transaction and for the future of the enterprise. Consider Enron for example. Several years before the revelation of systematic accounting and financial irregularities (endorsed by the accounting firm of Arthur Anderson) would a review only of financial records have been sufficient to uncover the hundreds of "special-purpose entities" designed to transfer Enron's debt to an outside company and get it off the books?

Looking beyond the financial assessment of Enron, it would have taken more than just a review of its documents and records to discover that Enron had been transformed from an old gas-pipeline culture into a swaggering, rule-breaking, deal-making cult that ultimately mislaid its analytical skills and perhaps its moral compass.[2] A comprehensive examination of the company would have been necessary to fully understand that pathological issues were embedded in the Enron company culture.

> *Due Diligence: The process of investigation, performed by investors, into the details of a potential investment, such as an examination of operations and management and the verification of material facts.[3] – Defined by Investorwords.com*

A due diligence effort conducted by a merger and acquisition team representing an investor or company is an effort to gather enough information necessary to make an informed decision regarding a proposed merger or acquisition. The effort must be an objective review of information presented by the target company and a review of information available through other sources. It would be ridiculous to rely just on the information provided by the targeted company to make a merger or acquisition decision. In other instances, one may want to conduct a due diligence and covertly research the targeted company before approaching the targeted company making an offer. After all, the targeted company may not want to merge or be acquired. Therefore, the acquiring company would want to ensure that a hostile takeover was feasible and worth the costs before going any further in the merger or acquisition process. Furthermore, the due diligence team should be performing within the boundaries of a formal company charter and process (Figure 6.1).

---

[2] See http://www.time.com/time/business/printout/0,8816,201871,00.html
[3] See http://www.investorwords.com/1596/due_diligence.html

CHARTER FOR A DUE-DILIGENCE TEAM

A company due diligence team may be established at the direction of the CEO for the sole purpose of conducting an assessment or investigation of a company targeted for merger or acquisition. The ultimate objective of this team is to determine the value of the target company. The due diligence team may also be established to prepare a business unit or portion of the company for divestiture.

The due diligence team, once established, will be tasked to review all aspects of the target business and prepares a formal assessment including risk identification and the impact of all observations and findings on the value of the target company. This assessment is to be delivered to the company CEO or company Board of Directors.

The due diligence team make-up must include the following representatives:

- Team leader – A business strategy executive
- Representative from the General Counsel's office
- Representative from the Chief Financial Officer's office
- Representative from the Chief Information Officer's office
- Senior Technology Expert
- Representative from internal Investment Banking
- Functional experts from the following organizations:
  - Consultant Investment Banker
  - Business management
  - Human Resources and Labor Relations
  - Risk Management
  - Strategic Planning
  - Security
  - Facilities
  - Company Communications or Public Affairs
  - Environment Health & Safety
  - Internal Audit
  - Others as needed

Figure 6.1   Sample charter for a company's due diligence team.

The due diligence effort leads to a critical analysis of data, assumptions, and conditions. Risks must be identified and subjected to a thoughtful review. The ultimate goal is to develop a comprehensive understanding of the target company's business. This understanding is the basis for making an informed decision as to whether to proceed with the merger or acquisition. This understanding begins with learning about the target company's obligations, which include:

- Financial statements
- Debt
- Business plans
- Pending and potential lawsuits

- Property and leases
- Warranties
- Long-term contracts, agreements (customer and supplier), and joint ventures
- Employment contracts
- Distribution agreements
- Compensation agreements
- Patents and trademarks
- Executive leadership (officers, directors, key employees)
- Related parties (collective bargaining units, consultants)
- Insurance and liability
- Governmental regulations and filings

Beyond the basic areas of examinations and considering the dangers of operating in today's global environment, companies have much reason to be cautious. Consider the following:

- *Globalization:* Companies need to be careful when doing business in the far corners of the globe. These areas are out of the immediate reach of the home office. Moreover, laws, customs, language, and expectations differ from country to country, which may make it difficult to communicate and cooperate, never mind the difficult task of making a profit.
- *Corporate scandals:* In the wake of corporate scandals, corporations must be careful with whom they do business. Even in countries with a mature and stable legal system, human beings continue to operate in an unethical or even illegal manner, thereby placing themselves and their companies at risk.
- *International terrorism:* The world is a dangerous place; well-organized and well-funded terrorist groups have targeted nations' global interests.
- *Legislation:* The effect of recent legislation, particularly the U.S. Patriot Act and the United Kingdom's (U.K.) Anti-terrorism, Crime and Security Act of 2001, has been to tighten and extend the vigilance and internal controls that companies must maintain. Companies operating within the United States and United Kingdom are potentially within the purview of this legislation and are subject to its provisions. Failure to comply could cause companies to have their commercial relationships within the United States terminated. Draconian as this measure may seem, it is a reality.

For businesses such as banks, brokers, dealers, investment and insurance companies, travel agents, money services, the gaming industry, and businesses engaged in vehicle sales, the antimoney laundering clauses of the Patriot Act drive them to much higher standards. The Patriot Act promotes a higher standard of vigilance than ever before seen or experienced. Companies must now be able to demonstrate they know who their customers are. There are also the privacy laws of many nations that must be considered when considering a merger or acquisition with a company headquartered in or with offices in a foreign country.

A due diligence is not an opportunity to study how an enterprise does business for competitive purposes. It is not an opportunity to trade information, nor is it an opportunity to discuss mutual planning. During a due diligence, information travels only one way—from the target company to the acquiring company. The acquiring company should not trade information. This can be dangerous if the deal does not go through and another company acquires the target. What might a successful buyer—one that is a competitor—do with the information you traded? Could the buyer use what it has learned to create a competitive advantage? If the deal ends up not occurring, having shared too much information could lead to a competitive advantage for the company one wants to acquire, thus leading to loss of market shares and profits

At the end of the day, a due diligence is only valuable if the acquiring company is prepared to walk away from the deal if the assessment reveals serious financial issues. A targeted company without the necessary personnel and operational capabilities and synergies, or other serious issues that may ultimately lead to a failed union, would have the opposite effect of what the acquiring company's intended merger or acquisition objective. The discipline to walk away from the deal is crucial. All too often merger and acquisition teams become so enamored with the deal that they focus only on closing it and fail to focus on the long-term objective of improving the strategic capabilities of their own company.

Is It always Necessary to Conduct a Due Diligence?

The answer to this question is always, Yes! The extent of the effort may vary, but it is always necessary to conduct a due diligence. First there is the fundamental obligation management has to the ownership of the company (private or public) to ensure the best interests of the owners and the company is served. Furthermore, there is usually some form of government oversight charged with reviewing mergers and acquisitions and their impact on the competitiveness of different industries and business sectors.

In the United States, the Securities and Exchange Commission (SEC) maintains oversight of mergers and acquisitions. Should irregularities occur, the Federal Trade Commission (FTC), or the Department of Justice, may also get involved. Much time and energy can be spent working with external oversight organizations to convince them that they should allow the proposed merger or acquisition to happen. This creates additional costs that must be considered in the costs of a merger or acquisition.

As critical as it is in the United States to conduct a proper due diligence, it is even more so in many other countries. For example, in China, a fast-growing market for mergers and acquisitions by Western companies, government regulations are inconsistently enforced.[4] Western companies need to be careful, as they pursue investment options there. Companies in China are not always compliant with statutory obligations, and since China lacks a culture of disclosure, obtaining enough information to make an informed analysis of any target company may be difficult at best. Generally, public information is limited and companies view investigations as intrusive. Furthermore, the trend is that the government will support its native companies over any foreign company.

The bottom line is that when pursuing a merger or acquisition, whether in North America, Europe, or Asia, conducting a due diligence is something that must be done. How extensive the effort is depends on many factors. The less known about a company or country where that company operates, the more critical the due diligence becomes.

An Area of Particular Interest

In the current global business environment, there are a few aspects of target companies that an acquiring company needs to take a close look at, but are often overlooked. One consideration in particular is the ethical practices of the company. Ethical practices are difficult to quantify and measure. Companies usually don't have a set of metrics that demonstrate how ethical they are, or are not. As difficult as it may be to measure ethics, it can be done.

The first place to start is to look for a published company code of ethics. Does the company state its values, what it believes, what it stands for, and how it operates? If so, is that code communicated throughout the company to all employees? And most important, do the employees buy into the company values?

During a due diligence, this type of information may be difficult to obtain, as the due diligence is limited in both time and the availability of information. Remember, the acquiring company does not yet own the target company, so the targeted company is not obligated to provide the acquiring company with every bit of information the acquiring company would like to know and have. If the due diligence is done in a more covert manner, this makes it much more difficult to obtain the information.

To learn as much as possible about the ethical behavior of the target company, the acquiring company's merger or acquisition team must take a close look at the target company's senior executives. How do they behave? The team can start with their resumes:

---

[4] See http://www.deaconslaw.com/eng/knowledge/knowledge_105.htm

- Are educational and professional histories accurately depicted? These are often available for publicly owned companies.
- Have there been any legal problems with any of the senior executives that may reflect on their integrity?
- Is their compensation above industry norms?
- Is there any evidence of nepotism within the company?
- Have there been complaints made from government authorities or employees about the behavior of any of the senior company executives?

The answers to these questions may provide enough information on which to draw a conclusion that ethical problems exist, or don't seem to exist. For example, if the company executives' compensation and reward program is significantly above industry standards, and management is aware of this, it may indicate a willingness to engage in other business practices where the outcome gives senior executives an unusual personal advantage. The willingness to take advantage of a process for their own personal gain is a possible indicator of the potential for unethical behavior.

WHAT IS SECURITY'S ROLE IN A DUE DILIGENCE EFFORT?

The role of the security representative on the due diligence team is to properly assess the security condition of the target company and evaluate the security organization. To do this requires the collection and analysis of information such as the competitive intelligence information discussed earlier.

It is important to remember that the time frame available for information collection is limited. If the target company does not track security costs, then that information will not be available. It may be estimated by using logical means such as the costs of like function within the acquiring company, but the information will not be precise. For example, to estimate security costs, a quick assessment of the security headcount (the number of people on the security staff) and their salaries will provide a rough order of magnitude cost for security labor. Again, if the due diligence is being carried out covertly, obtaining detailed information will offer increased challenges to the security professional.

Internal Security Assessment of the Target Company

To effectively assess the security condition of a target company, relevant data must be collected and analyzed. Generally, two types of data are needed:

- *Profile information:* This information depicts the size and shape of the security organization (e.g., size of security staff, cost of security).
- *Performance information:* This information depicts process or organizational efficiency (e.g., cycle times and external agency assessment or inspection reports).

With profile and performance information, the security manager should be able to conduct an analysis to determine the effectiveness of the security program and the efficiency of the security organization.

The next section contains relevant questions about security that are applicable to many different types of companies operating in different business sectors. In many cases, all of the questions will not be applicable and useful for every merger or acquisition target company. These questions are provided as a guide and, therefore, may be altered, modified, eliminated, or used to create different more applicable questions shaped to help any security manager more efficiently and thoroughly obtain relevant and necessary data. Some of the questions provided are targeted to companies doing business with the U.S. government. To the extent they are not applicable to a commercial transaction, ignore them or tailor them to your specific needs.

Most, if not all, of the questions below can be answered by reviewing documents in the possession of the target company and through an interview with the company security manager and/or other security professionals. If that is not possible, the security manager of the acquiring company should coordinate with other merger or acquisition project team members to see how they are obtaining their information. Maybe they can help, or their methods can be used to acquire the necessary information about the targeted company's security program. In addition, the security manager must be creative and use all ethical and legal means available to acquire the needed information.

In nearly every instance, an interview of the target company's security manager will be necessary to help elaborate on areas where the information is not sufficient or completely available. Moreover, the interview process usually expedites getting the questions answered with a higher level of detail. When considering time constraints, personal interviews help make the answers to questions as useful as possible.

Merger or Acquisition Security Questionnaire

1. Facility Information
    a) Identify the name and addresses of the target facility or facilities.
    b) What is the legal structure of the company? Are there subsidiaries involved? If so, how many?

    c)   Does the facility have a government facility security clearance? If so, with which government and at what level?

    d)   Does the company have government classified contracts? Identify the government agency and level of classification.

    e)   Obtain copies of all security requirements documentations (for classified work, obtain copies of all DD254s).[5]

2.   Facility Size

    a)   What is the total number of buildings?

    b)   How much space is dedicated to the office environment?

    c)   How much space is dedicated to the manufacturing environment?

    d)   What is the total amount of space dedicated to storage of raw material, supplies, and finished products?

    e)   What is the total amount of space dedicated to classified work?

    f)   What is the total amount of space dedicated to unclassified work?

    g)   Obtain copies of all approvals to operate in classified areas.

    h)   What amount of space is used for sensitive work where special security rules apply?

3.   Security Operations: Security Staff

    a)   What is the total number of full-time (or equivalent) security personnel on board?

    b)   What is the total number of uniformed security personnel (guard force)?

    c)   What is the total number of nonuniformed (professional) security personnel?

    d)   What is the total number of security personnel provided by a third-party security service supplier (e.g., contract guard force, security consultant, contract investigations)?

    e)   Do any security personnel work in high-risk areas or require highly specialized training (e.g., weapons, hazardous materials handling, driver, fraud examiner, protecting controlled substances)?

4.   Security Operating Costs

    a)   What was the total cost of security for each of the last three fiscal years?

    b)   What is the total security budget for the current fiscal year?

    c)   What are the projected security costs for the next fiscal year?

    d)   What is the dollar value of security work outsourced to a service provider?

---

[5] See: http://www.dss.mil/isec/nispom.htm: This site contains an electronic version of the National Industrial Security Program Operating Manual (NISPOM) used by the United States Government (USG) for classified contracts. It contains security guidance prepared for industry by the USG.

5.   Personnel Security
   a)   What is the total number of employees working for the target company?
   b)   What is the total number of employees with security clearances?
      •   Number of top secret clearances
      •   Number of secret clearances
      •   Number of special accesses
   c)   Security clearance backlog: What is the total number of employees in process for a security clearance or a periodic reinvestigation?
   d)   Are investigations for employees with special access current?
   e)   What is the impact to current business obligations due to security clearance backlog (if any)?
   f)   Is there a preemployment investigation process in place?
   g)   Is there a workplace violence prevention policy and program in place?
   h)   Have there been incidents of workplace violence?
   i)   Is there a security awareness program in place?
   j)   Is there a process in place to report adverse information to any of the following?
      •   External government agencies
      •   Senior management
6.   Physical Security (Surveys, Access Control Process and Alarm Systems)
   a)   Review the most recent physical security survey of the company, facility or site.
   b)   Identify all current threats and vulnerabilities.
   c)   Review risk assessment if available.
   d)   Obtain the number, type, and condition of all intrusion detection systems.
   e)   What type of access control system is used?
   f)   Are there any sites located in high-risk areas?
   g)   Are there any sites requiring specialized security protection (e.g., use of weapons, special security incident response teams)?
   h)   Identify any incidents, issues or trends of property theft.
7.   Information Security
   a)   Identify the number of information systems and networks used.
   b)   Identify the size of the information systems user population.
   c)   Are any information systems used for processing classified information?
   d)   Are any information systems used for processing highly sensitive company information?
   e)   Are there disaster recovery plans in place for all information systems?

f)   Are there appropriate intrusion detection systems, virus control, and firewalls in place?

g)   Have there been any security-related incidents during the past year?

8. Classified Holdings
   a)   Total number of classified holdings
   b)   Type of classified holdings (top secret, secret, confidential, special access)
   c)   Any issues or problems with accountability or compromise of classified holdings within the last three years

9. External Organization Security Reviews and Inspections
   a)   Review all government security inspection reports for the last three review periods.
   b)   Were there any significant security issues identified during that review? Identify the nature of all issues.
   c)   If there were issues, have they been corrected? If not, is there a corrective action plan in place?
   d)   What is the projected cost to correct all open issues?
   e)   Are there any open government investigations of the company or its personnel?

10. International Operations
   a)   What is the total number of offices located overseas?
   b)   What is the total number of employees stationed overseas?
   c)   What is the total number of ex-patriots and dependent personnel stationed overseas?
   d)   What is the total number of international travelers or total number of international trips taken within the last year?
   e)   Is there a contingency plan in place for emergency evacuation (for all high-risk countries)? Does that plan include events such as kidnap and ransom?
   f)   What is the total current year security budget for international operations?

11. Business Ethics
   a)   Is there a business ethics program in place?
   b)   Does the company have a "hot line" for reporting ethics or security violations?

INFORMATION SOURCES

Keep track of all sources of information. Invariably "information conflict" will develop, so it may be necessary to refer to original sources to resolve discrepancies either during the due diligence or during a later phase of the transaction.

The answers to the preceding questions should provide a security manager with enough information to make an educated assessment of the security condition of the target company and a rough assessment of the experience and efficiency of the security organization. There is no right or wrong answer to any of the questions asked. There is only the information.

That information must be analyzed within the context of the experience and capabilities of the merger and acquisition due diligence team and the level of risk the acquiring company is willing to take. What is learned through the analysis of information gained from asking the internal security assessment questions, as stated previously, should be coupled with what is learned from the external security assessment. Together, a characterization of the total security condition and environment can be made. That total security "snapshot" will become part of the analysis used by the team to make the decision to pursue a merger or acquisition.

External Assessment

Assessing the security condition of the target company goes beyond the internal review. Taking a look at the external environment is also necessary. For example, if a company operates in a high crime environment, it may be required to spend more on security than its competitors. Furthermore, if crime trend information suggests that crime is rapidly growing, that is an indication security costs may continue to rise. If one is looking at a company that manufactures high-demand electronic consumer products or produces pharmaceuticals in an area with a rapidly growing crime rate, there may be a problem.

Is such an environment a good place to run a business? This condition could affect the value of the target company and influence the decision of whether or not the deal should be made, or if the target company should actually be moved to another location after the merger or acquisition is completed. Such a move raises the possibility of additional costs and concerns: Move the facility to where? Will the current and needed employees of the targeted company also move or commute to the new location? Obviously, these types of issues will greatly increase the costs, albeit postmerger or acquisition, but increased initial costs that can be attributed to the merger or acquisition.

The following questions should help gather information relevant to security conditions and issues outside of the company:

1. Demographics
    a) What is the crime rate and projected crime trend for the immediate geographical area?
    b) What are the crime rate and projected crime trends for the adjacent geographical areas?

    c)   Does local law enforcement have control of the situation?

    d)   Is the city where the target company is located facing any economic issues that could drive a reduction in law enforcement support?

2.   Business Affiliations

    a)   Does the company have any risky relationships with other companies or individuals?

    b)   Is there any involvement in corrupt or criminal activities? A check of court records may prove useful here.

3.   Personal and Business Reputation of the Target Company and Its Executives

    a)   Have background investigations been conducted on all key persons and board of directors to determine if there is any history of criminal behavior?

    b)   Are there any issues of business or personal reputation of the target company and its executives?

    c)   Is there pending or threatened litigation against the target company?

    d)   What are the political affiliations and patronage of the target company?

    e)   What is the financial profile and lifestyle of key target company executives?

    f)   What is the media image of the target company and its key executives?

4.   Assess Associated Companies

It may also be necessary to conduct an analysis on associated companies. Areas investigated may include the following:

Business partners/affiliates – criminal links

    a)   Business ethics and past performance

    b)   Reputation within industry

    c)   Relations with labor unions

    d)   Litigation history

    e)   Financial profile

    f)   Media image

Some of the areas and concerns identified previously have to be handled by company lawyers. Some of them should be worked by the lawyers in concert with the security manager. Others are usually the responsibility of the security manager alone to assess and investigate. Regardless of what function has the lead in collecting the information, conducting investigations or making an analysis, these areas should be part of the external assessment process.

If the security manager knows from the start of the effort that the necessary expertise to perform a successful due diligence is not available within the company, it would be necessary to seek outside support. For the more complicated investigations, a security manager could hire the services of a reputable outsource provider specializing in conducting due diligence investigations.

Preparing for the Postmerger Integration

For the security manager, one of the primary areas of focus during the due diligence assessment should be to develop a thorough understanding of the target company's security organization structure and its associated costs. Each merger or acquisition brings with it an effort to improve efficiencies, increase revenue, and reduce costs. Security, like every other function, will be expected to make a contribution. Because security is usually not a revenue-generating organization and is almost always a cost center, the security manager can expect to be tasked with finding ways to cut costs during the postmerger and acquisition period. The more that can be learned about the new company during the due diligence process, the more it will help the security manager to move quickly and effectively in any effort to make postmerger organization and budget changes.

SUMMARY

The due diligence effort is all about learning as much as possible about the target company. This is not always easy to do, as time is usually limited, so the ability to gather relevant information as quickly as possible becomes essential. Using security personnel with experience in due diligence, information gathering, and analysis will be helpful. If necessary, the security manager can seek outside support from an organization with due diligence experience and capability.

Section III

Postmerger and Postacquisition Support

This section addresses the role of security and the security manager once the "deal is done" and the newly acquired or merged company is integrated into the acquiring company. Integrating the newly acquired company or business unit is a critical process, and the security manager plays an important role in its success. There are critical short- and long-term actions that the security manager must take to ensure an effective and efficient integration. Moreover, the security manager, in addition to completing security department activities, must support other organizations and the company in mitigating potential problems and vulnerabilities associated with each event.

This section also describes the strategy of divestment, that is, the sale of a company (by a larger company such as a holding company or conglomerate). As stated earlier, divestment is an opposite action of acquisition. When one company acquires another company, or a business unit from that company, a set of actions must occur at both the divesting company and the acquiring company.

Finally, a summary checklist is provided for the security manager to use when faced with a merger, acquisition, or divestiture in either the prephases or postphases.

Chapter 7

Short-Term Postmerger Security

He who rejects change is the architect of decay. The only human institution which rejects progress is the cemetery. – Prime Minister Harold Wilson[1]

INTRODUCTION

This chapter addresses security's role in integrating the newly merged or acquired company into the acquiring company's organizational structure. What must be done? What must be done first? What issues or problems will be encountered? How will the acquiring company's security manager ensure that the newly acquired company's security organization is fully integrated? What synergies can be achieved? These and many similar questions are asked and answered throughout this chapter.

The information provided in this chapter is all based on actual events and experiences of many mergers, acquisitions, and divestitures. It offers security practitioners guidelines for working their own specific or unique mergers, acquisitions, or divestitures projects. The general conditions encountered during mergers, acquisitions, and divestitures are similar from event to event. The specifics obviously vary depending on many factors. These include the size, type of business, condition of the acquired company, the experience of the acquiring company with integrating companies together, and many other factors that all contribute to the complexity and magnitude of the integration effort.

INTEGRATION OF THE ACQUIRED COMPANY INTO THE ACQUIRING COMPANY: WHY IT IS IMPORTANT TO THE ENTERPRISE AND TO THE SECURITY ORGANIZATION

Once the deal is done and the target company has been acquired, the job of any merger or acquisition gets bigger and in many ways becomes more

---

[1] Prime Minister Harold Wilson, speech to the Consultative Assembly of the Council of Europe, Strasbourg, France, January 23, 1967

complicated. The "sexy" part of any merger or acquisition is in the earliest stages. The chase or quest to identify a target, assess that target, and negotiate the deal is often viewed as the most interesting and exciting part of the process. Yet, as stated in earlier chapters, many mergers and acquisitions fail because of poorly planned and executed integration efforts. It is somewhat analogous to purchasing a new tool. No matter how much potential the new tool has, if it is not used properly, it will never deliver all of its capabilities.

The task of integrating the newly acquired company into the acquiring company requires the full attention of company senior management. It can't be assumed that the integration will occur naturally, nor can the integration be left entirely up to the various functions and departments to integrate at their own will and pace. Company leadership must establish a vision for the integration along with clear expectations and objectives. Goals and milestones must be established and progress must be closely monitored throughout the entire process. All problems and issues must be addressed as they arise. Senior company management needs to pay as much attention to the integration of the acquired company into the acquiring company as was paid to the target identification, due diligence effort, and negotiation processes.

With the deal done, the first phase, the premerger and acquisition effort, of the total merger or acquisition effort is complete. The final phase, the postmerger and postacquisition effort, now begins. In the postmerger and postacquisition phase, everything changes. During the premerger and acquisition phase, the target company was not the property of the acquiring company, so there were broad limitations on what could be accomplished. Laws regulating competition limited the exchange and sharing of information.

Good business practices dictated that any information exchanged be primarily a one-way transaction, from the target company to the acquiring company. The lack of ownership prohibited the acquiring company from providing guidance and direction to the target company. All target company-related business decisions were the prerogative and obligation of the target company alone. The acquiring company had no say in day-to-day business transactions. Once an agreement was reached, however, any major business decisions made by the target company required the support of the acquiring company, as it had the potential to affect the deal.

With the deal complete, the acquiring company (and new owner of the target company) is in an entirely different position. As the new owner, it now has the total control that comes with ownership. This control and ownership of the target company brings new obligations. These obligations demand the implementation of sound business practices. Company ownership, albeit public or private, and company stakeholders require and expect nothing less.

The Integration Process: How Does It Work?

The process of integrating the target company into the acquiring company must be systematic and comprehensive. It must be carefully planned and executed. It will not occur on its own, nor should it be allowed to. All aspects of the acquired business must be considered and reviewed to ensure a full and complete integration. Integration planning must take into consideration every element of the newly acquired company. Obviously, in some cases, there will be nonapplicable business areas or processes for which no planning or action is necessary. For example, if the acquired company does not have an external distribution capability but the acquiring company does, there is no reason for the acquiring company to plan for and integrate a nonexisting function into an existing one. However, it may be a good practice for the acquiring company to examine how the acquired company accomplishes external distribution and whether the practice is better (presumably an outsourced function) than that of the acquiring company. The acquiring company may want to conduct a cost-benefit analysis and, if the results are positive, consider adopting the distribution system as a best practice to use in the new company structure.

The extent of the integration process depends on how the newly acquired business unit will be expected to operate and the operating philosophy of the acquiring company. For example, if the new business unit, a vehicle rental company, was acquired as a new and separate service provider by a finance company, and the finance company had no other business units engaged in vehicle rentals, then the newly acquired business unit will likely be integrated into the acquiring company as a separate, stand-alone business unit.

In this case, the acquiring company may operate much like a holding company with different and independent product lines, with minimal linkage and commonality to the corporate entity. If a manufacturer of toasters acquired another manufacturer of toasters, however, it is likely that the acquired toaster manufacturer will be fully integrated into the existing toaster manufacturer's organization structure and day-to-day operations. In this scenario, the acquiring company likely intended to eliminate a competitor and expand its market share. With the vehicle rental scenario, the acquiring company likely intended to expand and diversify its products and services.

Each of the scenarios described next requires different levels of integration. A stand-alone business unit requires less change during the integration process than the combining of two business units with similar or the same product lines into a single business unit. In the following sections, each will be addressed. As a security professional, or one involved in a merger or acquisition, think what aspects would impact your organization and your functions. Then consider what you would need to do to support the merger or acquisition.

Integrating the Acquired Business as a Separate and Stand-Alone Business Unit

Integrating a newly acquired business unit into the acquiring company as a stand-alone entity requires a different process than does integrating a newly acquired business unit into the organization structure of the acquiring company or into other divisions or business units within the acquiring company. The integration process for a newly acquired stand-alone business unit attempts to leave the newly acquired business unit with a high degree of independence, particularly in its responsibilities for profit and loss.

This is not the case for the newly acquired business unit that is fully integrated into the organization structure of the acquiring company, eliminating its heritage organizational structure. For a company with a long-term strategy relying on mergers and acquisitions to achieve long-term growth and other objectives, setting up newly acquired companies as separate business units with responsibilities for profit and loss does have an advantage: they are much easier to divest. Separating an independently operating business unit is much easier than the complicated process of separating a product line or service that is heavily dependent on the infrastructure of the total company and fully integrated into its organization structure.

Objectives for Integration of a Stand-Alone Business Unit

The primary objective for the integration of a newly acquired business unit as a stand-alone entity is to prepare the organization and its infrastructure to be as self-sufficient and capable of operation on its own to the maximum extent possible. Naturally, the degree to which this occurs depends on the business operating philosophy of the acquiring company. For example, if the acquiring company operates as a holding company, the independence of the separate business unit will be quite extensive, with little more than financial and legal ties to the acquiring company. If the acquiring company has an operating philosophy in which the corporate office tends to be extensively involved in the operation aspects of all of its business units, however, the newly acquired business unit may be separate but dependent on the management of headquarters and the services and support of the company infrastructure.

> *One version of The American Heritage Dictionary defines a holding company as "A company controlling partial or complete interests in other companies." The important point in this definition is the reference to "other companies." A holding company generally maintains a limited operational relationship with the various companies or business units it owns or controls.*

Understanding the acquiring company's operating philosophy is important for the security professional. Usually, the extent of integrating the target company's security organization into the acquiring company's organization structure is consistent with the degree of integration of the acquired business unit into the acquiring company itself. What this means to the security professional is that the target company's security organization may need to be fully integrated into the acquiring company's organization structure, thereby creating a single company security organization, or it may be left as a separate organization providing support and service to its business unit independent, or loosely connected to, the acquiring company's security structure. Usually, what actually occurs is something in between both ends of this spectrum.

As a security professional in this process, would you wait to be told by executive management what you are to do? You should propose to executive management an assets protection security strategy or plan. This plan allows for you as the security manager to shape the new security organization. For example, the security function of the new business may also be stand-alone; however, it is obvious that some tasks would be redundant with your tasks. If, for example, you have outsourced your physical security guard force, quite possibly that contract can be expanded to include the new business entity and thus get a greater discount as a result of the contract expansion. Other such opportunities exist any time a company acquires and maintains a new business entity that is to be kept as a separate business.

Much like a due diligence effort, the integration of an acquired company into the acquiring company is usually led by an experienced team of professionals made up of experts from all affected disciplines within the company. Each will have specific tasks to perform to ensure that the integration is accomplished according to the expectations of senior company management (Figure 7.1).

The first action of an integration team is to develop an implementation plan. This plan will identify objectives, milestones, and schedules that must be met so a successful integration can occur. Part of the integration plan will include a subplan for communications. Communications during the postmerger and postacquisition phase are usually directed internally, targeting employees. The intention here is to keep employees as informed as possible and practical regarding the changes occurring within the company as a result of the merger or acquisition.

There will be some external communications primarily directed to the outside investment community if the company is publicly held. Company leadership wants to demonstrate to current and future investors that the merger or acquisition was a success and is proceeding as planned. And, if there are problems, company management is promptly working to resolve them. Maintaining the confidence of current shareholders and future investors is the desire and obligation for company executive

Postmerger and Acquisition Integration Team Membership
Supporting a Large Integration

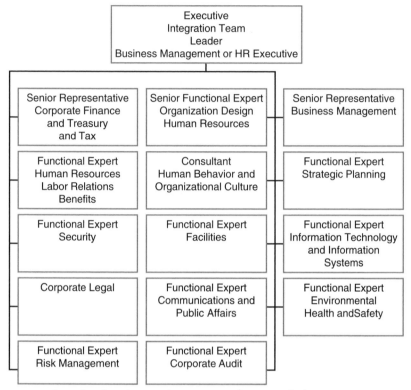

Figure 7.1   Sample of an integration team organizational chart.

management. For any formal communication, it is a good practice to have security as part of the review process. This is particularly important when there is a concern about protecting-company sensitive information from an unintentional release.

In support of the primary objective of integrating the newly acquired company as a stand-alone business unit capable of operating on its own, the integration team will work to achieve the following goals:

- *Stay on course with the current business plan.* As long as this plan does not conflict with future strategic plans of the acquiring company, the newly acquired company will be expected to keep current and future programs viable.
- *To ensure the current business plan is followed,* mechanisms must be installed to reflect and report fairly and accurately on the busi-

ness, programs, customers, performance, and people to the new corporate owner.

- *Conduct the integration effort in a timely manner with minimal disruption to other business areas and company elements.* This approach will cause the least amount of uncertainty for employees. Employees, particularly those directly affected by the integration effort, will pay close attention to what is going on. If the integration effort proceeds at a planned pace, with periodic progress or status reports provided to those employees, then their fears and worst expectations will be lessened. Should there be problems with the integration, sharing them (to a reasonable extent) with employees will ease their concerns as they understand what is happening; informed employees have little or no reason to develop rumors.

- *Retain key resources to sustain the business.* This action may be the most critical of all. When one company acquires another company, along with that acquisition comes the management team and its employees. In most cases, the management team of the acquired company will know much more about their business than does the management team of the acquiring company. Usually, the most prepared and equipped management team for leading the newly acquired business unit is its own current management team and its key employees. They know more about their business than outsiders do and are better positioned to do a better job. Retaining the acquired management team (at least the largest and most capable and critical component of it) and key personnel will help to prevent business disruptions while sending a message of stability to employees and investors alike. This also helps the security professional; during any transition period, it is much easier to work with an informed and experienced management team and informed employees than those who are not.

- *The ultimate objective is to create as much value as possible for the business.* Corporations are about creating value for shareholders and stakeholders. All actions taken will be done so with this goal in mind.

- *Bring the newly integrated business unit into compliance with existing and applicable company policy as soon as possible.* The sooner the newly acquired company comes into compliance with policies of the acquiring company, the less likely longer term problems will develop. Moreover, coming into compliance with company policy affects employee behavior that, in turn, becomes part of the company culture. Employees behaving in accordance with the written expectations of the acquiring company's values and norms is a necessary and desired result. This behavior (1) speeds the process of transitioning from how the company did business to how the company needs, and is expected, to conduct business, (2) supports regulatory requirements for having proper and effective business controls in place, and (3) facilitates a more expedient change of company culture from the separate cultures forced together to assimilate into the development of a new company culture.

In the Short Term, What Does the Integration of a Stand-Alone Business Unit Mean to the Security Professional?

Security must develop as part of the full integration plan, a plan of its own to ensure that all security-related actions and issues are addressed. This plan must be developed in such a way as to ensure that all security actions and issues are identified and handled in a manner that least disrupts the current day-to-day business. An exception to this practice may be necessary if there is a major security vulnerability that needs to be handled immediately, and to do so may require impacting day-to-day business activities. For example, if the acquired company has employees (and dependent personnel) working and operating in a hostile international environment with inadequate security protection and no contingency plans in place, rectifying this situation becomes an immediate priority. The safety and security of employees and their dependents operating in hostile or potentially hostile environments will, in the short term, override day-to-day priorities until the situation is corrected.

A major component of the security plan is to work to ensure that organizational attrition is kept to a minimum. Particularly, key personnel must be identified and kept. Mergers and acquisitions are disruptive events. How business is conducted changes during this process. Objectives and goals and even priorities change. Employees often become uncertain about their own future, particularly when reductions-in-force (layoffs) are anticipated. Even during a concerted effort to communicate with employees, uncertainty develops. When this occurs, employees begin to look for ways to protect their own economic interest. Sometimes this means looking for new work with another company. During the integration phase, this can be very problematic. The loss of key security management or highly skilled security professionals can be disruptive and will inhibit the organization's ability to effectively integrate a new business unit into the company while working to maintain normal, efficient day-to-day security operations.

To minimize the loss of key personnel and reduce the potential of them leaving, the following actions should be taken:

- Establish a transition period during which no employment actions will take place. This immediately provides a defined time frame within which all involved know they are safe.

- If reductions are necessary, and to some degree they usually are, identify key employees who will be asked to stay and offer them an incentive to remain. At this time, cash incentives are the only incentives that really work. They offer key employees a financial motivation and limited security to postpone their quest for new work. The value of incentives offered must be worked out with the company human resources organization and must be consistent with other incentives being offered to key employees in other areas. Offering an incentive to stay also serves as a gesture of good faith and recognition of an employee's worth. Surprisingly, employees can be motivated more by actions of good faith and appreciation than by the amount of money.
- Identify critical tasks and prioritize their completion so that they are finished while key employees are still with the company.

In some cases, it may be necessary for reductions in force to occur as quickly as possible. There may be immediate needs for large cost reductions, or management may believe it is necessary to act swiftly to protect the morale of employees left behind and to calm frayed nerves during the transition process. Much care needs to be taken to avoid laying off people who have knowledge and skills that could be crucial to the company's future.[2]

Objectives for a Full Integration

Fully integrating an acquired company into the acquiring company is a complete transformation for the acquired company. Essentially, in a full integration, the acquired company's structure disappears and it is absorbed into the acquiring company. Depending on the history of the acquired company, an attempt may be made to preserve events, products, or other significant elements of its success.

Employees of the acquired company face major changes. They lose their identity from the heritage company and are expected to adopt a new identity. They may face major changes in values and routine business practices as they complete the transition from values and routines of the acquired company to those of the acquiring company. The organizational structure they are used to will be eliminated or radically changed. Full integration usually means a complete reorganization from the way in which the acquired company did business to either the way in which the acquiring company does business or a hybrid version that capitalizes on the best both have to offer.

---

[2] *CIO Magazine*; CXO Media Inc., Farmington, MA; August 15, 2005. p. 76

> *This change is not unlike a divorce. The employee usually experiences a sudden and traumatic event (employees often don't know that the company they work for is being sold until the deal is announced by management) followed by a loss of identity and a forced transition into a new life. They are removed from their comfort zone and placed into an environment of uncertainty. How they conduct their daily activities will change to some degree. Most employees can make this transition smoothly, but some cannot.*

Periods of change and uncertainty can affect employee behavior. The short-term integration period—the time of the initial and greatest number of changes—is a period of particular concern to the security manager. With employees' anxieties riding high, the security manager must be concerned with the potential of workplace violence. Employees faced with losing their position or subject to change they can't or will not adapt to possess the potential to engage in violent behavior. Violent behavior can be extremely disruptive to the workforce and the business. Preventing it is a priority of the security manager. To successfully mitigate the possibility of incidents of workplace violence, the company must have in place an effective workplace violence prevention program.

PRIMARY AREAS OF CONCERN FOR THE SECURITY MANAGER DURING THE INTEGRATION PERIOD

During the early stages of the postmerger or postacquisition period, the security manager has many tasks to perform in support of the integration effort. Some of the tasks must be performed immediately; others need to be accomplished early in the integration period. The tasks range from managing identity and access control to preparations for an organization restructuring.

Identity Focused

Once the merger or acquisition becomes official, executive leadership of the acquiring company moves swiftly to integrate all new employees into the new company construct. An emphasis is placed on shedding the identity of the acquired company and adopting or embracing the identity of the acquiring company. This change manifests itself in many ways. For example, during the last decade, many people experienced a change in the bank where they conducted their personal business. When one bank acquired another, one of the first actions taken was to eliminate all vestiges of the acquired bank. After they were acquired, it seemed as if some banks disappeared as they changed their name and the signs on their buildings seemingly almost overnight.

In Southern California, during the 1980s and 1990s, Brentwood Savings became Glendale Federal Savings; they then became California Federal, which later became Citibank.

An internal mechanism used to reinforce the change of identity for all employees is through the use of one of the most common and visible security tools: the employee identification badge. The employee identification badge is primarily a security tool used for positive identification management. However, senior company management may often view the identification badge as a visual reminder of each employee's individual and organizational identity. In a sense it is a cultural icon.

In large companies, it is one of the few items all employees have in common. The employee badge is unique to both the individual employee and the company. Requiring all employees to wear and use a single, common company badge reinforces, in the eyes of management, the employees' association and identification with one company. It is interesting that a security tool would be co-opted by management as a branding and unification tool.

It is important for the security manager to recognize this fact and act to ensure that whatever changes management seeks with use of the employee identification badge, that those changes do not degrade the primary value of the badge, that is, its usage as an identification management tool to assist in the control and authorization for access to company sites and facilities. In some cases, it is a tool used for approved access to company information systems. The use of the identification badge as a tool to manage logical access to information systems requires technology (smart chip) more sophisticated than technology generally used for most physical access control systems (magnetic stripe and bar code) and readers.

For the security manager, the bad news is that it requires much time and effort to reissue, and perhaps even redesign, new badges for all employees. The good news is that periodically it is good to change the look of the company identification badge. It renders those lost badges totally useless and allows for adopting new technologies or capabilities of the badge at one time. It may also be easier to obtain funding for planned changes if accomplished as part of a major management directed change. Should this happen to security professionals, they should use it to their advantage.

Vetting New Employees

Many companies have in place preemployment background investigation processes used to establish suitability for hire for applicants to whom they are planning to offer permanent employment. This process is used to provide the hiring company some degree of assurance that the employees they are considering for employment:

- meet company standards
- have truthfully communicated skills, education, and experience
- are not a potential problem or threat to the workforce

Obviously all investigations are conducted within the provisions of all applicable laws and company values. Many preemployment screening programs implemented over the past decade were instituted at the urging of legal guidance for the purpose of preventing negligent hiring and because of the potential for litigation. In this case, operating in a litigious society has led to companies knowing more about employment candidates before they are hired today than ever before.

When one company acquires another, along with that company comes all of its employees. If the acquired company did not have in place an acceptable process for prescreening all candidate employees, then there is no guarantee that all of their employees were suitable for hire when they were given permanent employment. Knowing this causes the acquiring company to make a decision—to accept the risk of potentially having a large population of new employees who may not meet the hiring and employment standards of their company (grandfather them in) or to incur the added cost of conducting a background investigation on each of the acquired company's employees.

The latter can be a costly proposition. For example, if the acquired company has 5000 employees, and it costs $100 dollars to conduct a single preemployment background investigation, then to do so for all of the acquired company's employees would cost $500,000. Regardless of the cost, this is an issue that must be addressed and a decision made. The security manager must weigh in on this decision. Usually legal and security are the two functions that will weigh in on the issues associated with negligent hiring. All too often, others with a say in the matter focus on issues of cost or inconvenience only. Here, security can force the broader issues that must be considered.

Short-term Operating Procedures

In the early stages of the integration immediately after the completion of the merger or acquisition, it may be necessary to implement some short-term operating policies and procedures. Employees from the acquired company will be used to working in compliance with the policies and procedures of the acquired company, which they see as their own. Some of those policies or procedures will no longer be applicable, may actually be in conflict with those of the acquiring company, or may need to be changed immediately to come into compliance with various regulations or laws. Moreover, senior company management may want immediate policy or procedure changes, and the best way to direct and communicate them is through the creation of a short-term operating policy or procedure.

A short-term operating policy or procedure should be created only for those areas of critical or immediate importance or to address a specific problem, risk, or vulnerability. It should not be established for all areas or as a means of forcing immediate compliance with the acquiring company's current policies and procedures. It will take time to make the transition from the acquired company's operating practices to compliance with the policies and procedures of the acquiring company. Full transitions and integrations do not occur overnight, nor should there be an expectation that they will. The short-term operating policy or procedure is purely an interim step.

The short-term operating policy can be created in whatever format a company chooses, including a routine office memorandum, as long as that communication is made to all affected employees and clearly states the policy change and duration. It should last long enough only to allow enough time for a smooth transition to compliance with all company policies and procedures. It is a temporary, not a permanent, vehicle. The short-term operation policy or procedure is an expedient way of implementing key or critical policy changes. The longer term objective is to bring the new entity into full compliance with the existing company policies and procedures of the acquiring company over a period of time deemed reasonable and appropriate.

Employee awareness classes or training classes may be necessary to uniformly bring the acquired employees into the new company. If these are necessary, security and asset protection matters should also be integrated into the classes.

Customer Communications and Notifications

For companies doing business with the U.S. Government engaged in classified defense and national security contracts, there is a requirement for company security to notify the cognizant government security agency of the merger, acquisition, or divestiture transaction. Major changes, such as changes in ownership and key executive personnel, must be reported. In some cases, the cognizant security agency will expect assurance that the acquired company will continue to operate to premerger, acquisition, or divestiture approved procedures and processes until a transition plan is developed and reviewed by the government customers' representatives.

Expansion of Data Collection and Analysis

During the due diligence period, the security manager collected as much data as necessary and possible about the security condition of the target company and its security operating practices. For many reasons, this data collection effort had limitations that prevented the security manager from developing a full picture and understanding of the target company's security profile and operation. During the postmerger and postacquisition period, all limitations are removed. The acquiring company now owns the target company, so both responsibility and prerogative exist for detailed data collection and analysis.

Data collection and analysis is the biggest step forward in developing an understanding of the newly acquired organization. Without data, the security manager can't fully understand the workings of the organization he or she may be about to change. Expanding on the collection effort done during the due diligence phase should begin immediately during the integration phase. This will enable the security manager to establish a baseline understanding of the organization and begin planning for any needed changes. Changes should not be made without data analysis unless there is an immediate compelling need such as a compliance or vulnerability issue. It is with this complete data profile that the security manager can move forward with future budgetary and organizational reviews.

The security professional should have already developed a plan for the postmerger or postacquisition phase. In that plan, checklists and questionnaires should have been developed and be ready for use when the postmerger or postacquisition phase is initiated.

Budget Analysis

The old adage of "follow the money" is also applicable in an environment where one needs to learn about an organization. Knowing the amount of money spent and how it is spent can tell much about operational priorities and efficiencies. As part of the data collection effort, particular attention should be paid to budgets and expenses.

To better understand what the costs of security are and to identify opportunities for cost reductions, the security manager should first learn how much money has been allocated for security in the target company. This information should be compared with how much money has actually been spent. The difference between the two, if any, may be very telling. If the difference is significant, it may indicate that the current security management poorly managed its budget, or it may indicate that an unplanned event occurred that required additional funding. Unplanned events should be carefully assessed, as they may be indicative of existing problems.

It would not be unusual for an acquired company's security manager, in the middle of a budget cycle, to spend the remaining security budget, assuming that the acquiring company will provide security services with a new budget. Therefore, it would behoove the acquiring security manager to immediately get control of the acquired company's security budget to prevent the "draining" of that budget; this budget can then be integrated into the overall acquiring company's security budget.

Budgetary data may also be analyzed to assess comparative levels of efficiency. Determining the efficiency of a security organization as it delivers its services is not a simple process, nor is it "rocket science." The cost of security can be benchmarked (compared to) with like companies to provide a "ball park" assessment of operational efficiencies and adequacy of funding. For example, if the cost of security is compared to that for a company within a similar industry, of a similar size, and known to have a solid security program, and the cost of security varies significantly, this could be an indicator that something may be out of line.

If the target company is spending much more on security than other comparable companies, perhaps too much money is being spent on the security program, and more security is being applied than what is needed. Or, the security being provided may be delivered inefficiently. If the opposite is occurring, perhaps too little funding is available for security. Only a detailed analysis of the security program will reveal what is and is not needed. In any event, budgetary analysis is warranted and can be very telling.

Process Analysis

After the data collection effort and the budgetary analysis, the next area of review should be with key security processes. Specifically, major security processes should be examined for redundancy, efficiency, and need for improvement. Security processes are the vehicle any security organization uses to deliver its security services or products. Processes are the means by which security performs its work and fulfills its responsibilities.

Redundant processes should be consolidated or the best process chosen and adopted for the new operating environment, while the less effective process should be eliminated. Any and all remaining processes should be assessed for efficiency and the potential for improvement. When two companies come together, it should not be assumed that the acquiring company has a monopoly on efficient and effective ways of delivering security services. The security manager of the acquiring company should never be so arrogant as to assume that everything his or her organization does is better than the target/acquired company. With acquired companies come many capable and bright people who know their business and do many things well. Failing to recognize this may mean that some of the potential gains in efficiency will be lost. The acquiring company security manager must look at all processes and capabilities of the target company and where they do things better, adopt that practice. It has been purchased and paid for, why not use it? Use the best of the best processes. After all, security professionals, like other company employees, are paid for results, not for whether or not the results were based on a new or adopted process. The "not invented here" syndrome and acquiring company arrogance can cost money and adversely impact productivity—the very reasons that some businesses fail to realize the planned gains of a merger or acquisition project.

During the early stages of the implementation period, the security manager should determine what security processes exist and prioritize them in order of criticality to the organization. That is, which processes are the most critical in support of its internal customers in their effort to deliver products and services? Moreover, which processes are most important to external customers in fulfilling their requirements and expectations? All security processes can't be examined and improved during the early stages of the integration period. They must be prioritized and examined in order of their importance. Part of the criteria for assessing importance may include potential for cost savings or cost avoidance.

Generally, security processes can be categorized into three types:

- *Core:* These processes must be completed or performed to meet obligations such as regulation, law, contract, company policy, and customer expectations. Moreover, they include the processes that support the fundamental aspects of a good security program. They include the major processes for the protection of people, information, and other company assets. For example, the process of preemployment screening for all potential new hires may be a core process that must be performed to support the hiring and staffing process. Further, it contributes to the successful implementation of the macro-process for protecting people, in that preemployment screening is a tool used to establish (to a company-declared standard) the suitability for employment of a potential candidate.

- *Oversight:* These processes are implemented to assess and ensure compliance with all obligations. For example; in a heavily regulated industry, an oversight process may be used to ensure compliance with those regulations. An internal audit process may be considered an oversight process.

- *Hotel services:* Processes used to deliver "hotel services" are those that support the "care and feeding" of employees located on company sites. For example, building lock-and-key services ensure that proper controls are in place to prevent unauthorized access to a company site and to provide a means for employees to secure company (and limited personal) property in their work area. This supports the employees of that specific site.

Core and oversight processes are more critical than basic service processes. However, on a day-to-day basis, site employees will demand quality support for their needs and may do so with such emphasis that their needs get addressed before more compelling needs. This is what is often referred to as the "squeaking wheel gets the oil" syndrome.

Organization Structure and Redesign

The two most costly areas of security are capital equipment (i.e., access control systems, alarm systems, and other technologies and security systems) and labor. The security organization structure is made up of employees. These employees perform the needed security services and provide security products. When two or more organizations are combined, there is an expectation that redundancies will be eliminated, best practices adopted, and efficiencies gained. That translates to an expectation for cost reductions.

Cutting the cost of security usually means reducing the number of security employees on staff. Eliminating employees will impact the organization's ability to deliver security products and services. If the number of employees is reduced, so too will be the level of services they provide. Another approach to reducing cost is to outsource selected security services to a lower cost provider. Outsourcing may lower the cost for implementation of some processes, which may in turn provide enough cost savings to preserve other processes staffed by some of the more high-skilled security employees. With any approach, cutting cost from a security organization usually entails some degree of organization redesign.

The extent of any reorganization redesign varies. If the acquired company is integrated into the acquiring company as a stand-alone business unit, with anonymity for profit and loss responsibilities, its security organization may need to remain as it is to properly support the stand-alone business unit. However, "buying" some security services from the parent company may be possible. Any cost reductions may need to be achieved through efficiency gains. The security organization should be analyzed to determine whether it is operating as efficiently as possible or whether some of the services it has provided can be eliminated, changed, or provided in a different way.

If the newly acquired company will be fully integrated into the acquiring company, eliminating most if not all of its infrastructure and support services, then the security organization, too, must be integrated. In essence, the security organization structure of the acquired company will be disestablished and integrated into the security organization structure of the acquiring company. Depending on the size of the acquired entity, this may or may not be a simple task. If the acquired company is small, with little need for security support, then it may be a matter of the acquiring company absorbing the additional workload and eliminating some number of security personnel. However, if the acquiring company has a large security statement of work, then an organization redesign may be needed.

The first step to be accomplished in preparing for integrating the acquired security organization into the company and to understand where cost reductions can be made is to conduct an analysis of the statement of work. The following questions must be addressed:

- What is the current (preacquisition) statement of work of the acquired security organization? What is it really doing? Are the security services and support they provide needed by the organization they support?
- What are the security needs of the newly acquired business unit? Does it have a need for security support at all? If so, what type of support is needed and how extensive is that need?
- Can the security needs of the newly acquired business unit be fulfilled by the existing security organization of the acquiring company? If no, what security services need to be provided, and what additional resources are needed to provide them?
- Can the security needs of the newly acquired business unit be met buy purchasing additional services from a security service provider, or must those services be provided by or fulfilled from within?

When considering outsourcing security services to a security service provider, it is usually the lower skill functions or the transactional processes that best lend them to outsourcing. For example, functions such as guard services, preemployment background investigations, or technical security countermeasures assessments lend themselves to outsourcing, as there are many service providers for these processes, the need for them is occasional or periodic, and some require low skill levels or minimal expertise to complete.

Processes requiring more sophisticated skills, such as information security and information assurance or contingency planning, should not be outsourced. Those processes require the skills and sophistication of well-trained and experienced security professionals. These individuals are difficult to find and keep. So letting them go is not a prudent approach. Once they are in-house, part of the company's security organization, and performing at a high standard, they should be kept for as long as possible. One of the problems of outsourcing the highly skilled security processes is their limited availability and the constant pressures on the outsource provider to move high-demand, skilled professionals to assignments paying more. Using an outsource provider for security processes requiring highly skilled professionals usually does not provide the security manager with the same leverage and advantage as does keeping them within the company.

Staffing

Staffing a security organization occurs after assessing the security state-ment of work and then determining what resources are needed and whether those resources should be obtained through a service provider (outsourced) or provided from within. The decision to outsource is really part of the classic business decision "to make or to buy." "Make" is to pro-vide the service from within the company; "buy" is to purchase the serv-ices from outside the company. Subsequent to the analysis of the security statement of work, a budget analysis must be performed. Often the secu-rity support needed does not match the available budget. When this is the case, further analysis is needed to determine what services may be omit-ted, delayed, or redesigned. In an ideal world, the security manager would not be faced with this problem; in the real world this is almost always the case. Furthermore, security managers often encounter the budgetary con-dition of limited available resources. A security manager may be faced with owning a budget established on the basis of affordability. That is, the com-pany has only a certain amount of money to spend on security regardless of the level of support needed. Working within the confines of an afford-able budget will impact staffing and the security manager's ability to pro-vide adequate security support.

Workplace Violence Prevention after a Merger or Acquisition

Over the past few decades, workplace violence has become a significant issue. In response and due to legal pressures to maintain a safe work envi-ronment, many companies have put in place workplace violence preven-tion programs. These programs are designed to mitigate the potential for violence in the workplace and seek to achieve the following:

- Protection of employees
- Protection of customers, visitor, and suppliers
- Prevention of business disruption
- Preservation of good company reputation
- Prevention of litigation for negligent hiring

Workplace violence may be caused by a variety of factors, many of which manifest during the stressful period of a merger or acquisition.

Mergers and acquisitions are most stressful on the employees of the acquired company.

During the early stages of a merger or acquisition and on into the integration phase, the acquiring company is learning more about its acquisition while it develops plans for its future. Until these plans are developed and communicated, employees can only speculate as to what the future will bring them. Will they continue to have a job? Will that job be the same as it is now, or will it change? Will their plant or facility be closed? How will their benefits be affected? Until these and many other questions are answered, they contribute to the heightened anxiety of employees. Anxious employees can create a negative work environment.

Imagine how you would feel if you got a lay-off notice based on the rationale of "saving the company money," and then it is announced that the CEO or others in executive management just got a bonus of several millions of dollars for saving the company money as a result of the merger or acquisition. Even a calm and sane person would at least become upset, possibly to the point of considering whether to move on or take some form of revenge. If the economy is good and another job is readily available, that is one thing. It is quite another in times of an economic slowdown or recession where jobs are scarce. The security professional involved in a merger or acquisition where layoffs are imminent should also analyze the economy and jobs available. This may provide some indication as to the increased threat level resulting from the merger or acquisition and subsequent layoffs.

Heightened employee anxiety, if not addressed, can lead to unacceptable forms of behavior, including violence. Some of the most common causes leading to workplace violence are:

- The perception of being treated unfairly by the company
- Job instability
- Instability in the business environment
- Pressures at work
- Depression
- Personal problems, including financial, family, or marital problems

After a merger or acquisition, there is much change and much uncertainty. Regardless of how extensive the effort to communicate to employees, keeping them abreast of integration and organization plans, it is never enough. Rumor and speculation often develop to fill information voids. Uncontrolled, rumors feed the fears and uncertainties held by employees, making the environment more stressful. It is management's role to quell those fears and make the workplace less stressful.

The six factors listed as common causes of workplace violence all exist during the postmerger and postacquisition period. These factors can contribute to changes in individual employee behavior. Changes in employee behavior can be, and usually are, observed by others. Recognizing behavioral changes and reporting them to management, human resources, security, or an intervention team will help reduce the likelihood of violent behavior. First, all employees need to understand the types of behavioral changes that signal a potential change for the worse:

- Loud, angry outbursts in reaction to normal everyday situations
- Abusive verbal or physical actions toward co-workers
- Isolation, a decrease in social connections and support
- Degradation of personal appearance and hygiene
- Destruction of personal or company property
- Stalking
- Preoccupation with weapons
- Chronic complaints and expressions of dissatisfaction with work

---

The American Heritage Dictionary's definitions of violence include the following: (1) Physical force exerted for the purpose of violating, damaging, or abusing. (2) An act or instance of violent action or behavior. (3) The abusive or unjust exercise of power; and outrage; a wrong. (4) Vehemence of feeling or expression; fervor; fanaticism.[3]

What can be done to prevent incidents of workplace violence during the postmerger or postacquisition period? There are six major components to a workplace violence prevention program that need to be in place during this period:

- The foundation for any workplace violence prevention program begins with management's declaration of a zero-tolerance policy. Zero-tolerance means that threats of violence or acts of violence will result in disciplinary action, up to and including termination of employment. This policy must be in writing and its existence shared and communicated with all employees.
- Ensure that the company has in place a workplace violence prevention program. A workplace violence prevention program is an organized and institutionalized approach to identifying potential workplace violence situations and behavior and dealing with them before they escalate. Furthermore, should a situation escalate, the company must have in place an established intervention team trained in how to manage a crisis, particularly a violent situation. The intervention team should include members from several disciplines such as security, human resources, employee assistance program (this may be a

---

[3] Morris, William (ed.). *The American Heritage Dictionary of the English Language.* Boston, MA: Houghton-Mifflin, 1981, p. 1431

company employee or an outside licensed professional), legal, and management.

- Have available for employee use a formal grievance process. Employees must feel they have a legitimate and accessible process to address their grievances. If they do not, they may choose to seek other avenues for resolution.
- Provide all management and employees with basic workplace violence prevention training. All managers and employees should be trained to recognize signs or indicators of behavior changes that have the potential to lead to violence. Furthermore, they must be trained and required to properly act on their observations to ensure that potential violent situations are addressed immediately.
- Offer all employees access to an employee assistance program where they can get assistance in handling or coping with serious personal problems and issues. Often employees need a place to go for assistance in dealing with issues too large to successfully handle on their own. Professional and licensed counselors should be made available for all employees who seek or need them.
- Provide an outplacement employment service for those employees who may be displaced from the company. Helping those employees who will lose their jobs as a result of the merger or acquisition find future work will go a long way in helping reduce their anxiety and fear. Facing uncertainty is difficult. Facing it without assistance is more difficult. Providing employees with support to help them make the transition from the loss of employment to new employment will help reduce their anxiety and, therefore, reduce the possibility of workplace violence.

Such a program is generally the primary responsibility of the human resources staff. However, the security manager, along with the legal staff, must play a major role in the program's development. Preventing workplace violence is not the sole responsibility of any one organization but rather all employees, including managers.

The security manager must be an active participant in the workplace violence prevention process and a key member of the intervention team. Since one of the major responsibilities of the security function is to respond to emergency situations, it is likely the security manager will be the most experienced person on the team with handling emergency or crisis situations. Furthermore, the security manager, in concert with the human resources staff and legal staff, is in a good position to develop and deliver workplace violence prevention training to the management team and to employees. As emergency responders, security personnel offer first-hand experience in dealing with emergency situations as part of the training process. The ultimate objective of any prevention training is to identify the potential workplace violence situations and resolve them before they develop.

Beyond the responsibilities of the security manager and the other members of the intervention or crisis management team, company management (all company managers) has an important role to play in preventing incidents of workplace violence. Some of the actions managers can take to help prevent situations of work place violence from occurring are the following:

- Learn to recognize and document the signs of a significant behavior change. Documentation is important, as it may provide a record of behavioral change and can be used to track patterns of behavioral change.
- Listen to employees and be receptive to their work-related and personal concerns. Sometimes, employees just need someone to consult with or to acknowledge their concerns. Moreover, listening to employees may be enlightening, allowing for early recognition of issues and problems.
- Establish an environment in which employees can express themselves confidentially.
- Know the appropriate actions to take when confronted with potentially violent behavior and the support systems available for employees to help them deal with their problems and issues.
- Seek advice from security, human resources, employee assistance specialists, other intervention team members, and even other managers to discuss concerns regarding individuals who pose a threat. Behavioral changes and the actions of employees may be difficult to assess. When there is doubt, advice and counsel should be sought from other skilled professionals.
- Consult with human resources for guidance in taking proper disciplinary actions in response to threats and acts of violence. It is important to ensure that disciplinary actions are commensurate to the unacceptable behavior.
- Promptly notify human resources and security of any reports or threats of violence.
- Work with security to ensure that all alleged, reported, or potential threats of violence are investigated and assessed. These events should never be dismissed or discounted without a complete investigation.

All employees can make a contribution to the prevention of workplace violence. It is not merely the responsibility of management and trained professionals to work toward preventing workplace violence. Every employee can play a critical role in defusing serious situations or incidents with the potential for workplace violence. By expressing concern over the welfare of their co-workers and observing changes in the work environment, employees can make a difference. Some actions employees may take to prevent violence include:

- Being aware of a co-worker who has demonstrated a sustained behavior change.
- Discussing any concerns with a supervisor, human resources representative, or security manager. It is better to err on the side of caution than to ignore an issue to avoid getting involved or dismissing it as a one-time event.
- Promptly reporting any threat of violence or any violent act to management, human resources, and security.
- Avoiding a confrontation with a violent person.
- Avoiding any acts of retaliation or what may appear to be retaliation.
- Notifying security when emergency situations arise.

As stated earlier, all threats, perceived threats, or alleged acts of violence must be investigated. If they are determined to be real, a response appropriate to the activity must be taken. Employees who violate the workplace violence zero-tolerance policy must understand that they are subject to disciplinary action. Furthermore, disciplinary action must be administered swiftly and fairly.

The disciplinary action should be commensurate with the behavior exhibited. It may be as simple as counseling, or it may be as severe as termination of employment. Each situation should be independently handled and actions taken based on the severity of the situation. If an employee is suspended from work as a result of an act of workplace violence, before returning to the workplace that employee should undergo a fitness-for-work evaluation. One must try to ensure that such disciplinary action does not further provoke an employee to act out with violence.

TRANSITION INTO A LONG-TERM POSITION AND PERMANENT ORGANIZATION

Any effort to reorganize the security organization should be done with the idea that future changes will be necessary. Regardless of how well planned the first attempt at reorganizing, further changes are inevitable. As the company shrinks or grows, during normal business cycles or through additional acquisitions or divestitures, so too will the security statement of work. Designing an organization and staffing that same organization in such a way as to facilitate contraction or expansion will serve the security manager well for the future.

For example, a small security department does not have the luxury of having a staff of security professionals with high degrees of expertise in the many disciplines within security. It is important to staff a small security organization with experienced generalists. These generalists should have skills and experience that is a "mile-wide and a few inches deep." That is to say, they need to be familiar will all aspects of security they may encounter yet not be an expert in but a few, if any. When they do encounter a situation requiring a high degree of expertise, they need to know where to find that expertise.

Larger security organizations have an advantage with staffing. They usually can afford to have security professionals with high levels of expertise in very limited or focused areas. Generally, the security statement of work is sufficiently large to keep such professionals busy full time.

FOR COMPANIES DOING BUSINESS WITH THE U.S. GOVERNMENT

Most companies do not engage in business with the U.S. government. For those that do, particularly those that engage in classified contractual work, several security-related actions need to be accomplished as part of the postmerger or postacquisition period in order to continue to maintain compliance with the obligations of the national industrial security program.

The first action is a notification of change. A change of ownership is a major event and must be reported to the cognizant security agency of the U.S. government. Initially, a written notification alerting them to the change will suffice; however, as the integration period progresses, it may be necessary to submit additional change notification.

One requirement of particular interest for the cognizant security agency will be the degree of "Foreign Ownership, Control and Influence," as required by the U.S. Government National Industrial Security Program Operating Manual (NISPOM). More precisely, formal documentation must be submitted advising the cognizant security agency of the degree of foreign influence and control now affecting the acquired company. It could be little or none, or it could be quite extensive. In any case, the documentation must be submitted and reviewed. If there are issues, the cognizant security agency will work with the company representatives to resolve them. Specific instructions regarding how to accomplish this can be found in the National Industrial Security Program Operating Manual.[4]

Major operational changes driven by the merger or acquisition may also require approved security plans and procedure revisions to be in place. It may be necessary to revise these documents and resubmit them to the cognizant security organization for approval. In some cases, the pace of change after the merger or acquisition is so rapid that it may be necessary to seek a waiver from the cognizant government security office to operate with interim or temporary approvals.

---

[4] See http://www.dss.mil/search-dir/isec/ch1-1.htm

SUMMARY

During the due diligence period, the security manager's effort was focused on applying security to the effort itself to protect it from unauthorized disclosure and on the physical protection of the due diligence team. The security manager also worked to assess the security condition of the target company, helping the due diligence team value the target company. During the postmerger or postacquisition phase, the role of the security manager changes. Many more of the tasks to be accomplished are routine management tasks such as assessing organizational performance, sizing the security statement of work, and ensuring that sufficient resources are available to accomplish that statement of work. Processes such as budgeting, organization design, and staffing require most of the security manager's attention and effort. However, there are some important security issues that must be handled. During this period of much change and uncertainty, the security manager must be sensitive to the work environment, and the company must have in place a workplace violence prevention program to mitigate the potential for violence.

The short-term postmerger or postacquisition period is a busy time for the security manager, as much needs to be accomplished fast. The longer term phase of the postmerger or postacquisition period is less hurried but no less important. Actions will be taken during that period to better position the organization for future success.

Chapter 8

Long-Term Postmerger Support

In achieving culture, man's first steps were doubtless the hardest, like the first pennies that lay the foundation for a fortune. – Lewis Mumford, The Transformations of Man

INTRODUCTION

In this chapter, long-term security issues and activities in a postmerger (or acquisition) environment are addressed. Much of the chapter is directed toward the "how and why" of bringing two different security organizations together, and the issues a security manager faces during the process. Most important, suggestions are offered on how to overcome those issues.

Furthermore, the chapter addresses one of the most complicated issues facing any merger or acquisition—dealing with culture clash and creating a new company culture. We will consider what that means specifically to the security organization and the security manager in terms of the manager's role for providing support to the company, and in integrating the security department from the newly acquired or merged company into the acquiring company.

CULTURE

Culture is usually thought of as a general, shared social understanding, resulting in commonly held assumptions and views of the world among organizational members. Culture is developed in an organization through joint experience, usually over long periods of time.[1]

The clash between the cultures of combining organizations in mergers and acquisitions has received growing attention by practitioners and

---

[1] Weber, Roberto A., and Cramerer, Colin F. Cultural Conflict and Merger Failure: An Experimental Approach, *Management Science*, Vol. 49, No. 4, April 2003, p. 403.

academics. Culture clash influences the effectiveness of the postmerger integration process, the integration of information systems, and the financial performance and shareholder value of the acquiring company.[2]

It can be argued that the most significant obstacle to the successful integration of companies after a merger or acquisition is organizational culture clash. Each company has its own culture. Each has its own way of doing things and conducting business. This includes what it values, respects, and stands for. Moreover, each has a heritage and a belief that the work it does is as good as it can be. This may or may not be true. It may purely be perception. Let us not forget that one's perception is another's reality. Generally, organizational capabilities are a mixed bag. Some things are done well while others are not. In any event, the culture of an organization, if not one already accustomed to change, will resist change, particularly if the required changes are inconsistent with the norms and standards the company is used to. For company and department management, getting employees to make the transition into a new way of doing business offers a difficult challenge. This, too, is true for security managers, as they try to combine and shape their organization.

In the early stages of the integration, it may appear that the employees of the newly acquired company are easily transitioning into their new roles. There may be signs of acceptance, indicating that employees are comfortable with their new environment and identity. Be careful not to be fooled. Acceptance of a new identity and a new way of conducting business does not come easily. Often resistance will manifest itself in passive ways. While events appear to be proceeding as planned, it may not be until an audit or other significant events occur that the real situation is revealed. For example, an internal audit may uncover a failure to comply with company policy and procedures well after the integration was declared complete and a success.

Plans may have been in place with the appearance that all is well, but the audit uncovers conditions to the contrary. Passive and subtle resistance may have led to the noncompliant condition of failing to follow policies and procedures of the acquiring company. Employees from the acquired company continued to do what they were comfortable with in spite of direction and a commitment to the contrary. To correct the problem(s) may require the firm direction and involvement of senior management. All of management, including the security manager, must be aware of issues related to culture change. To prevent behavioral and cultural problems from developing in the various phases of the merger or acquisition, plans

---

[2] Webber, Yaakov and Menipaz, Ehud. Measuring Cultural Fit in Mergers and Acquisitions, *International Journal Business Performance Management*, Vol. 5, No.1, 2003, pp. 54–55

to deal with these issues must be part of the process in both the premerger and postmerger or preacquisition and postacquisition phases. For the security manager, these company "macro" issues must be addressed within the security "micro" organization.

DOING BUSINESS DIFFERENTLY: COMBINING SECURITY ORGANIZATIONS

In Chapter 7, we addressed some of the immediate reasons for reorganizing security when two companies come together through a merger or acquisition. Early in the integration phase, the primary drivers for organizational changes are alignment with the statement of work and reducing the cost of security.

> *Use of the term Statement of Work refers to all of the work that the security organization is responsible for and must accomplish to properly support the enterprise.*

Alignment with the new statement of work is necessary to more clearly understand not just what needs to be done, but what resources are needed to execute the statement of work. It is an assessment of the work that needs to be accomplished to support the business, along with the coupling of the appropriate resources to do the work.

Having to control costs also contributes to the shape of the new organization. The need to control costs by eliminating redundancies, adopting best practices, and becoming more efficient supports one of the primary objectives of the merger or acquisition, that is, bringing the two companies together into a single organization that is expected to become more productive, more capable, and more efficient than the two were alone. Reducing costs helps shape the organization, as management must seek ways to conduct business with fewer resources. Improving existing processes, outsourcing, eliminating redundancies, and even redefining the role of security are methods to reduce cost and are actions that shape an organization.

More severe resource limitations and budgetary constraints also contribute to shaping the security organization, particularly if the company budgetary and resource allocation philosophy for security is to use an affordability model. An affordability model for budgeting considers funding for security support bases on what senior management has determined to be available. An amount is established and the security manager is expected to provide security operating completely within the parameters of affordability.

Affordability budgeting is not a process that assesses the statement of work and then allocates an appropriate level of resources; it is just the opposite. A budgetary value is established with an expectation that the security organization will do what it can to provide the best level of security within the confines of the affordability target. Threats or risks are not the primary driver in establishing the budget. However, the security manager is expected to plan for and provide sufficient support to address the most critical or compelling security needs. Beyond that, it is a "do what you can approach." Affordability budgets usually manifest themselves under two common conditions:

- Management has serious cost issues to deal with and is taking strong measures to solve them.
- Management has a high tolerance for risk and is willing to take risks with security (e.g., protection of assets).

For the longer term, there are other compelling reasons to bring the security organizations from the two companies together into one.

LONG-TERM REASONS TO COMBINE THE SECURITY ORGANIZATIONS INTO A SINGLE DEPARTMENT

The security organization should not be fractured; it should operate as a single entity. The macro level responsibilities for security are to protect people, information, and all other physical assets of the company. Security, effectively applied, is an integrated process with interdependencies between different security subprocesses. Security is applied in layers, with one security process supporting the others. For example, physical security controls are the building blocks used in support of developing controls for the protection of information systems. Even the best tools and processes used for protecting information systems would be seriously weakened if the physical controls for protecting information systems hardware were not in place, thus providing a secure foundation.

To be successful, security must be applied in layers. To be successful and efficient, security must be applied in a manner by which "the left hand knows what the right hand is doing." That is, security must be planned and implemented in a deliberate way; it is not a happenstance occurrence. To best ensure this condition, security should be organized as a single integrated organization, with all elements operating together toward a common objective and with a single responsible authority. A fragmented or split security organization runs the risk of its many parts not working together efficiently or effectively for the good of the enterprise. In the long run, this condition does more harm than good.

Develop Common Operating Philosophy

There is an old cliché about everyone in the choir singing from the same sheet of music. If they are not, the music sounds terrible. It is much the same with a security organization or any other business organization. Everyone on the team needs to be moving in the same direction and working toward the same end. Anything less will degrade performance, diminish consistency, and lead to conflict.

Any security organization needs to have singular leadership with a clear and shared vision and common mission. Shared is the critical element. Leadership establishes the vision and operating philosophy for an organization. It must be communicated throughout the organization, and its members must buy in. Thus, the framework is established for operational expectations and performance. Without clear expectations and defined operating parameters in place, employees or elements of the organization will move in their own direction. Vision, mission, and operating philosophy are to be supported by common policies, procedures, and processes. With this structure in place, all elements of the organization have an enabling construct in place to cause them to work toward the same purpose.

With fundamental organizational elements in place, the leader can help shape the development of the organization's culture. With expectations defined, performance measures in place, and a reward system that encourages behavior consistent with organizational expectations, a culture can be shaped over time. Assuming that the leader is following the company's vision and operating philosophy, the culture of the security organization can be similarly shaped.

If the two security organizations coming together from a merger or acquisition are never united, each will follow its own leader. Unless the relationship between the two is collaborative, there will be differences in how they operate, friction between them, and even competition. Competition can be, and usually is, beneficial but not when unity is what is needed.

Without strong company executive leadership in place to drive the organization in a unifying way, many employees and managers will move off in their own direction. Separate organizations will follow different paths. If the security organization is fractured into two or more sections, it, too, will develop cultural differences. Each security organization will follow its own direction. An example of this can be seen within the U.S. Defense Security Service (DSS). Over the past five years at least four different executives have led the DSS. To date, the organization struggles with many operation problems from the timely processing of security clearances and background investigations to reciprocity (recognizing and accepting the work and authority from one element of the organization by another element of the organization) within its own regions. Many factors contribute to the current struggles of the DSS. Lack of consistent leadership and the differing cultures from one geographical region to another are major contributors to current problems.

> *"Honeywell Security Products Group acquires Olympo Controls s.r.o and Olympo Bratislava spol s.r.o: This acquisition will allow Honeywell to solidify its distribution base in central Europe."*[3]

Better Management and Control of Resources

Combining like organizations after a merger or acquisition helps a company better manage and control professional resources for long-term usage. It can be argued that the singular most important resource for any organization is its people. Having the flexibility to deploy resources from a larger single pool best serves the organization and the company at large. From within the construct of a single security organization the following critical areas can be addressed:

- *Identification and retention of key employees in high-impact positions:* In every field of expertise, it is important to get and keep the best people for the tasks at hand; this, too, is true for security. When a merger or acquisition occurs and the time comes to begin reducing costs, which usually translates to eliminating people, the best performers with the most critical skills must be identified and protected. The needs of the organization must be evaluated against the available talent, and those security professionals best prepared (skills and performance) to perform the necessary work must be kept. Those on the other end of the spectrum, the professionals least prepared to meet the needs of the organization, can be let go. As mentioned earlier, any reduction in force must be completed in accordance with company policy and standards and take into consideration the needs of the person being discharged. Help them transition out of the company and find new opportunities. There is no reason to make their departure any more difficult than it already is.
- *Deployment of personnel and skills:* Organizational changes made after a merger or acquisition are a good time to reassess the current deployment of personnel based on their skills and performance and to realign with future organizational needs. Much change occurs with a merger or acquisition, and with change comes opportunity.

---

[3] ASIS Magazine, *Security Management*, January 2004, p. 119.

Use the assessment made as part of a reduction in force initiative to evaluate the skills and performance of all security professionals. Rank them in order of the most valuable to the least valuable, and prepare to assign them matched by skills and needs. If a performance assessment and ranking was not accomplished in preparation for reductions-in-force in the early stages of the integration effort, now is a perfect time to complete one. Take advantage of this period of change. Assess the professional staff, align them with the security obligations and statement of work to support the company, and make the changes.

- *Opportunities and talent development:* Any merger or acquisition immediately increases the size of the company and thereby expands the security statement of work. Integrating the security organization from the acquired company into the acquiring company creates a larger security organization. An increase in size alone will generate opportunities for security employees to develop their skills and advance their career. In a larger, more diverse company, employees will encounter situations that differ from those experienced in a smaller company. Each experience will differ in magnitude, complexity, and even frequency. The postmerger or postacquisition period is a different learning environment from what was experienced in either company before the merger or acquisition.

- *Realigning the security statement of work for those processes not properly assigned to the security function:* In some instances, traditional security functions will not be handled or managed by security but are managed by another discipline. For example, it is not uncommon to find human resources organizations with responsibility to deliver services such as preemployment background investigations or even all investigations. Typically, in many companies, investigative functions are delivered and managed by security professionals. Traditionally, investigations are a core competency and skill set of security organizations and a large part of their statement of work. When a process is misaligned, the integration period is a good time to correct the alignment and move traditional security processes back under the control of the security manager. Such moves must be based on business-sense logic and not "turf grabbing." In other words, the security manager must make a "business case" for the realignment.

Recognition of Longer Term Opportunities for Synergies and Cost-Savings Changes to Larger Security Systems and Technologies

As stated earlier, the short-term action for large cost reductions is to downsize the workforce. Downsizing translates to the layoff of employees. The long-term effect of layoffs is to reduce costs; however, in the short –term, costs may rise as severance packages may be required depending on company policy. Furthermore, reducing the size of the workforce, including the security workforce, has long-term implications for security. When reductions in force occur, what becomes the priority are the routine day-to-day security needs. Money and resources are not available for upgrades in systems and expenditures on new security technologies. This can lead to the degradation of the security infrastructure. Furthermore, training needs may be considered "nice-to-have" and eliminated. Thus, security professionals may not be able to keep up with progressive changes that may, in fact, save the company money.

Additional cost reduction opportunities may be achieved through outsourcing low-skill or transactional security processes, that is, if the security manager has not already outsourced as much as possible. For the longer term, however, other potential ways of reducing costs must be identified. They rely on the use of technology to eliminate activities normally performed by people. Below are several areas where change may lead to reductions in cost.

- *Information systems:* Can be used for more than data storage and retrieval. Information systems can be designed to deliver workflow. Certain tasks can be automated, thereby eliminating the dependence on the human in the loop and allowing the system to manage the work process. For example, if security awareness training sessions are conducted by a security professional, the security manager can automate that process by creating a web-based presentation where employees, at their convenience, can go on line, review the briefing material, and even take a test to assess what they learned.

- *Expand the use of video surveillance and monitoring (alarm) systems:* Again, security technology allows for the reductions of people by having the task performed by sophisticated equipment. Further savings can be achieved by using technology solutions with open architecture. Open architecture allows for the expansion of systems without having to be concerned with the replacement of incompatible equipment. It also allows for different makes and models of equipment to be integrated into the same system. It is a bridge, bringing the incompatible together to be compatible.

- *Best of the best processes:* A thorough assessment and comparison can (and should) be made of the major security processes from each organization and of how they work. Invariably, each security department will do some things better than others. Adopting the best practices and processes for the combined organization should make an immediate impact on performance efficiencies.

- *After the adoption of best practices and processes, changes will need to be made to security policies and procedures.* This action will institutionalize and standardize the changes adopted. Furthermore, reviewing all policies and procedures could prove beneficial, as updates and changes may allow for new ways of doing business more efficiently and further identify other areas of potential conflict.

A Single Security Voice and Face Presented to Internal and External Entities

The work and responsibilities of the security manager and the security organization require interface with other internal departments and organizations external to the company. Security professionals regularly interface with local, state, and federal law enforcement agencies, regulatory agencies, government security agencies (when doing business with the federal government or business in other countries), attorneys, security service providers, courts, and many others.

Internally, security professionals are likely to interface with the management and employees of every department within the company. As such, delivering a consistent message and being able to represent the security organization, and its positions with a single voice for the company is crucial. This is difficult to do with a fractured security department. The ability to have one consistent position and speak with a single voice is reason enough to drive the consolidation of the two security organizations from both companies into one.

Issues with Restructuring the Security Organization

Restructuring the security organization to combine two departments into one, for the purpose of reducing costs, becoming more efficient through better deployment of skills, adopting best practices and processes, will be difficult even under the best of conditions. It is much more complex and demanding when other factors, such as the following, are involved:

- *Geography:* Global companies have facilities and offices in many parts of the world. They operate where their customers are located and where the markets take them. Security professionals may be spread out and assigned to different regions of the globe or assigned to a central home office and deployed to other locations when needed. Small, geographically dispersed sites seldom have security professionals permanently assigned to them, and security is often an extra duty for another professional. Often a country manager, the senior company person on assignment in a particular country assumes additional duties of security. Regardless of who is providing security support, it must be coordinated through, and in concert with, the oversight of the company security manager.

Having many small sites dispersed to the corners of the globe makes it difficult to consolidate and deliver security services; nevertheless, it needs to be done. Anyone providing security services and support in the company must be connected and accountable, in some way, to the company security manager. Ideally, everyone providing security support should report to the security manager. If for some reason that alignment will not work, the site person responsible for security must be indirectly connected to the security manager and accountable to them for the application of basic security practices and accomplishing security goals, objectives, and fulfilling security responsibilities.

In some situations, the security manager does not have full control over the company security program and all security resources. These resources are assigned to other organizations, but are used to perform a fundamental security task or deliver a security service. This is not an ideal situation, but it may be a practical one. To change this paradigm, much persuasion and patience on the part of the security manager will be necessary. A heavy-handed approach to drive change will more than likely have a negative effect. Changing this paradigm requires the application of influence. The senior company executives with the authority to cause this change must be convinced that it is best for the company. Homework (building the business case), patience (taking the time to educate), and persistent influence (don't give up) are needed.

- *Diversity and culture:* In this context, diversity and culture refer to the differences in security philosophy and security operations between different types of businesses operating in different environments and different countries. Local laws, customs, and values differ from business to business, from country to country, and from culture to culture. For example, a North American security professional may view the problem of kidnapping and ransom in South America quite differently than a South American security professional sees the same problem. The North American may view the problem as totally unacceptable and will work diligently to ensure that systems are in place to prevent kidnapping. The South American may view the problem as another security eventuality that must be prepared for, particularly by having a process in place to meet the demands of the kidnappers and obtain the safe return of the victim. Both understand the problem, but their approach to preventing or managing it differs.

To the security manager, these differences may seem to drive inconsistency in the security program. Inconsistency is a problem when employees view it as an unfair application of standards or contrary to their own expectations and beliefs. To eliminate differences and inconsistencies, security processes, policies, and systems need to be as common as possible. This is difficult to do in a construct held together by persuasion and influence. It is much easier to do under an organizational structure in which all of security is part of a single organization with a single reporting structure.

OUTSOURCING SECURITY

In addition to the many challenges of consolidating security departments subsequent to a merger or acquisition, the security manager is also faced with another long-term operational decision, that is, to "make or buy" security services. To *make* is to provide security services from within, using company employees to deliver all security services and products. To *buy* means to purchase security services from another source that expertly delivers security services and products. Under the new company construct and within the newly formed security, the security manager must decide whether to provide security services from within or to outsource some or all security services to a company with the capability to deliver the needed support.

The acquiring company just spent a fortune (large or small) to obtain the target company. Company leadership will be looking to demonstrate to company ownership, whether private or public (stockholders), the value of making this acquisition. The two immediate priorities will be to increase revenue and decrease costs, thus demonstrating the acquisition to be worth the cost as it contributes to increasing the value of the acquiring company. For the revenue-generating entities within the newly combined company, there will be pressures to increase revenue. For all cost centers (including security), there will be pressures to reduce costs.

The security managers must continually be aware of the need to cut costs after a merger or acquisition. For most companies, providing security costs money; therefore, security is a cost center. In most cases, the security function does not generate revenue. Therefore, as with all support or enabling functions, there will be constant pressures to keep costs low while maintaining quality of service and support. For small, medium-size, and many large companies, security is not a core competency. It is not one of the key capabilities of the company that enables it to be successful, differentiating itself in the marketplace, or generating revenue.

There are, however, some exceptions in which security is a core competency. Companies in the business of selling security services and expertise rely on security as a core competency. Security is the product and service they market and sell. Selling security services is how they generate revenue for their owners. Many other large companies, such as those in the energy and defense industries, have huge complex operations dealing with many risks and threats. To effectively mitigate those risks and protect their assets, people, and information, they, too, must maintain a core competency of security. However, these companies don't sell their security services. Quite often, they purchase many security services from expert providers.

Small and medium-size companies often outsource their security work to security service providers who can provide the services and expertise many small and medium-size companies can't afford to maintain. These companies may also purchase limited security support for a particular security service or capability needed only occasionally, such as investigation services. It would be far too expensive to maintain that capability in-house if the need for it is only occasional. The most common security services outsourced are plant protection services; these are predominantly guard and fire protection services.

Companies outsource these services for many reasons including the most compelling of them all—security service providers can generally provide the needed services at a lower cost than the company itself can deliver from within. Moreover, outsourcing to a security service provider eliminates the need for maintaining a related process support structure. For example, to maintain an armed proprietary guard force, a company will need to also maintain weapons, ammunition, equipment, training capabilities, and other associated support mechanisms. If the service is outsourced to a security service provider with an expertise in delivering armed guard services, that provider will handle all of the associated support mechanisms.

Large companies primarily outsource to keep their costs low. Large companies usually have the capability to maintain a large security service and its support structure, such as guard and fire prevention services along with many others, but they find it to be more cost-effective to use a skilled service provider who maintains security-specific services as its core competency and can deliver those services on a large scale with high levels of efficiency. Furthermore, large companies will sometimes outsource for limited periods to augment their proprietary services and capabilities in support of special events or changes that occur during normal business cycles.

What does this mean to the security manager who is working to combine two security departments into one after a merger or acquisition? Faced with the task of consolidating the two departments or redesigning the security organization, company management's expectation will be that this is accomplished swiftly and effectively while reducing costs and improving efficiency. Moreover, company management may not exhibit patience as they are expecting to see benefits very early in the integration phase. This is not easy to accomplish.

Generally, the quickest way to reduce costs in security, since security is a labor-intensive process, is to reduce the size of the security workforce.

The problem with reducing the workforce is that there is still work to be done and, without a sufficient number of security professionals to do the work, it will not get done. A quick solution to this dilemma is to outsource work to a security service provider. For the reasons stated earlier, a service provider can deliver the same level of service but at a lower price and, it is hoped, just as efficiently.

Outsourcing is not an easy thing to do when it leads to reductions in the internal workforce. To contribute to the goals and objectives of the company, however, a security manager may have no alternative. If managed properly, outsourcing to a quality service provider can be a positive and value-added experience. A mistake commonly made by security managers is assuming that once they have outsourced, their work is done. Outsource providers still require oversight and to be held to the provisions of the contractual agreement. The performance of any service provided needs to be regularly measured and managed to ensure the level of service meets the buyers' standards and the provisions of the contract.

POST POSTMERGER: WHAT LESSONS WERE LEARNED?

In every activity, in order to improve, a performance analysis must be accomplished on the results and of the steps taken to achieve the end result. The grand question is "Was the desired end result achieved?" Athletes continually measure their performance and adjust their training routine in order to improve. Students have their performance measured in school in order to advance to higher levels. Businesses are excellent at measuring some areas of their performance, usually financial goals, but not necessarily as effective at measuring other critical and enabling processes.

A merger or acquisition is a critical endeavor for any company, using it either as part of a strategy for growth or survival. For such critical processes, performance measures must be used, and management must react to them in a manner that causes improvement in the steps taken to achieve the end result, along with the end result itself. As a critical business process, security must also be measured by answering these questions:

- Did the security organization perform at the expected level?
- Were its processes effective and efficient?
- Were the expected security goals and objectives achieved?

These and other questions must be part of an "after-action assessment" to determine how effective security was in supporting the effort. The following section identifies critical security processes in support of the merger or acquisition and how they may be evaluated in terms of performance.

From the Premerger Activity

Competitive Intelligence Gathering and Use

How can the value of competitive intelligence be measured? Did the competitive intelligence produced prove valuable during any phase of the merger or acquisition effort? These questions must be asked and answered at the conclusion of the merger or acquisition to better understand the effectiveness of gathering and producing competitive intelligence. If they are not, the team will never truly know whether the competitive intelligence used was of any value. When competitive intelligence is produced and applied, it cannot be assumed that the results were useful or made a difference. An evaluation must be made to determine if the specific intelligence gathered actually led to an improvement in the merger or acquisition team's understanding of the potential target or business sector. Did the competitive intelligence enhance the decision-making process of the merger or acquisition team members? Here are some areas to focus on when attempting to measure the success of the competitive intelligence processes and products.

Knowledge of the Target Company

- Did the competitive intelligence produced actually increase team knowledge of the target company?
- If so, was the increase in knowledge minimal or significant?
- Was that knowledge useful in the decision-making process, or was it just interesting to know?
- Did having this information provide an advantage over a competitor also interested in the same target for acquisition?
- Did having this information contribute to the acquiring company's ability to negotiate a better price for the deal?
- Was the cost to produce competitive intelligence about the target company less than or greater than the value of having and using that same information?
- Did the competitive intelligence uncover or make apparent any vulnerability or issues that helped assess the value of the target company or led to a decision not to pursue the target company?

Knowledge of a Market

- Did the competitive intelligence gained actually increase team knowledge of the market segment examined?

- If so, was the increase in knowledge minimal or significant?
- Was that knowledge useful in the decision-making process, or was it just interesting to know or possess?

Team Success

- How successful would the merger and acquisition team have been had they not had the benefit of using competitive intelligence produced by the competitive intelligence team?
- Would that information have been readily available to the team from other sources?

If the competitive intelligence gathered and produced did not contribute to the effectiveness and success of the team, the process should be analyzed to determine if and how it can be effective. If the intelligence products were useful, knowing how useful they were will allow the team to assess the value (e.g., was the intelligence gathered worth more than it cost to produce). Conducting this assessment will provide a basis for continually improving the competitive intelligence process.

Protecting the Effort

Was the premerger or preacquisition phase properly protected? This is the most basic question that must be answered. However, other questions must be asked and answered to fully understand the degree of success or failure of the effort to protect. Some of the questions can be easily answered, but others may be much more difficult. In any event, to continue to improve the process, a postevaluation must be made. The following are questions to consider as part of the assessment:

- Was the target company acquired?
- Was the existence of the merger or acquisition effort exposed to unauthorized persons?
- If yes, how did that exposure occur? Unauthorized exposure is a common problem.
- Was there competition for the target company?
- Did a competitor successfully acquire the target company?
- Was competitive information compromised? (This may be difficult to assess.)
- Were the intentions of any team members exposed to unauthorized persons?
- Were any of the team members harmed?

- Did company executives encounter security or protective issues related to the merger or acquisition?
- Was team leadership satisfied with the protective effort?

Getting and analyzing answers to these questions will help the security manager find ways to improve the protective processes. Invariably, something will go wrong. Learning from mistakes and making appropriate changes will lead to improvements with the protective processes.

Conducting the Security Assessment of the Target Company

- Was the premerger or acquisition assessment of the target company's security condition accurate?
- Did a further review during the integration period support the analysis made during the due diligence?
- If it did not, why not?

These questions must be asked and answered to assess the effectiveness of the security assessment and its impact on the team's effort to value the target company. In support of this assessment, some other questions must be asked and answered:

- Was the data collected useful in making the assessment?
- What was learned after the merger or acquisition that would have been valuable to know during the due diligence?
- Was that information obtainable, or were there reasons it could not be obtained?
- Were there any major surprises?
- If yes, what were they and why did they occur?
- What could have been done to prevent these surprises?
- Was there sufficient time to make an accurate assessment?
- Was the assessment team effective in their analysis of data?
- Did they use what they knew properly?
- Was there information gathered and used for the assessment that had no value?

Asking and answering these questions will provide the security manager with enough information to analyze the effectiveness of the security assessment process for potential targets. Understanding the effectiveness of this process is important and could be critical. If a major issue was overlooked or not revealed, it could have a significant impact on the value of the target company, causing the acquiring company to pay more for the target than the target is worth. As stated in earlier chapters, one of the contributing factors of failed mergers and acquisitions is paying much more for a target company than it was worth.

From the Postmerger Activity

Integration Assessment

Measuring the success of the integration phase is much more difficult. Some aspects of the integration are easy to quantify, but others are not. For example, financial expectations are easy to assess, as items such as revenue targets, cost reductions, and market share growth are easily captured and tracked. Actual performance data can be compared to stated goals and objectives. Other areas of the integration are more difficult to measure:

- Were the security procedures and processes sufficiently analyzed to determine the best of the best?
- Were the best practices adopted and implemented?
- Have the practices been measured sufficiently to make that determination?

The best criterion is to measure the integration performance against its stated goals and objectives of company leadership. What did the company CEO or Board of Directors declare to be their expectation for the merger or acquisition? During the early stages of the premerger and preacquisition period, undoubtedly the merger or acquisition team's analysis produced short- and long-term expectations that were presented to the CEO before proceeding with pursuit of the target. These expectations, once approved by the CEO, were communicated to the owners or Board of Directors and subsequently became the strategic goals and objectives for the acquisition. The criteria and any expanded expectations provide a basis from which to measure performance.

Culture

Cultural issues related to the integration of a stand-alone business unit tend to be less frequent and less complex than those encountered when an acquired company is fully integrated into the acquiring company. The stand-alone business unit will have less day-to-day interaction with the acquiring company than the business unit whose heritage company and identity are eliminated as they become part of the fabric of the acquiring company. Nevertheless, in both cases cultural issues and conflict will be encountered and may have an adverse effect on the success of the integration. Preventing cultural conflicts, or at least mitigating them, must begin at the onset of the merger or acquisition effort.

Cultural fit is a critical factor, particularly among the senior management teams, and should be considered in all stages of any merger or acquisition. As much attention should be paid to issues of cultural fit as was to issues of strategic fit and financial and operational analysis. Failing to do so greatly increases the chances of failure. According to a KPMG study, 26% of mergers and acquisitions are more likely to be successful if the acquirers focus on identifying and resolving cultural issues.[4] Moreover, culture must be looked at in a broad sense. Obviously, corporate culture must be considered, but in the global marketplace, national issues of culture must also be considered. If an American firm were to acquire an Indian software company, are there not both company and national cultural issues to contend with?

If the merger or acquisition team did not consider the cultural fit and issue resolution from the very early stages of the premerger effort, it failed. The lessons learned by many others are that consideration of culture must be part of the process. If the premerger planning did take into account issues of culture, then how is success measured? How are positive changes in culture measured?

Perhaps the best indicator in determining successful cultural integration is to track the number of culture-related incidents. To do this requires a merger and acquisition team to be conscience of what constitutes cultural issues and to know how to intervene to resolve them. Resolving cultural conflict is a complicated process, as cultures may differ vastly. The best approach for planning for and resolving cultural issues is to have, as a member of the merger or acquisition team, an expert in human behavior and conflict resolution. Considering the high rate of failure for mergers and acquisitions where culture is not considered, the added cost of a cultural expert to the team may be insignificant.

Understanding the importance of planning for and dealing with culture issues is just as important to the security manager as it is to any other member of the merger or acquisition team. The security manager must consider culture, as it will impact the security organization. Bringing two security departments together will generate as much culture clash as does bringing any other two organizations together. However, when conflict escalates, the potential for incidents of workplace violence also increases. The security manager is a key person in the workplace violence prevention program. The security manager not only serves as a member of the intervention team but also leads any emergency response effort. Therefore, issues related to culture are of heightened importance to the security manager.

---

[4] KPMG, "Unlocking Shareholder Value: The Keys to Success," *Mergers and Acquisitions: Global Research Report*, 1999, p. 17

SUMMARY

Mergers and acquisitions are not short lived. The postmerger period requires much support from the security manager as the newly acquired company becomes integrated into the acquiring company. The process of integration may lead to major organizational changes, redeployment of resources, improvements in processes, and practices facing the need to do business differently. Reducing the cost of security and increasing organizational efficiency will occupy much of the security manager's time. Dealing with issues of organizational culture may cause much of the pain.

One of the major obstacles to a successful integration of two companies is the issue of organizational culture. Culture clash can unravel all of the expected gains and benefits of a merger or acquisition. Culture clash can occur at macro levels (throughout both companies) or within departments (e.g., the two separate security departments). If the issue of culture clash is not planned for during the very early stages of the premerger or preacquisition period, then it will be difficult to handle these issues and resolve them as the integration moves forward.

For a variety of reasons, the security manager must be concerned with issues of culture clash. Problems stemming from culture clash may impede the security manager's ability to effectively implement change within the security organization and also adversely impact assets protection. Culture issues may also delay any gains expected from combining organizations. Culture clash can also lead to incidents of violence in the workplace. As conflicts develop, they have the potential to escalate into violent behavior. As a member of the violence prevention intervention team and the owner of emergency response program, the security manager must always be concerned with preventing proactively incidents of workplace violence.

Chapter 9

Divestitures

So, the question is, do corporate executives, provided they stay within the law, have responsibilities in their business activities other than to make as much money for their shareholders as possible? And my answer to that is, no they do not. – Milton Friedman.

INTRODUCTION

This chapter discusses security support for divestitures. Why does a company divest any part of its business? What needs to be done to prepare for a divestiture? When a company does spin-off a portion of the business, what role does the security organization and security manager play? How can the security manager contribute to a successful divestiture? What are some of the key security issues faced during a divestiture? All of these questions are addressed in this chapter.

> *Divestiture: The disposition or sale of an asset by a company. A company will often divest an asset that is not performing well, which is not vital to the company's core business, or which is worth more to a potential buyer or as a separate entity than as part of the company.*[1]

WHY DOES A COMPANY CHOOSE TO DIVEST ANY PART OF ITS BUSINESS?

There are many reasons why a company chooses to sell a portion of its business. In business, cash is king. Divesting a portion of a company is not a decision that is made lightly. Much time, effort, and resources must be dedicated to the process. A decision to divest a portion of the company is made at the highest levels of the company. It is usually a strategic decision with a focus on long-term growth and opportunities; however, it may be a

---

[1] See: http://www.investorwords.com/1508/divestiture.html

decision of survival. It may be necessary to convert assets into cash. Any company that chooses to divest a portion of its business has determined that the potential divestiture is to its advantage. Some of the more compelling reasons to divest are described next.

A Need for Cash

A company may need cash for many reasons including these:

- Sales and profits may be down.
- The company may be in the downward portion of the business cycle.
- The company may want to raise additional money to invest in research and development.
- The company may need to reduce debt and eliminate high interest payments. It may want to purchase a product line or business unit from another company, so in order to raise the money to take that action, it must divest a portion of the business it no longer needs or is not in line with its long-term strategic objectives.

The sale of an asset, particularly an unwanted or unneeded asset, is always a good way to raise cash. If an asset has real value, it can be sold. The company must find and match a buyer whose interests are aligned with what the company wants to divest. Sometimes the asset divested is in the form of a plant or equipment. Sometimes it may be a piece of real estate. Other times it may be a product line, a single business unit, or even a technology. For the purpose of this chapter, we will discuss divestiture in terms of divesting a single stand-alone business unit that is one of several within a company. In any event, the sale of the asset occurs for the purpose of raising cash to be used in whatever way best suits the selling company.

Not Part of the Company's Long-term Strategy

Another reason to divest an asset or a stand-alone business unit is driven by changes in the marketplace. As consumer demands change, so too does the marketplace. As a result, companies will change and focus on what they perceive to be the demands of the marketplace. Moreover, as companies grow and mature, they may choose to enter and exit different markets. As they do, the change can be slight or completely transforming. For example, during the 1990s, Westinghouse Corporation, which owned such diverse businesses as a defense systems division producing products for military and government use, nuclear power plants for generating energy and broadcasting, and media companies, chose to divest itself of all businesses except those involved in media and broadcasting.[2]

Westinghouse even went so far as to drop its long time brand—Westinghouse—and adopt the highly recognizable and well-established media and broadcasting name *CBS*. It did this after acquiring CBS and divesting its other diverse business interests. This was a complete transformation of the company, as the Westinghouse CEO and Board of Directors chose to exit certain business sectors and move into the media and broadcasting sector. Clearly, this was a major change in its long-term business strategy. It strategically reshaped the company from a conglomerate involved in many markets and businesses to a company focused on media and broadcasting.

Not all companies engage is such drastic strategic restructuring. Sometimes a company will divest a specific product line simply because it no longer fits into its long-term strategic plans. In October 2003, Bayer AG announced that it was initiating a process to divest its plasma business.[3] Bayer AG decided this was a product line they no longer wanted to pursue. Divestment is a common strategy that many companies use to help shape their product portfolio to meet long-term strategic objectives. As companies mature and develop or acquire new technologies taking them in different directions, it is common for them to divest those elements of the business that are still viable but no longer part of their future strategic plans.

Asset Sale

Asset sale is another form of divestiture. Although a stand-alone business unit is considered an asset, here we are referring to smaller assets. These assets are used in support of a stand-alone business unit or the development, production, and distribution of a specific product line. These assets are the tools that enable a company to produce and sell products. For example, when the production of widgets winds downs as the demand for them wanes, or when producing the widget is no longer profitable, a company will choose to phase out the widget product. Ideally, it will have a product line to replace the widget and that product line may not need the same tools and resources to make it work and keep it going. As part of phasing out the widget product line, the company may sell all related resources and tools (i.e., assets). This is particularly true if the assets cannot be used in other ways to generate revenue.

---

[2] See: http://hope.journ.wwu.edu/tpilgrim/j190/190structurelist.html
[3] See: http://www.press.bayer.com/news/news.nsf/id/95FE860DE7C50D5CC1256DB30041FBF4

What Must a Company Do to Find a Buyer for Its Divestiture?

When a decision is made to divest a portion of the business, the first action is to find a prospective buyer, that is, to identify who may be interested in purchasing what the company intends to sell. In some cases, this may not be difficult. A quality internal competitive intelligence function may have done sufficient market analysis to determine what other companies, whether or not they are competitors, may have an interest in the stand-alone business unit being sold. It is also possible that a competitor or another company may have approached the divesting company and expressed an interest in the business unit being considered for sale. If neither occurs, it will be necessary for the selling company to find a prospective buyer on its own.

The most likely and obvious pool of potential buyers usually comes from within the same business sector and marketplace. Competition is often most interested in acquiring business units being sold by competitors. They operate in the same marketplace and have the best understanding of the potential value of the business unit up for sale.

To divest a business unit requires a communication to potential buyers that the business unit is for sale. A description of the business unit must be provided to potential buyers that communicates the following message:

- *Value drivers:* What makes this particular business unit valuable? Why would another person or company be interested in buying it? How would acquiring this business unit add value to the acquirer? What are the long-term earning prospects for this business unit? To generate interest among potential buyers, the seller must help them understand the value of the divested business unit. Furthermore, it is important to help buyers understand how they would benefit from owning the business unit being divested. The value needs to be expressed in ways beyond financial performance. For example, the divested unit may possess a unique technology that has potential beyond its current usage, or the business unit may bring with it highly skilled people in a unique area.

- *Outline financial performance for a potential acquirer:* What is the financial value of the entity to be divested? More important, what is its potential to generate future revenue and profits? Any potential buyer will seek immediate answers to these questions. Before they become serious interested buyers, they must first understand the financial potential of the business unit being sold.

How Is the Business Unit "For Sale" Message Communicated to Potential Buyers?

The divesting company needs to tell its story. It needs to put together a package that highlights the business unit, explaining its attributes directly and as simply as possible. It must communicate a complete and accurate representation of the business. To do this the package should contain the following information:

- *High-level product line descriptions:* For potential buyers to develop an interest, they must fully understand the products and/or services provided by the business unit for sale. Preparing a product line description with sufficient detail for buyers to understand but not so much as to overwhelm them is important. Descriptions should be kept initially at an executive (overview) level. If the potential buyer is seriously interested, additional information can be shared later. It is important not to share too much before a potential buyer commits to a purchase. Sharing too much information may reveal sensitive competitive information to a competitor who may not buy. (*Note*: If sensitive competitive information is released, the potential buyer should sign an agreement not to use that information if he or she does not proceed with the purchase.)
- *Market drivers:* What are the drivers for the products or services being marketed by the business unit up for sale? Why does anyone want those products and services, and how would they benefit a prospective buyer?
- *Competitive discriminators:* What differentiates the business, its products, and services from its competitors? Are competing products and services available? If so, who produces them? Is this a niche market?
- *Human resources and facilities highlights:* What type of human talent comes with the business unit being sold? Is there a highly skilled labor force? Are there organized labor issues? Will the employees of the business unit being sold be motivated to move to a new company? What special skills and expertise do they bring to a potential buyer?
- *Top-level financial data:* This information will be of critical interest to any potential buyers. They will want to know the financial benefits to them if they proceed with purchasing the business unit for sale. Financial data must be clearly and accurately communicated.

SEPARATING THE BUSINESS UNIT

After the deal is completed and the business unit is divested, the separation effort begins. The difference between a merger or acquisition and a divestiture depends on what side of the deal you are on. Throughout this book, we've mostly addressed the actions and issues associated with merging with or acquiring another company. Now we look at a similar transaction, but from the perspective of the divesting company. When a company acquires another business unit it must integrate that business unit into its company. The selling party must physically separate that business unit from the company. This process requires an opposite set of actions than does the integration process. Moreover, the degree of complication varies depending on how integrated the business unit is into the company divesting that same unit.

Divesting a single stand-alone business unit that operates independently from the company is an easier separation than that of a program or product line that is fully integrated into the structure of the company. It is much like the process of integrating an acquired business unit into the acquiring company as a stand-alone business unit. Because the stand-alone business unit operates with a great deal of independence, there are fewer systems and processes to integrate or separate. If the separate stand-alone business unit's infrastructure is independent of the company infrastructure, then the actual separation process will be less complicated and will take less time than separating a fully integrated business unit.

The fully integrated business unit, which is highly dependent on the infrastructure and system of the company, is a much more complex and time-consuming process to divest. For example, if the divested business unit is fully integrated into the company wide area network (WAN), the primary information systems structure for the company, that separation alone will be time consuming for the divesting company and could be expensive for the acquiring company. The extent of the expense will depend on whether or not the acquired business unit is

---

The New York Times said MCI also tapped Greenhill & Co. and law firm Davis Polk & Wardwell to help canvass for buyers. MCI hopes to fetch more than $6 billion, according to the newspaper. MCI and its rival AT&T Corp. (T.N: Quote, Profile, Research) have been slammed by competition from Baby Bell local telephone companies that have pushed into the long-distance market with discounted packages of services.

Although MCI's shrinking sales and bleak growth outlook may make it difficult to find a buyer, it boasts a lucrative base of corporate customers and a global high-speed Internet network that could allow a Baby Bell to quickly leap-frog competitors, analysts have said.[4]

---

[4] http://www.reuters.com/financeNewsArticle.jhtml?type=bondsNews&storyID=6281882

being connected to the acquiring company's WAN, or whether an entirely new WAN is to be established. The security managers from each company (acquiring and divesting) must be part of this process, as there are major information assurance implications and issues associated with this transition.

WHAT ROLE DOES SECURITY PLAY IN THE DIVESTITURE?

How does security contribute to the success of the divestiture? When a business unit is divested, the selling company wants the transaction to occur as quickly as possible and without incident. This is no different than the sale of any other product. The seller always wants to move goods and services as quickly as possible and collect payment right away. With the sale of a single business unit, there are certain actions the security manager must take to support this divestiture.

Speedy Separation of the Divested Business Unit

People

Once the business unit is sold, things change. Employees from the divested business unit begin to see themselves as employees of another company. They understand they are separating from their heritage company and moving on. Some will look forward to the change, while others will not. Most will be apprehensive. The faster the separation occurs, the fewer number of problems will develop for the divesting company. The business unit has just been sold. From the perspective of the divesting company, any problems that develop are the problems of the acquiring company. A speedy separation will help. The security manager must support this. One means of doing so is to facilitate the employee transition to a new identity. Two areas requiring the immediate attention of the security manager are:

- *Badging:* The security manager of the divesting company must work with the security manager of the acquiring company to change the badges of each affected employee. Employees separating from the company should be identified as such. Their company identity has changed and acknowledging this by making the transition from one company badge to another will encourage the process to move forward. The worst situation that can occur is to let the transition linger. That will only heighten the anxiety of the affected employees and lead to discord, neither of which are good for the workplace environment.
- *Physical controls:* Executing the complete separation of a divested business unit takes time. During that time period, physical controls

need to be established for segregating employees of the divested business unit from the divesting company. Employees going with the divested business unit no longer have a need –to know for any of the business of their heritage company. In a subtle way, plans need to be developed and implemented that separate these two groups of employees during the early stages of the divestiture as a permanent separation is implemented.

Protection of Assets and Information

Only those assets and information that were identified as part of the divestiture should be removed from the selling company. The terms and agreement of the divestiture spell out specifically what part of the company is sold. Those assets (physical and information) not identified as being sold must stay with the selling company. If not closely watched, assets and information not part of the sale will find their way out of the company and into the possession of the new owners. This may occur unintentionally or intentionally. It is the security manager's responsibility to work with company management to ensure that this does not happen. The separation plan must address the protection of information and delineate what goes as part of the sale and what must stay. Of course, it is difficult to prevent the employee with dishonest or criminal intentions from stealing information. The focus must be on preventing an inadvertent transfer of information that is not part of the sale to the acquiring company. All employees must be cautioned to ensure that they take with them only those assets and data defined by the terms of the divestiture agreement.

In July 2003, Lockheed Martin filed suit against The Boeing Company, alleging proprietary Lockheed Martin documents regarding that company's plan to bid for contracts for the Air Force's Evolved Expendable Launch Vehicle (EELV) program, which were in the possession of McDonell Douglas (which became part of Boeing through a merger), were misused during bidding for Air Force contracts.[5]

Getting Costs out of the System

Another way the security manager contributes to a successful divestiture is to eliminate those segments of the security organization that existed solely in support of the divested business unit. The security manager must move

---

[5] See: http://www.spacetoday.net/Summary/1711

quickly to reorganize the security organization in concert with a reduced statement of work resulting from the divestiture.

Separation from Security Infrastructure

In addition to the responsibilities of the security manager already described, there are infrastructure actions that must also be handled. Separating a business unit requires the separation from all company support systems. For the security manager, this will include the following security systems:

- *Access control:* If the divestment of a stand-alone business unit includes the sale of facilities and buildings, the supporting security systems must also be separated. Unless the access control system for the sold business unit is totally self-contained, that is, separated from the company access control system, it has to be dis-integrated. To accomplish this action requires the reconfiguration of both hardware and software. Affected facilities must be disengaged from the system and established as separate, independent systems.
- *High security alarm monitoring services:* In companies with high-security (and fire alarm) alarm systems, the alarms usually terminate at a single point. It may be an internal security control and monitoring center, or it may be at a service-provider location that monitors system alerts and dispatches response personnel in the event of an alarm activation. Single monitoring stations tend to be the most effective and efficient operation. When a unit of the business is divested, much like the access control system, it must be disengaged from the divesting company alarm monitoring structure.
- *Security information systems:* Large security organizations use information systems for a variety of reasons. Some systems are used to help deliver security services such as web-based security awareness training for company employees. Other systems are used to help the security manager manage the company's security program, for example, maintaining up-to-date files on employees. Here, security records are kept for each employee. The records contain information such as the results of a preemployment background check and/or individual security training records. When a business unit is divested from the company, all affected employees must be identified and removed from that system. Their records are transferred to the acquiring company's information system. Moreover, departing employees who have access to security information systems must have their access terminated, as they no longer need to know the information contained in these systems.

- *Statement of work changes:* Divesting a business unit generally leads to a reduction in the size of the security statement of work. This reduction may also affect the statement of work and contractual agreements made with security service providers (outsourced). Depending on the contract structure, new agreements may need to be negotiated. This is particularly true for those contracts and agreements with volume-based cost structures. Types of services affected could include plant protection services, investigative services such as preemployment screening, and leased equipment agreements. A divestiture could lead to a large reduction in the need for certain types of security support. A contract based on volume usage may need to be restructured, as large reductions in activity may increase costs.

The security manager of a company divesting some portion of that company must work closely with the security manager of the acquiring company to ensure an efficient and effective transfer of assets and processes. It is in the best interests of both security managers to successfully work together toward that end.

SECURITY EMPLOYEES

The security manager of a company that is divesting a portion of itself must address several key areas:

- What is the fate of the security employees whose role it is to support the divested business unit?
- Do they lose their jobs?
- Do they go along with the divested business unit as part of the cadre of all employees moving on to the acquiring company?
- If they do, which employees transfer to the new company and which employees do not? Who makes that decision, and do the security employees have a choice or say in the matter?

All of these questions must be asked and answered by the company divesting its business unit and the security manager. The answers to these questions depend on many variables. Each situation is different and requires analysis by the security manager and coordination with the acquiring company. Keep in mind, once the deal is complete, the acquiring company makes decisions about the newly acquired business unit. Any security-related actions not specifically defined in the sale agreement may ultimately be the decision of the acquiring company's security manager.

> *Boeing may sell Canadian plant . . . Explaining the move, ... message reiterated by Boeing's strategy to focus on 'large scale systems integration.' That strategy has led to a series of divestitures of part-making plants as the company focuses on design and final assembly . . .* [6]

An example of an issue the security manager will face that was not addressed in the sale agreement occurs in the area of security staffing. If the acquiring company has in place a security staff skilled enough to absorb the additional statement of work, then they may choose to not to take with them the security employees from the divesting company. Those employees, if no work can be found with either company, may be faced with a lay-off. Security employees usually have little to no say in the employment decisions created by a divestiture. The divesting company will work to keep its best employees and look to transfer others with the sale. The acquiring company will plan to use its current employees to fulfill the expanded security statement of work to the extent possible, taking on additional security employees only as needed. Invariably, reductions in the security workforce will occur. How they do depends on the decisions made by security managers from both companies.

ISSUES FACING COMPANIES DOING BUSINESS IN AREAS HIGHLY REGULATED BY THE GOVERNMENT

For those companies doing business in sectors that are subject to the requirements of stringent government security regulations, security-related issues must be coordinated with the cognizant government security organization when the company is involved with a divestiture of a business unit. Industries and business sectors such as the defense and national security sector, the pharmaceuticals industry, the banking industry, and the maritime sector are subject to regulatory requirements beyond those faced by companies in most other business sectors. Security managers for these companies must be aware of their obligations to coordinate with their respective government agencies charged with regulatory oversight to ensure all necessary actions are taken to satisfy them and to ensure there is no disruption to the divestiture. For the acquiring company, it may be necessary to seek approvals before any changes can be made to security procedures, processes, and plans.

Changes also usually require support from the legal staff and the contact staff, as they are the experts in the laws and contract interpretations.

---

[6] See *The Seattle Times*, Business Section (D), August 10, 2004. p. 1

The security manager should not take on these tasks but should rely on the guidance of these professionals. Failure to do so can lead to serious consequences, for example, breach of contract charges by the customers. The security manager's job is difficult enough without facing such charges that may ultimately lead to dismissal. Security managers should always rely on the experts in the various specialties for support and not think of themselves as experts in anything but security and assets protection matters.

SERVICE LEVEL AGREEMENTS FOR CONTINUATION OF SUPPORT

Large and complicated divestitures don't happen quickly. It may take months to make the deal and when it is finished, it may take even longer to complete the separation of the business unit from the company divesting. How much time and effort involved depends on many factors. The extent to which the divested unit is integrated into the company infrastructure is the primary factor. The provisions of the divestiture/ sale agreement also play into the length of time it may take to separate. For example, a company may choose to divest a stand-alone business unit but makes an agreement to continue providing services to that business unit for an extended period of time. The acquiring company may not have the capability to relocate the acquired business unit or provide the necessary business infrastructure to provide basic support. The acquiring company may choose to purchase services, ranging from leasing buildings and facilities to providing security services, from the divesting company. This is not an uncommon practice, as it provides a financial advantage to both companies. For the acquiring company, it may delay the need for capital expenditures or for the delivery of services they have not usually been provided. For the divesting company, it may buy time to find alternative uses for resources they would otherwise need to eliminate.

Awareness of this possibility is important to the security manager. The security manager needs to be involved during the early stages of divestiture negotiations to better understand what services and support will need to continue for the divested business unit during the separation period and beyond. It is possible that these services could continue for months or even years.

Whatever services and support will continue to be provided to the divested business unit after its sale, those services and support activities must be clearly defined in the sales agreement and any subsequent lease agreements. *Do not operate on assumptions.* Providing services costs money. To ensure that all costs are recovered, the services need to be clearly defined, from a description of the statement of work to the duration of time they will be performed. A failure to do this could be costly to the divesting company.

It is easy for a security manager to continue supporting a business unit just because they have always done so. Knowing exactly when to terminate services and support, if not clearly defined in contractual agreements, can be difficult to pin down. The tendency for service providers is to continue to provide support for periods longer than required. This condition obviously has an adverse impact on controlling costs.

The security manager must be aware of the type of security support likely to continue on into the separation period and beyond. It generally occurs in areas where change is slow to occur. Furthermore, the costs of each task, function, and process must be qualified and quantified so that the divesting company's security manager does not provide services at a loss.[7] The following services and support activities are likely candidates for continuation:

- *Plant protection (guard services):* Because guard services are so closely tied to facilities and buildings, it is likely a divested business unit that remains in the same building or facility (leased back for some period of time) will, for at least a short time, choose to purchase back this type of support. Generally, doing this allows the acquiring company more time to decide how they would like to deliver this type of service.
- *Security (and fire) alarm monitoring:* Generally, if the acquiring company chooses to lease back buildings and facilities, it will, for a period of time, also choose to purchase alarm monitoring services. This is particularly true if the acquiring company does not have the capability to monitor alarms itself. Purchasing back the service allows sufficient time to establish a longer term plan. Building an alarm monitoring capability requires a large capital expenditure, and outsourcing the service takes time to select the best provider and then transfer the alarm lines from the divesting company infrastructure to that of the chosen alarm monitoring provider. This is neither a simple nor quick job.
- *Emergency response services:* This service is similar in nature to plant protection and alarm monitoring in that it is closely associated with buildings and facilities. Emergency response services, by the nature of what they are and the need to be able to respond in minutes, must be established and maintained within or close to the locations they support. If the acquired business unit in far from the operation of the acquiring company, it is likely this service will be purchased back from the divesting company until enough time is allowed to develop an alternative approach.

---

[7] See Butterworth-Heinemann's book, *Security Metrics Management* book, written by these authors, for guidance on how to measure security costs (publication scheduled for late 2005).

SUMMARY

The security manager plays a key role in the divestiture of a business unit. To successfully support the divestiture, the security manager must focus on the following areas:

- *Support a speedy separation of the divested business unit:* People and systems must be separated from the divesting company and transitioned to the acquiring company as quickly as possible. The longer it takes to complete the separation, the more cost the divesting company will incur.
- *Protection of the assets of the divesting company:* During the separation period, people, physical assets, and information leave the divesting company and migrate to the acquiring company. The security manager must ensure that a plan is in place to ensure that only those assets declared as part of the sale move on. Any assets not identified as part of the sale must stay with the divesting company.
- *Security employees and infrastructure:* The security manager may have to identify employees who, in essence, become part of the sale and move to the acquiring company. Furthermore, security systems may need to be reengineered or reconfigured to carve out those elements supporting the divested business unit.
- *Continuation of support:* The security manager must be prepared to continue delivering services to the divested business unit for an indefinite period of time. This approach may be advantageous for both companies, and the security manager's support is necessary for success.

Chapter 10

Mergers, Acquisitions, and Divestitures Summary by Checklists

After all, the chief business of the American people is business.
– President Calvin Coolidge

INTRODUCTION

In this chapter, we review the major activities and responsibilities security has in any merger, acquisition, or divestiture. A checklist is provided for each major activity as tools and samples. It is hoped that this checklist will help to guide the security managers or business executives tasked with supporting a merger, divestiture, or acquisition in creating their own checklists specific to their activities and events.

PREMERGER AND ACQUISITION CHECKLIST

During the premerger or preacquisition phase, the high level objectives for the security manager are to protect the effort and to participate in the due diligence. During this phase, the security manager has many distinct tasks to perform that contribute to the overall success of the effort. The checklists in this chapter are useful to security managers and merger, divestiture, or acquisition team leaders as they develop their plans.

Protect the Effort

Develop an operations security (OPSEC) plan that includes guidance and requirements for the following areas:

- Maintain confidentiality of the effort's existence and activities
  - Nondisclosure agreements to be executed by all participants

- No public release without team leader approval
- Identification of designated project areas
- Confidentiality of the team's work
  - Brief team members on:
    - Need for strict compliance with need to know
    - Requirements for protecting information
    - General procedures, requirements, and other obligations
    - Protection of information
      - Define information sensitivity: what must be protected and why
      - Identify Information Administrator: control and tracking of project documents
        - Create an information control plan addressing the following areas:
        - Handling of information (paper and electronic)
        - Creation of documents (paper and electronic)
        - Distribution of documents (paper and electronic)
        - Electronic transmission of information and documents
        - Reproduction of information and documents (paper and electronic)
      - Destruction of documents (paper and electronic)
- Protection of all M&A team members
  - Conduct general threat and vulnerability assessment
  - Identify all team executives and members
  - Prepare for international travel
  - Obtain country risk assessments
  - Provide team members with travel safety briefings
  - Develop and brief the cover story for all team members to use

Due Diligence

During the due diligence effort, the security manager has two primary goals:

- Continue to protect the effort, particularly of team members, as they move from location to location.
- Conduct the security portion of the assessment on the target company.

The results of the due diligence assessment will be used by the CEO and/or Board of Directors to assist in making decisions relative to proceeding or not proceeding with the merger or acquisition.

- Competitive intelligence assessments: Security must be a member of the competitive intelligence team providing information and investigative support for the following assessments:
  - Market sector
  - Target companies
  - Competition intentions
- Background investigations are to be conducted as needed on the following:
  - Target company executives and board members
  - Target company affiliates and associates
  - Target company key supplier executives
- Evaluation of the target company's security profile
  - Assess current security condition
  - Collection of data for organizational analysis
  - Identify potential operational synergies
  - Identify any major vulnerability
  - Identify any deal breaking issues

POSTMERGER AND POSTACQUISITION CHECKLIST

The major activity of the postmerger and postacquisition period is combining organizations. The newly acquired company or business unit must be integrated into the acquiring company. Each functional leader must participate. The security manager is responsible for integrating the security department from the acquired business unit into the acquiring company. In the process, there are tasks to accomplish and issues to address.

- Develop plan to combine security organizations
  - Leadership: A single leader needs to be recognized and tasked
    - Create a single security department
    - Establish common vision, operating philosophy, goals, and objectives
    - Analyze and define new security statement of work
- Security operations
  - Implement a common operation: common and consistent application of security services and requirements is essential
    - Process: analyze all processes; adopt the best, improve the others
    - Operational synergies: identify areas where savings can be achieved
    - Best practices: identify practices from both companies and adopt the best, discard or improve those that are inefficient

- Policies and procedures: review all policies and procedures. Ensure that they are revised to properly reflect changes made during integration and take advantage of the best both companies have to offer
- Budget analysis
- Staffing requirements: are they aligned with the security statement of work?
- Reorganization: to ensure security professionals are best matched with security tasks
- Cost control: identify ways to improve the efficiency of department processes and procedures
- Company-wide security issues
  - Identity issues: badges for all new employees
  - Vetting of new employees: consider for target company employees never before subjected to a preemployment or suitability for hire background check
  - Workplace violence prevention: ensure that a prevention program is in place and staffed and that all intervention team members are trained
  - Customer notifications, as needed

DIVESTITURE CHECKLIST

When a business unit is divested, the security manager has two primary actions to take in support of the activity. One is a protective effort; the other is a management action to separate out those security systems and employees that go with the divested unit. The protective effort could include providing support to the divested business unit if the company decides this is in its best interest.

- Separation of the divested business unit
  - Identification of employees' badges: collect company badges from departing employees; work with acquiring company to establish new identity process
  - Access controls: ensure departing employees have access only to that information and those areas for which they have a need to know
  - Cost containment: ensure separation occurs as swiftly as possible; delays translate to added costs and expenditures
  - Ensure only those assets defined as part of the deal go with the divested company. Anything not part of the deal, stays.
- Security infrastructure
  - Systems: separate the departing business unit from the security systems being used.

- Alarm systems: remove from divested buildings and facilities
- Access control systems: reconfigure systems to accommodate operational changes
- Security information: remove divested employees from the security information systems database. Transfer data to acquiring company (if appropriate)
- Employees: be prepared for employee issues in the following areas
  - Unauthorized removal of assets and information
  - Potential for workplace violence
  - Seeking general security guidance about rapidly changing events
  - Maintain regular communication with employees advising them of changes, security concerns, and events

LESSONS LEARNED CHECKLIST

Many companies choose to shape their strategic direction through the use of mergers, acquisitions, and divestitures.The number of mergers, acquisitions, and divestitures continue to increase throughout the global business environment. The likelihood that they will occur more than once in any company is increasing. Therefore, it is a prudent action to learn from one transaction in order to better prepare for the next. Below are areas to consider when reviewing lessons learned.

- Use of competitive intelligence
  - Did the competitive intelligence produce added value?
  - Did it increase team knowledge of the target company?
  - Did it increase team knowledge of the market?
  - Did the intelligence contribute to the team's success?
- Was the effort properly protected?
  - Were there any security failures?
  - Was the effort exposed to anyone without a need to know?
  - Were any team members exposed, embarrassed, or harmed?
- Assessment of target
  - Was the target company properly assessed?
  - After the deal was closed, was anything significant about the acquired company learned that could/should have been learned earlier?
  - Did the assessment lead to a realistic valuation?
  - What problems developed?
- Integration success
  - Were the goals and objectives of the team, the CEO, and the Board of Directors met?
  - Did the team perform as expected?

- Were cost objectives met or exceeded?
- Did any issues of culture develop, that is, culture clashes?

SOME THOUGHTS ABOUT THE FUTURE OF MERGERS, ACQUISITIONS, AND DIVESTITURES AND THEIR IMPACT ON SECURITY MANAGERS

It is expected that mergers, acquisitions, and divestitures will continue on a global scale. They will increase and decrease depending on the economic conditions of the global marketplace, nation-states, and companies.

Thus, today's and tomorrow's security professionals must understand the global marketplace and environment in which their company's assets—facilities, people, and information—will be located. A security professional cannot operate in a global vacuum and wait to be told by the company that, "Oh, by the way, we need the help of security, as we are acquiring a company" (or merging with another company, or divesting of portions of the company). The security professional must begin now to plan for future changes in the company that will be the result of a merger, acquisition, or divestiture. This can be done by continually analyzing the company's business and competitive environment, outlining security plans, and preparing some security checklists for such events, as well as by communicating with the company's specialists who would be involved in such matters.

Security managers in the twenty-first century can no longer concern themselves only with physical security such as guard services, locks, and alarms. We are fully into what the Tofflers called the Information Age, and we are beginning to step into the Knowledge Age. Yet, it seems that most security professionals still have not taken on their responsibilities for information security as a holistic function. Although the physical security for assets protection are in place and the documents are under security control, the automated information and the systems that store, display, process, and transmit vital and often sensitive company information need to be addressed? They are today's most vital assets.

Security professionals continue to leave such tasks to the information technology staffs who may or may not even understand the problems, let alone how to mitigate them. Today's cell phones, faxes, notebook computers, and personal digital assistants (PDAs) allow for information to be released outside controlled channels without a trace, while security professionals concentrate on the physical aspects of information protection. This must change!

As part of a merger, acquisition, or divestiture, this vital function plays an integral role in the success or failure of any merger, acquisition, or divestiture. The security manager must continue to work today's problems and also must set aside time to look into the future, predict future security and assets protection problems, and have plans in place to solve them. This should be included in all contingency planning functions. After all, isn't contingency planning based on "what will we do if such and such happens?"

To be truly considered professionals, security professionals must keep up with many factors including::

- World events
- Global marketplace conditions and trends
- Technology
- Threats, vulnerabilities, and risks to assets

Some security managers will say they are too busy to keep up with trends, plans for the future, or possible future events, as they are too busy "putting out fires." If that is the case, they should join the fire department. For all others, it is a time of excitement and challenges in one of the most rewarding professions there is.

So, enjoy yourselves!

SUMMARY

Mergers, acquisitions, and divestitures are activities of strategic importance to the companies engaged in them. They may bring great benefits to a company or great loss. Mergers, acquisitions, and divestitures are such important and significant events that they must be executed by skilled and experienced people. Anything less will produce less than desired results.

The security manager must be part of the merger and acquisition team. Much is at stake and, without expert security advice and participation, the likelihood that serious issues and problems will develop increases. For maximum value, the merger, acquisition, or divestiture needs to go according to plan. Deviations from the plan can lead to increased costs and other problems. Planning is critical. Embarking on an effort of the magnitude of a merger, acquisition, or divestiture without proper planning is a serious mistake. One a company may not survive.

As a security professional, plan now for the future. Don't wait, as the future is always upon us!

Index